29 5

~~~~, ~~ . ~~

# TALKING TO ZEUS

# TALKING TO ZEUS

## My Year in a Greek Garden

Jane Shaw

**WINDSOR**
**PARAGON**

First published 2010
by Pocket Books
This Large Print edition published 2010
by AudioGO Ltd
by arrangement with
Simon & Schuster UK

Hardcover  ISBN: 978 1 408 48810 2
Softcover    ISBN: 978 1 408 48811 9

British Library Cataloguing in Publication Data available

For dad—always an inspiration

Printed and bound in Great Britain by
CPI Antony Rowe, Chippenham and Eastbourne

# Contents

# PROLOGUE

# Joy Strataki's Letter

*Helikion Garden*
*Attica*

*Dear Jane,*
  *I'm pleased to tell you that your application for the job as my assistant has been accepted. Some of the applicants had very substantial CVs, much more experienced than you. However, I was impressed by your references from Hyde Park and Chelsea Physic Garden—they stressed how hard you work, even in poor conditions. Your life as a WREN in the Royal Navy no doubt got you ready for it! Work on a steep-sided five-acre garden such as this is demanding, especially in the heat of summer and cold of winter. I hate to tell you but no UK student horticulturalist has ever managed to last the intern year. I fear a lack of TV/internet, having to wash up outdoors and a generally monastic lifestyle disheartens the lily-livered youth of the UK. I hope you're not inclined to this disposition and will be the first to survive the year.*
  *As you know, the garden has always been a stalwart advert for organic and water-wise gardening. With each passing year water is becoming more scarce. We have an annual rainfall barely more than a desert and now we're suffering from fiercely hot summers, with many fires sweeping the country. It's so hot the agapanthus's leaves have turned*

white! This has never happened before.

I have enclosed a copy of the American owner's gardening diaries, written when she first started the garden in the seventies. It will help you to understand more about the garden's history, our mission here and the trials and tribulations incurred since we began. She turned an arid, treeless, windy, stony hillside into a garden with little more than a pickaxe and a few seeds. She visits once a year for a month and is due to arrive next February, so you will meet her then.

Now, to the business end of things:

Your wage will be 600 euros a month. Board and lodging is free. Telephone calls are billed. The contract extends from October 2007 to October 2008 and is final, subject to a three-month probationary period. We don't bother as they do in England about health and safety. No need for steel toe-capped boots. But do get health insurance—the occasional poisonous adder slithers around the garden, although they are, unfortunately, becoming a rare occurrence. And bring thermals—it can be like the North Pole here and there's no central heating or double glazing. You have the use of a small electric heater in the outhouse.

My dear friend Charles, who lives at the top of the hill, deals with the garden's emails and will answer any of your questions. I'm a useless technophobe.

I look forward to meeting you at Athens International Airport. I have enclosed a *photograph of myself so you can recognize me.*

*With best wishes,*
*Joy Strataki*

*P.S. I have two dogs, a cat and a scarlet macaw. They are all rescued strays and can be a tad too demanding. If you're not an animal lover or are allergic I would strongly suggest that you think twice about coming— if this is the case, let me know promptly.*

# 1

# Queen of the Night

*Epiphyllum oxypetalum*
'Queen of the Night'
Gr. ĕpi, upon - phyllon, a leaf. The flowers
are borne on flattened green leaf-like
stems are thought to be leaves. CACTACEAE

The sun shone low into the arrivals hall. I grasped the straps of my rucksack, eased it off my shoulders and squinted into the crowd.

I recognized Joy Strataki from the photograph she had sent. In the fading print she wore the same taut expression as the elderly lady now tip-a-tap-toeing towards me, lean and vital like a whippet about to bolt the traps. From underneath a battered straw hat, strands of long, grey hair fell to her shoulders. A robust man with a black, swirling beard strode beside her. She tapped his arm and pointed at me.

I felt queasy. Too many free drinks on the plane. One too many last night.

My instinct was to turn and bolt for the flight home. I was an habitual runner, my CV to date a smorgasbord of abandoned jobs. My greatest escape had been from the clutches of the Royal Navy. Having served Her Majesty for a mere nine months of a four-year contract I'd persuaded my father, a playwright, to write a letter to the admiral stating that my patriotism had been compromised by depression brought on by the burden put upon me by my forebears, all brave soldiers of the Queen. The admiral must have reached for his hankie, since I was given an 'honourable discharge' forthwith, my character assessed as 'exemplary'.

Back in 'civvy street' I dosed myself with Seroxat and tinkered with my CV to make it look as if I'd served the mandatory four years. Guilt now all-embracing, I skulked in new workplaces: the darkroom of a photographic agency, then the gardening section of a bookstore on Charing Cross

Road. There, one quiet morning, I perused the pages of a book by Monty Don and was hit by a eureka moment—the great outdoors, physical exercise, toiling the earth. Why hadn't I thought of it before?

In a trice I enrolled on a Royal Horticultural Society Level 2 certificate, secured a gardening job in Hyde Park and volunteered at Chelsea Physic Garden.

I told myself that my application to Helikion, which is visited by enthusiasts and plant scientists the world over, wasn't based on a whim, but a way of restoring my self-respect. It would boost my horticultural CV, help me towards my goal of working at the Royal Botanic Gardens, Kew. I was no longer a dreamer who flipped from job to job, relying on my parents to bail me out when the going got tough. No. I was . . .

'Welcome to Greece, Jane!' Joy's stentorian tones jolted me to near sobriety.

I shoved a hand out in greeting. She patted it away, grabbed me by the waist and kissed me firmly on each cheek, then reached up to put a wiry arm on the man's broad shoulders. 'This is Pavlos, my knight in shining armour. For a friend, he'll turn over the deepest compost heaps.'

He chuckled. Loose curls of black hair bobbed above warm eyes the colour of dark chocolate. '*Ya sas*,' his voice rumbled. 'After digging heaps of Helikion, you eats Joy's cakes of honey.' He enfolded me in a bear hug. 'Heaps not that deep.'

'Thank you,' I mumbled into the soft creases of his denim shirt, adjusting my ear to his lilting English.

'Cakes take fillings out though,' he added with a

wink as he released me.

Joy raised a hand. 'Rush hour,' she said commandingly.

We made a ramshackle dash for the car park. Any lingering preconceptions I harboured about Joy were soon banished when, at the boot of an old Jeep, she suddenly bent from the waist and surveyed her footwear. 'Will you look at that! My village shoes, scuffed to kingdom come. That wretched Winston will keep masturbating on them.' Her grey-green eyes twinkled beneath hooded lids, like crumpled tarpaulin over a shop full of secrets.

I glanced at her slip-on shoes, the soft brown leather plucked and stained. Pavlos noticed the bemused look on my face and laughed as he tossed my heavy rucksack into the boot of the Jeep. On the front passenger seat a small, dirty-grey dog sucked on the face of a toy teddy.

'Say hello to Winston,' Joy said.

The dog lifted his head and glared at me. A stained incisor poked between bits of frothy teddy and saliva. One eye looked like a plum, a blue bloom over it, the other was dark brown and full of venomous contempt. I reluctantly patted his sweaty dome, and mumbled a greeting. Apparently satisfied, Joy plonked the grumbling dog into Pavlos's arms. 'You two, into the back. Jane, in the front.' She grabbed the teddy, a Greek flag stitched over its belly, and tossed it onto the backseat. 'The rest of my menagerie are waiting for you at home.'

I discreetly wiped away a clump of Winston's gloopy debris and gingerly sat down, glancing over my shoulder. 'I've been looking forward to meeting them,' I replied in what I hoped was a convincing manner.

Pavlos was staring into a clear plastic box, inside which a fat lizard sneered, flicking its forked tongue in and out. 'This is Gordon,' he said. 'Don't mind him. He's all gums and no bites. Joy's looking after him for a friend.'

'That's nice,' I said, pining for a reassuring cuddle from my cat, Bubski.

Joy settled into the driver's seat, threw her hat towards me and put on a pair of heart-shaped, red plastic sunglasses. 'Now, Jane. Let's get you to the garden and settled in.' She theatrically grabbed the gear stick, crunched the gears and missed the exit twice before finally zooming out of the car park.

Against a rising wind, we were soon speeding along the six-lane Attiki Odos highway, its sides and ditches full of builders' rubble and litter. Beside the road, large advertising boards touted brands of cigarettes, coffee and sports goods, their tall stilts rooted in the ancient wine-producing land of the Mesoghia.

Joy jabbed my shoulder, jolting me out of my reverie, and pointed out of the side window. 'Mount Hymettos, Jane. Odysseus used to hunt boar up there. Thank heavens only a few fires. But the poor Peloponnese . . . people dead . . . ancient olive groves and forests destroyed.' She looked to the skies. 'We've been praying to the gods for rain. Even drought-tolerant plants need water at some point.'

I sat upright to look at the mountain that loomed over Athens' urban sprawl, displaying its tarnished crown of twisted metal, radar installations and mobile-telephone masts. As the sun set and a deepening twilight took hold, the mountain's hue imperceptibly shifted from a bluish grey to a bloody violet.

'I'm desperate for a cigarette.' Joy looked in the pocket of the car door, fumbling through its contents. 'Do you smoke, Jane?' The Jeep veered into rough ground at the side of the road.

'No. Sorry.' My eyes were fixed rigidly ahead.

'I'm afraid I'm doomed.' She leaned forward, stretching her long neck upwards, and peered through the rear-view mirror. 'Stop teasing Gordon, Pavlos. Have you got any cigarettes?'

'I've given ups yesterday,' declared Pavlos. 'Keep eyes on road, Joy. Gordon is dizzy with sway.'

I noticed the speedometer creeping upwards and gripped the door handle.

We soon left the highway and sped along a tortuous road. Halfway along a rolling hillside, our headlights illuminated a series of roadside shrines. The last housed lit candles and vases of dried flowers. Soft toys huddled at its base, cards from the bereaved pinned to their synthetic chests.

Joy flicked the indicator and slowed the Jeep down. 'Bit of a dodgy turning, this,' she said.

We waited for a gap in oncoming traffic. Suddenly, back wheels squealing, she propelled the Jeep in front of a lorry. I grabbed the sides of my seat, sighing with relief as we turned up a steep, rutted track, the hard tips of Spanish broom rat-a-tapping over the car's sides. We passed a large gate with CCTV cameras perched above it. Security dogs leapt onto its bars, snarling and barking, as we rumbled by. Joy sniffed and tutted. 'I'm friendly with all of my neighbours apart from that one. A Neanderthal. Expat. Made his fortune

13

out of other people's miseries and ripped off a charming Greek couple to buy that place dirt cheap. Both dead now. Cancer. The beast destroyed the natural vegetation to build terraced lawns. Blasted sprinklers on them all the time. I could quite happily tar and feather him.' She scrunched the gears around a sharp corner. Cigarette ash rolled around the gear stick, dusting my flip-flopped feet.

'Nearly home. I've prepared us some dinner and there's a bottle chilling in the fridge,' she added.

I perked up somewhat and let go of the door handle to rub the blood back into my hand, desperate to get out of the Jeep, eager for another drink.

Above, a long squat house nestled within layers of shadowy vegetation. Spiky black outlines of yuccas and prickly pears punctured the night sky. With a spray of gravel, Joy brought the Jeep to a rattling halt, inches away from a duck-egg blue moped with a leather jacket and helmet hanging off its handlebars. 'Here we are. Home.'

I climbed out of the passenger seat into a pool of flickering light. Hanging from the front door's alcove, two cast-iron holders held a plethora of flaming candles. Cicadas chirruped softly in the undergrowth. Stepping out of the light I caught my head against the branches of a mastic tree. Joy and Pavlos laughed and told me to mind my step. I rubbed my ear and looked down the hillside. Tall cypresses, their jagged outlines imitating offbeat skyscrapers, painted the inky twilight a deeper black.

Pavlos walked towards the moped. 'I go get cigarettes for you, Joy. And a first aid kit for you,

Jane.'

'Oh, you lovely beast,' called out Joy. 'Don't go buying that Turkish stuff you *used* to smoke!'

Pavlos chuckled and said he'd see us soon.

'Come on in then, Jane, before you do yourself another mischief.' Joy waved her skinny arms around grandly.

I lugged my rucksack through the alcove and entered the open-plan house. There was a smell of garlic and dusty corners. Opposite, a huge sofa creaked and groaned under the massive weight of a black Rottweiler. Seeing me, he stretched out an iron-clad neck, bared a few hefty teeth and turned onto his back. Offloading ballast, the sofa spewed out yellow foam from its stitching.

'This is Titan, Jane.' Joy went over to tickle his velvet belly. 'He's a big softy . . . oh, yes you are . . . look at you, all delicious. Come and stroke him!' Titan flexed his breeze-block paws and sighed a rank, meaty breath. Winston, teddy clamped in his jaws, scuttled over my feet and jumped up onto a Zulu warrior stool standing beneath a large framed print of Hieronymus Bosch's triptych, *The Garden of Earthly Delights*. Beside it a large birdcage hung from a metal pole and stand, its door open.

'Now,' said Joy. 'Cigarettes. I know there's a packet around here somewhere.' She cast a hand over a cluttered table next to the sofa. 'Ah, found my specs at least.' She held up a pair of spectacles, put them on and scanned the table. Three Arabian hookahs, candles strewn with rivers of wax and an upturned wooden cross sat on its top. 'That pesky macaw.' Joy turned the cross upright. 'I'll hang you upside down one of these days, Wizard!' She

15

tipped her head back searching the thick wooden rafters for any signs of the bird. 'He's mentally ill. Should be sectioned. The Devil long since left his mark on that one. He's probably outside tormenting the bats. Now, where are those cigarettes?'

Joy trotted to the kitchen. I could hear her stirring pots and pans, opening doors and cupboards. 'Ah, in the fridge. Who put them there? Bugger. One left.'

I heard her sigh and strike a match. A plume of smoke shot into the room. Seconds later, two village shoes flew out of the kitchen's open entrance and landed with a thump on the dining table. Barefooted, Joy poked her head out and glared at their upturned soles. 'Oh my, that's bad luck. Usually I get them near the shoe rack at least.'

She stared at me, inhaling deeply from the cigarette clenched between her fingers. For the first time since we met she had stopped talking and stood motionless. 'Now, do you drink and are you punctual?'

'Er . . . definitely yes and almost always,' I said.

'Then an ouzo is in order, Jane.' She wafted back into the small kitchen. I carefully picked up the village shoes and put them on the shoe rack, then turned to survey the room.

Antique furniture crouched across the sunken marble floor. Along the length of one wall stood a faded, twisting, floor-to-ceiling bookcase. Stuffed into its wooden frame were thick, yellowing tomes on philosophy, history, Greek mythology, poetry, gardens, botany, travel and cookery. From its lower shelves I picked out *Recipes of Baghdad*.

16

Pencilled notes, shaky and slanting, straddled each recipe.

Joy sidled up to me with two tall glasses of cloudy ouzo. 'The most interesting recipe,' she declared, 'is on page thirty-two. Udders and bladders boiled in an unmentionable liquid. Quite fascinating.' She handed me the ouzo and clinked her chipped crystal glass against mine. 'Welcome to the garden, Jane!' I took a swig. Ice picks hammered into the back of my skull.

Joy's thick spectacles glinted. 'It's an acquired taste. I buy, or filch, it from Pavlos.' She finished her drink with one long swallow, the ice cubes hardly touching the sides of the glass. 'By the way, ask if you want to borrow a book from the library. It may look a complete farce, but from chaos comes order.' She took the book from my hand and put it back in its slot.

'There are six things that sustain me in my old age, Jane. The garden. My pets. Books. Ouzo. Cigarettes. Friends.' Joy ticked them off on her fingers, frowning darkly. 'If anyone gets in the way of these, I get ex-treme-ly angry.' Each syllable fell hard as whips. Her eyes bored into mine. 'They told me at Chelsea Physic Garden that you were one of their hardest-working volunteers. As my intern, I also expect you to be knowledgeable. How's your plant ID?'

She sniffed at my hesitation, pulled another book from the shelves and thrust it into my hands. 'You *may* borrow this book—*Wild Flowers of the Mediterranean*. Every week I shall test you. We'll start with the *Lamiaceae* family. Thymes, mints, teucriums—we have a lot in the garden. Learn their botanical names. There are roughly nine

17

hundred species in the *Salvia* genus alone. That's enough to be getting on with.'

She broke into a grin as I took a large gulp of ouzo. 'And don't worry if you see geckos running around the bookshelves. They live there.' Her face plummeted. 'Oh my Lord, Gordon!' she shrieked. 'He's still in the Jeep!' She slipped on a pair of shabby Jesus sandals and dashed outside to retrieve the forgotten lizard.

On her return, Joy topped up my glass of ouzo.

'It *is* an acquired taste, isn't it?' I said, coughing, my throat burning.

'You'll get used to it. Four years in the Navy must have toughened you up. All those assault courses and scrubbing the decks. I've had interns here who can't get out of bed in the morning. The welfare state, they must be warm and comfy, you know the sort?'

'Mmm, terrible,' I said, cringing inside, wishing she would stop talking about the Navy.

'You look strong. Are you?'

'Yes, I am.' This time I told the absolute truth and felt better for it.

We heard a spray of gravel outside. A minute later, Pavlos walked through the unlocked door. He gave Joy three packs of Silk Cut. From the top of his shirt pocket poked another, its cellophane cover still intact. Pavlos caught us looking at it. He shrugged and splayed his hands out. 'In case of emergencies.'

Joy chuckled. 'Yes, of course—emergencies. Like the time when you accidentally drove over Mrs Koliopoulos's foot. I hope you like octopus, Jane.' Joy walked to the kitchen, talking all the while. 'And I hope you like digging. The ground is tough.

18

Only pickaxes will do the job. Sometimes I'm tempted to use dynamite, but then the soil structure would be buggered.'

I laughed, relieved that the Navy was no longer a topic of conversation, and followed her into the kitchen. Saucepans rested on an old stove, their contents bubbling and simmering. She picked up a pair of pliers from the counter and turned one of the knobs for the gas, its plastic cover missing.

\*       \*       \*

After the meal, munching on warm honey cakes, with Titan sleeping on my feet, I stared at the bookcase, hoping for a gecko to emerge from its gaping cracks. I was tired and about to ask Joy to take me to the outhouse when the telephone rang. She picked up the receiver, which would not have looked amiss in the 1970s section of The Design Museum—the computer sitting next to it looked equally outdated. 'Hello, Charles . . .' She lowered her voice and turned her back.

After a few minutes of quiet conversation, Joy returned the phone to its cradle and lifted her glasses to massage the drooping bags under her eyes.

'Everything all rights, Joy?' Pavlos asked.

Joy put out a hand to a snoozing Winston. Slowly and pensively she scratched the top of his head.

Suddenly, she looked up at me. 'Oh Jane, I'm sorry.' She grabbed a wooden chair, swivelled it around and sat down legs akimbo, arms resting over the backrest. 'Tragedy,' she said, pouring herself another ouzo. 'That was Charles. Just had an email. Marilyn's died. The owner. Heart

19

attack.' Joy's voice cracked and faltered. Pavlos laid his hand over hers. 'She's left the garden to Tom, her son.' She looked thoughtfully at the few discarded octopus lumps at the side of my plate. 'He came over with his mum a few years ago, about to start a Classics degree at Emmanuel. He wasn't that interested in the garden,' she mused. 'Head always buried in a book.' She paused, deep in thought, then looked at me, slammed her glass on the table and pointed. 'But you're not to worry. I've got you for the year.'

I looked into her fiery, red-rimmed eyes and recalled the words of one of the few successful interns at Helikion whom I had tracked down from contacts at Chelsea Physic Garden. From Barcelona, she had warned me in broad Catalonian tones: 'It's tough. Up a steep, windy hill, nowhere to walk to. Stuck with an old dragon.' She had told me about a student of Joy's who, shocked by the conditions in the outhouse, rang for a taxi to take him back to the airport just an hour after arriving.

A shaft of moonlight forced its way through a mass of windowpanes, flooding an oak and ebony writing table. Joy went to it and rifled through its drawers, banging them shut. 'It's in here somewhere,' she mumbled. Plant cuttings tumbled over its worn edges, brushing bronze mask inlays of Socrates and Plato. An ancient microscope with a rusty stem wobbled on top of a stack of well-thumbed gardening magazines, diaries and sketchbooks.

'Bingo!' She brandished a small book, its paper cover ripped at the edges. An angelic smile caressed her face.

She began to read: 'Through winter-time we call on spring . . .'

Pavlos delved into the pocket of his crumpled chinos, brought out a set of black amber worry beads and lazily tossed them to and fro. She continued to read, oblivious:

'. . . And after that there's nothing good, Because the spring-time has not come, Nor know that what disturbs our blood . . .'

She abruptly lifted her arm up to the wooden rafters, her voice dropping a few octaves.

'. . . Is but its longing for the tomb.'

She dropped her head to her chest, paused and looked up. Titan gave a mountainous yawn and rolled over, the released springs of the dilapidated sofa pinging with relief.

Pavlos clapped and called out, 'Bravo! Bravo!' his eyes full of shadows and sparks.

Joy laughed, then looked at me sternly. I was sitting quietly, thinking of friends, wishing I could be with them in a London pub.

'Do you read poetry, Jane?'

'Er, yes, sometimes. Doom-laden stuff. Philip Larkin, Sylvia Plath, Billy Childish.'

A rush of wind swept through the veranda's open door, scattering papers, upending Winston's ears. Swaying oil lamps cast light into hidden corners, illuminating Minoan statues and abandoned cobwebs. Joy laid the poetry book down on the table and tottered over to close the banging door. Her attention was caught by one of the potted plants that populated the veranda's warped decking. Outside she stepped over a row of kalanchoes sprouting from recycled olive oil tins and closely inspected the plant's flower buds.

21

'Pavlos, Jane. Come here.' She stood, legs apart, scanning the night sky, her long grey locks whipping in the wind. 'Of course. A full moon. You've arrived just in time.' Joy plucked up Winston and rushed back into the house. 'We need to gather the troops. Raid the cellar. We are duty bound to toast this garden.' She kissed Winston on the snout. 'The Queen of the Night is flowering. A party is in order.' She raised her upturned palms to the heavens, Winston falling to the floor with a yelp. 'A party to the garden!' Her splintered tones lifted a few decibels. 'To Marilyn! We must do it tonight!'

I thought about the boy who had left after spending only an hour with Joy and rooted in my rucksack for the leaflet that listed the telephone numbers of airlines and taxi services.

# 2

# Up a Steep Hill

Arisarum
vulgare
'FRIAR'S COWL'
Tuberous perennial
herb mentioned by
Dioscorides.

It was 8 p.m. I sat on the veranda staring listlessly at the Queen of the Night's unfurling white petals, its buds drooping and pendulous like meerschaum pipes. I could hear Joy on the phone, gathering guests for her party. Strong gusts of wind whipped across the veranda, clanking the chains of the oil lamps. A cloud barred the moon's soft light, transforming the wall creepers and vines from a ghostly blue to a menacing black. I reached for the doorpost to steady my entrance into the house and found Pavlos staring at the print of Bosch's triptych.

'That bit's hell,' Pavlos murmured, pointing to the triptych's right panel. 'Warns sinners about pains to come,' he chuckled, glancing at Joy.

She dropped the phone in its cradle and rose abruptly, issuing forth orders. I had to join Pavlos in washing up the dishes, then brush up the dog hair and wipe up the feathers and droppings from around Wizard's cage. Finally I had to prepare snacks. I stared at her in weary dismay as she vanished through a rustic door I hadn't noticed before. Immediately she opened it again, letting in Titan. At the same time she chucked a plastic bag to land at my feet.

'And blow these up,' she said. 'A party without balloons is a plant without roots.'

Pavlos laughed and nodded at Bosch's painting. 'With Joy we're all in hell.' He gathered up the dirty dishes on his arm and took them to the kitchen. 'I do work, Jane.' His voice softened. 'You do balloons and rest. When did you last go to beds?'

25

I couldn't help breaking into a smile at Pavlos's mix-ups with plurals.

'Can't remember. I went to a party in London last night.' I broke off, picked up the packet of balloons and sank down on Titan's sofa. A spring jabbed into the back of my knee. 'The lily-livered youth of the UK'—Joy's phrase penetrated my nauseous haze just as a tinny burst of jazz music hissed from her room. Winston sat on his Zulu warrior stool and eyed me up and down.

I shuffled back to the veranda and sat at its edge, dangling my legs over a lemon-scented pelargonium. The moon was now shining bright, the wind reduced to a gentle breeze. Moths pinged against the oil lamps, providing a gentle counterpoint to 'Twelfth Street Rag'. Pavlos brought out a mug of strong coffee and placed it gently beside me. I gnawed into the knot at the top of the packet of balloons and gazed at the moon, like ET, dreaming about home. I had promised to call my parents, let them know I had arrived safely. I couldn't face it. I would either end up a blubbering mess or talk myself into leaving. I started to blow up the balloons.

The music stopped and Joy brought out a gramophone, her face scrubbed ruddy underneath her straw hat, a fresh slab of blueberry lipstick applied. Titan and Winston barked and scrambled to the sound of knocking and voices at the front door.

'Guests, Jane,' Joy said, and gestured for me to follow her.

Two men approached me. One, tall and all angles, his arms cradled under a crate of champagne, the other rotund and bald. He carried an earthenware bowl.

'Ah, Joy's fresh gardening blood,' Daddy-long-legs said in a varied accent of Greek and American. 'I'm Demetri.' He studiously inspected my face over a pair of half-moon spectacles then nodded at the other man. 'My partner, Vassili.'

Vassili hopped forward and kissed me twice on both cheeks. 'Now, my darlings. The true Queen of the Night has arrived!' He offered me the earthenware bowl and chuckled. It was brimming with pink sherbet lollies and chocolate bars. I couldn't help but smile and quickly picked one out. Demetri urged Vassili to the dining table, snacks and drinks arrayed on its top, while Joy hustled me back onto the veranda.

'Don't mind Vassili,' she whispered. 'He can be sooo home-oh-sexual at times.' She pointed at the Queen of the Night, its long strap-like stems climbing the wall. 'It was a gift. From a Mexican visitor. He said if its flowering isn't celebrated at full moon then Montezuma's revenge will follow.' She cupped one of its opened flowers in her hands and urged me to inhale its scent. It was as big as a dinner plate and let out a heady aroma, an unusual blend of spices, sweet and sour. 'Its botanical name is EP-EE-FIE-LUM OX-EE-PET-A-LUM. Remember that, Jane.'

Demetri and Vassili had rejoined us and began to dip into the bowls of stuffed grapevine leaves and nuts. Pavlos followed with a tray of charged champagne flutes. I tried to repeat the plant's name through a fog of twisted vowels and consonants. 'Ep-ee ...' In exasperation Joy thumped one of the balloons that I'd tied to canes stuck in the olive tin pots.

27

'*Epiphyllum oxypetalum*!' she barked, making me step back in shock. 'And it's in the Cack-ta-ace-eye family. Botanical names only, Jane. I don't want to hear any of the common names.' She swept back into the house, swirls of terracotta dust following in her wake. I dipped into a bowl of nuts to hide my shock and embarrassment.

Vassili handed me a champagne flute. 'Gods, she can be such a bitch. Ignore her, darlings.' He raised his glass. 'Welcome to Helikion.' I took a gulp of champagne and managed a small smile.

Joy returned, poking a botanical book into my free hand. 'Read it, Jane. Learn. And write down the titles of the books I've lent to you on a sheet of paper and sign. Put it on my desk. I don't want them to go missing.'

Pavlos put a hand gently on my shoulder, directing me back to the Queen of the Night. 'Nature is amazing, no? Joy tolds me that hawk moths of the night pollinates it.' He looked into the depths of one of its long flowers. 'They grow their proboscis exactly same size as flower tubes so they can get nectar at bottoms.' He shook his head in wonder and gently patted my shoulder, a warm and calming gesture, and I turned to smile at him in gratitude. Was my reception, I wondered, a 'bad cop, good cop' routine as part of my initiation ceremony into the world of Helikion? Pavlos—was he as sweet as he appeared? I put my drink down. If I had any more I might say something damaging or ridiculous.

An elderly man and woman strode onto the veranda, their backs ramrod straight. The woman, wearing a red linen vest that threatened to split with the weight of her huge bosom, handed Joy an open Tupperware box. Inside were thick slabs of cake. 'Our septic tank hasn't been emptied yet. Not a phone call. Nothing.' She stood with her hands on her hips, chest thrust out, lips pursed.

'Bloody people don't know their arses from their elbows,' the man mumbled, adjusting the tension of the red braces clipped to his white linen trousers. The woman stared at me then thrust out her hand. 'You must be Jane. Pleased to meet you.' It was like being gripped in a vice.

'This is Rachel,' Joy said, 'and her husband Charles. Your emailer, Jane.' She dropped her head. 'Such a tragedy about Marilyn.'

'Yes. We must soldier on, though,' he replied, pushing back a lock of white hair from a face that looked as though a blowtorch had been wafted over it. 'Now, Jane. Are you ready to dig?'

'What, now?' I wasn't sure if he was joking or not—his tone was serious enough. Encouraged by their laughter, I told them about my last day as a gardener at Hyde Park. 'I had to weed borders covered in frost. It was impossible. The contractors I worked for didn't make any allowances for the weather. Nothing for the soil, the temperature, wet or dry. Amazing.' Joy stared at me. I couldn't decide whether she was impressed or just wanted me to shut up. I chose the latter.

'Jane,' Joy said, 'Charles and Rachel published educational books in India. Met in hospital— Charles bitten by a snake, Rachel with Delhi belly.'

'We live at the top of the hill, Jane. Ten dogs, three cats. The odd wild snake,' Rachel said, patting her hair to ensure it wasn't coming adrift from the ramparts of clips and combs holding it in

29

place. She was telling me about an unusual plant that she'd grown in India when suddenly there was a loud angry screech.

I snapped around in shock. A large bird was at my head, thumping the air with its wings. It whacked me around the ears, then powered into the night sky, strands of hair caught in its talons.

'Wizard!' shouted Joy, pointing above my head. 'Leave her!'

'You should have that thing castrated, Joy!' Rachel barked.

'Devil bird,' Joy cried, her fist bunched at the wheeling macaw.

I dropped on a pile of large tasselled cushions and felt my skull. Pavlos bent over me to extract a downy feather gently from my hair. I checked I wasn't bleeding and held back an urge to run out of the front door and head for a bus stop. Joy's driving here had been dangerous enough. Now her parrot seemed to be programmed from the dark side. What next?

Joy spotted a new arrival, a thickset woman with silvery hair as wiry as a scouring brush, and rushed across the decking to greet her. She handed Joy a small painting, hugged Vassili and Demetri, then waddled over to Pavlos, raising her hands to pull down his shoulders and kiss him on the forehead. 'Pavlos! *Erhomaiedo edo sas panemorfi pragma!*' She then turned her attention to me and put out her hands, bracelets jangling.

Oh God, I had to take hold of them. It would be rude not to, and everyone was looking. Legs set apart for leverage, she hoisted me upright and into her arms for a hug that was so tight the gold cross hanging from her neck nearly took root in my skin.

30

'*Ya sas*. Welcome Greece!' She gestured to her side. 'This my Spiros.' She gestured at a barrel-bodied man moving into the light, his brow furrowed beneath a grey cloth cap. He flicked a set of worry beads, put them in his waistcoat pocket and turned suddenly, raising his head and whistling through his mighty moustache. Wizard swooped out of the darkness, banked sharply and dropped onto the man's fist with a gentle squawk.

'Bravo!' Charles boomed, and took a step backwards away from the bird's outstretched wings. 'Spiros,' he said, 'which cowboys empty your septic tank?'

Joy took my arm and drew me aside. 'Spiros and Eleni, Jane,' she whispered. 'Spiros is my handyman. Does the plumbing and helps with Wizard. Eleni paints.' She looked affectionately at the couple. Eleni lit a fat cigar and popped it through the hedgerows of Spiro's moustache. Joy handed me the painting and frowned. 'One more for the toilet wall, I'm afraid. Now then, everybody!' Joy clapped her hands for silence. 'Raise your glasses. To Marilyn. To Ep-ee-fie-lum ox-ee-pet-a-lum!'

'To Marilyn,' I wearily answered, joining the cries of the guests, holding aloft an empty glass to toast the nine white blooms of the Queen of the Night.

'Pavlos. Time for a tale,' Joy commanded. Pavlos drained his glass and stood under the thick vines of a wisteria. 'I gives you the bloody rites of the great goddess, Cybele.' He spread his arms wide, the moon and stars glittering behind him.

'Oooh, I love bloody rites, darlings,' Vassili piped, grinning at me. I sat at the back of the group, lulled to sleep by Pavlos's honeyed tones. Titan, a balloon tied to his metal-studded collar, placed his head softly on my knee.

*       *       *

'And so!' Pavlos declared, waking me. 'To become priests men had to go through bloody rites. They chop off dicks with rusty knives,'—he sliced through the air with the cutting edge of his hand— 'run through streets, throw bloody bits into houses. Home owners dress the bleeding men in women's clothing and at last they are Priest of Cybele.'

'The things men have to do for a woman,' Vassili commented, rolling his eyes.

'I've no food for Gordon!' Joy cried suddenly. She grabbed my hand. 'Come along, everyone. Worm hunt.'

I found myself following Joy up a narrow, rocky, moonlit path, clutching an empty marmalade jar and trowel. Pavlos whistled a tune behind me, a tray of drinks balanced on the end of his fingertips. Croaking, clicking and humming sounds came from out of the whispering undergrowth. Sharp leaves and thorns scratched at my arms, insects flitted in the warm air. Titan gave a sudden bark.

The path opened onto a small plateau. A barrier of kermes oak and buckthorn shielded rows of potted plants. I slumped on a boulder. A toad bounced out from between my feet and hopped between Demetri's legs into the shadowy shrubs. Vassili dabbed at his head with a spotted handkerchief and took the champagne flute that Pavlos offered him. 'I was built for the horizontal, darlings,' he gasped, and sat beside me.

32

Joy turned on the potholer's light strapped to her forehead and strode towards a small shack underneath the dipping branches of an umbrella pine. She beckoned me to its door made of chicken wire and bamboo cane. Overhead a sign painted on a wooden plank read 'Potting shed'.

'Look around. Tell me what's wrong?' she snapped, arms folded.

I hesitated. Despite feeling exhausted and bewildered by everything since my arrival, I wanted to give the right answer.

'Well?'

I lifted the string latch. Inside were bags of compost, buckets, stacks of empty plant pots, jars, cardboard egg-holders and yoghurt pots with seedlings spurting out, and a trug on a makeshift table. 'How do you mean?' I said.

'Look.' She stared grimly at a slowly dripping tap that stood sentry at one side of the door. 'We're not in England. This is life and death here.' She tried to tighten the faucet. 'Bugger. Spiros, do something.'

Spiros fiddled with the tap then grunted and slowly shook his head. 'Tomorrow.'

'I can't bear it. First thing tomorrow.' Joy quickly put a bucket underneath the drip and shook her head to get rid of her annoyance. 'Right, best place to look for worms is under these pots.' She paused and cupped her ear with her hand. 'Ah, Jane. Do you know what's making that noise?' I listened to what sounded like the steady sonar-blip of a submarine and shook my head.

Charles, Eleni and Pavlos laughed and held their drinks aloft. 'Scops owl! Botanical name, OAT-US-SCOPS. Like snakes and hoopoes, he's bothered by climate change. Becoming a rarity around here. Name, Jane?'

'*Otus scops*,' I said quickly, fearful I'd forget, and picked up a pot.

Joy knelt down next to me, jabbing at the earth with her trowel, muttering to herself. I pinched myself hard and breathed in deeply, disjointed thoughts tumbling through my mind. What was I doing looking for worms on a steep hillside in Greece at nearly one o'clock in the morning—Joy was clearly mad—I wondered if I'd ever see my friends and family again—I wished I'd stayed in the Navy. This was God's way of punishing me for lying on my CV.

I looked under another pot. Whatever happened I must not run away.

'The shame. An organic garden and no bloody worms,' Joy croaked, after ten minutes of scrabbling in the earth. Charles held up what looked like wriggling pieces of string.

'Victory!' he cried. Pavlos clapped, accidentally dropping his cigarette onto tinder, dry pine needles and twigs.

'Pavlos,' raged Joy, pointing. 'Fire!'

He looked down in horror and leapt onto the smouldering butt, then immediately cried out in pain and clutched his ankle.

*　　*　　*

A pink and blue sky wrapped itself around the moon and slowly the trees and shrubs slipped out of their black, shadowy overcoats, leaves twitching in the emerging sunlight.

Pavlos lay asleep beside Titan on the sofa, a bag

of iced peas melting over his ankle, while I sat at the table clasping my head. The guests had left, tired, dusty and soporific with drink. A sated Gordon sat on his water dish idly flicking his tongue in and out. Wizard rocked gently back and forth, the repetitive squeak of his metal swing filling the room. When Joy disappeared into the kitchen he cackled at me. I slowly stuck my tongue out at the bird, closed my eyes then reached for my rucksack. Surely now Joy would show me my living quarters?

When I opened my eyes again I found a cup of coffee at my side, Joy smiling down at me.

'I'm going to take you on a tour of the garden. Only five acres. We'll take Wizard,' she said, reaching into the cage. 'Good way for him to get to know you.'

In a stupor I followed Joy through a swathe of irises, their leaves brown-tipped and toppling over. Winston yapped and chased insects then raced into a dark green mound of pistacia. Joy talked, pointed, hollered and jabbered, Wizard swooped and clattered. Balled plants, shaggy plants, dense thorny masses, olive trees and the tall spears of cypress trees whirled through my vision.

'I call this area the phrygana. Technically it's not. Look it up later.'

I was too tired to speak, although I knew it was a low-growing open plant community of mainly spiny cushion plants, dotted with bulbs and annuals.

Joy stopped underneath a tall yucca near to the Neanderthal's fence of spiked iron bars from which there was a long drop to the bottom of the hill. I yawned. Wizard batted me lightly around the

35

head with his long wings. Joy looked up at the yucca's drooping head, the scruffy, dead leaves underneath revealed like the undergarments of a can-can dancer.

The rest of her words scattered through my head like grapeshot. I squinted around me, eyes painful. Insects crawled through my hair. Seeds armed with hooks and spikes crunched under my feet.

'Jane!' Joy barked. 'Are you listening?'

I looked dumbly at her. She was pointing at a rosette of wavy-edged leaves that resembled a mutant cauliflower dipped in a vat of glue. I smiled and nodded, desperately trying to look intelligent.

'*Mandragora officinarum*. Its forked roots look like a human. Remember it. People used to believe that if you pulled it out of the ground it would scream and strike you dead.'

She took me on to stop under a Judas tree. Near to the base of its trunk, white flowers appeared rootless as though hovering above the earth, their stems ethereal, supplying life through the most delicate of passages.

'*Narcissus serotinus*. Their scent is heavenly. Smell one.'

Slowly, I put my nose towards the yellow corona of one of the flowers and pulled back in a wave of nausea. Joy, laughing, dragged me to the rear of the house, leaping steps, charging along the narrow gravel paths of the terraces, calling out the names of plants, her questions never-ending. 'The botanical, Jane?'

Was she really mad, this old woman who had the energy of a Greek god, drank like Oliver Reed and smoked like a chimney? I was less than half her age and couldn't keep up. As if in a nightmare, I ducked under branches of myrtle and pomegranate trees, scraping my legs against the sticky leaves of cistus, lavender and rosemary shrubs.

'*Homalocladium platycladum.*' Joy caressed a cascade of long tapering leaves. 'I was in an old sea-dog's garden. Snipped a cutting of this while he wasn't looking. Hid it in my bag. When I left he handed me another cutting. Said it was in case the one I'd stolen didn't grow. Who said crime doesn't pay?'

I smiled weakly, took a deep breath and followed her to overlook three sunken compost beds above a narrow track and a steep drop to the Mesoghia plain. She pointed into the first pit, which was covered with eggshells and dog hair. 'I pee into it to spark the rotting process. Mid-pee, trousers down, Charles once drove past and . . .'

A truck resembling a fuel tanker lumbered up the track, knocking branches, its wheels teetering over the edge. 'The honey wagon,' Joy said, and flagged it down. The driver leaned out of the cab's window and exchanged bullets of Greek with Joy, his hairy arm gesticulating, a tattoo of barbed wire around his wrist. Finally, Joy lit a cigarette and came back to me as the truck trundled up the hillside towards Charles's house.

'Honey?' I said, baffled.

'The septic-tank lorry. Ours will need emptying in a month or two. I got him down a euro or two. He'll be back. Tool shed next. Nearly done.'

Joy pushed me back up towards the house. In its shadows was a small shed. She removed a plank of wood slotted through a rusting metal clasp and heaved open the door, hinges groaning in protest.

37

Inside, broken spiders' webs covered a rusting scythe and a pair of old skis. Heaped on leaning shelves were baskets of stones, driftwood, rope, wire and old secateurs without their springs. She lifted a burlap sack from an electric shredder on wheels. 'Come asphodel time, Jane, this will be your friend—as a rifle to an infantryman.'

I stared bemusedly at two words painted above copper rods hanging from a nail. 'For Dowsing.' Outside stood regimental rows of old watering cans, their metal spouts pointing in the same direction.

Joy marched me back up the path to the hilltop. Split logs edged along the path had ants tumbling out of their dry interiors. Above the nursery and its border of kermes oak and buckthorn we came to a cemetery for dead pets. Stones and marble slabs marked their resting places. Wizard launched himself from Joy's shoulder and swooped over a lumbering tortoise.

'Stop bullying, Wizard!'

Further up the hill, picking our way through balls of wild thyme and teucrium, we stopped at a rusting racing bicycle, its back wheel half buried in the stony ground, front wheel supported over a boulder. Tenderly, Joy stroked the faded red tape around the handlebars. My head throbbed. Faintly, I heard the words, 'My husband's bike ... long dead now. Sculpture to his memory ... blast ... can't remember his name ... bugger.' She left the bike to stride through a river of carob and olive trees. 'Christos!' she suddenly cried, turning to face me in triumph. 'He was Christos.'

The gravel in her voice had softened. She stopped to peer into my eyes. 'Are you all right,

Jane?'

'No,' I groaned. 'Knackered, to be honest.'

She laughed and picked a brown seed pod from a carob tree. 'Suck on this. Gives you energy.' At the top of the hill, we reached a round stone cistern. 'This is our lifeblood. Each week water is pumped up here from a licensed well at the bottom of the hill.' She put out the palm of her hand as if taking an oath. 'We, Jane, are water-wise. Underground aquifers are drying up. And why? Rising population, tourism, drought, and . . .' She shook her head in disgust, spitting out her next words. 'Illegal boreholes. Used to soak ridiculous lawns and fill swimming pools.' She jabbed a finger down the hillside. 'The Neanderthal has one. I'm convinced that he's—'

I lifted my arm in the air to get her attention, my mind tottering, the need to sleep overwhelming.

'Joy, could you please take me—'

Joy waved a hand to quieten me and carried on talking. In an act of desperation, I reached for the trunk of the nearest olive tree and clutched my belly, as if in pain.

'Oh dear, Jane,' Joy said, walking to me. 'You should have said something. Let's get you inside.' She guided me down a path, its width no more than a rake's head. At the path's end I could see a small stone outbuilding perched drunkenly on the hillside. The walls were washed a faded blue and its shutters blistered by sunlight. An umbrella pine threatened the roof, branches pushing beneath orange tiles.

'OK?' Joy peered at me. 'One last circuit. You're living on the wild side. Has its own beauty.'

She led me around mounds of sage and unkempt

39

phlomis, their old seed heads black and upstanding, then suddenly stopped.

'*Urginea maritima*. Big as babies' heads.' She pointed at a patch of large bulbs poking out of the ground. 'People used to hang them over their doors as protection against evil spirits. Just one-point-five grams of a pulverized bulb is lethal to adults.'

Finally, beside a fallen wheelbarrow bursting with straggly herbs, she took my arm and guided me onto the outhouse's stone veranda. I dropped into a wooden chair, the slats cracking underneath me like gunshot. A black cat leapt off the veranda's awning and charged around a shrub resembling a bunch of barbed wire.

'That's Orwell,' said Joy, and turned on a tap above a marble trough balanced on an old fridge. 'Spits out his worm pills. Stupid cat.'

Brown water trickled, gurgled, then spattered out in a rush, gradually clearing. Joy picked out a glass from the trough, filled it and handed it to me.

'Make you feel better.' She wrestled with the handle of the wooden door, a dinner fork twisted in a hole once occupied by a lock. 'Can be a bit sticky.' She barged her shoulder against the door, opening it with a grunt.

'I'll get your rucksack. Make yourself at home.'

The sign of a cross had been roughly made out in soot above the door. Wondering what evil spirits it was warding off, I ducked my head into a murky yellow twilight and looked beneath a small barred window. What I saw had me gasping in horror.

# 3

# Alcatraz

Joy arrived back with my rucksack and found me staring at a large, stuffed lion.

'Ah, I should have warned you about Zeus. He was in our zoo.'

'Zo-zoo?' I stuttered, gaping into the lion's glass eyes.

'We ran a small zoo from our home in the Peloponnese. Christos played with him—once too often. Zeus knocked him over. Left Christos injured.' Joy paused. 'Couldn't manage the work on my own. We packed up. Kept Wizard, sold the rest of the animals. Zeus had to be put down.' She stroked the lion's mane, her voice barely a whisper. 'Christos adored him so much, I had him stuffed.'

I faintly registered Joy's story as being both bizarre and sad. I tried to form a word or two of sympathy, but ended up raising a tired hand in acknowledgment. Joy continued to stroke the lion, muttering to herself. I pushed apart bead curtains hanging to the left of the door and revealed a tiny cubicle. An old shower head and its cracked rubber cable were coiled around the taps of a small sink. A large yellow plastic bowl rested against a toilet minus its seat. A fly buzzed around one of Eleni's paintings hung alongside the cistern.

'Work tomorrow. Nine a.m. sharp. You've got food,' Joy shouted, and left, the door rattling in its frame. A second later the dinner fork clattered to the floor.

I opened the door of a small fridge decorated with gaudy magnets of the Acropolis. A bottle of retsina, milk, a tub of feta cheese and butter nestled inside its door. Next to the fridge were a few dilapidated cupboards, one door hanging off its hinge. On a tiny worktop an encrusted kettle, a bread stick and a jar of coffee and Marmite were pushed against a camping stove. I put the books that Joy had lent me onto a shelf beside a radio, then delved into my rucksack for my pyjamas and, finally, crawled into bed. The thin mattress provided little cushioning against the narrow wooden slats of the bedstead. It didn't matter. I could have slept on a bed of rocks. I was slipping into merciful sleep when suddenly the crashing sound of machinery blasted through the room. The camping stove vibrated and rattled.

Dogs barked. I stared at Zeus. He glared at me. I pulled the sheets over my head.

*       *       *

'Wizard's lost his mind.'

The macaw hung upside down from the top shelf of the bookcase. The wooden cross was in his beak and his wings were outstretched. Joy offered him a walnut. 'Quite insane. It's that racket. I've called Spiros. Did it keep you awake?'

'No. I was out like a light.' I gave Joy a quick smile, wondering what she would have said if I had said yes.

On waking I had climbed the hilltop—the only place where my mobile received reception—and called my parents. After telling them about my first night, they had laughed, told me that Joy sounded 'a character' and in no uncertain terms told me to 'stick it out'. I hadn't told them of my drab outhouse compared with my living conditions

44

in London or their home in Derby. Instead I called a friend, Leslie, to tell her the truth. She'd been both brutal and sincere in her reply. 'Don't be a loser all your life. Come on, you can do it.' I felt that my walk to the house that morning was like that of the condemned walking to the gallows.

Joy picked up a cutting that lay on the writing table and, along with the walnut, put it in my hand. 'I want a report. Genus. Species and natural habitat. Next week, plant ID test.' She put on her hat. A sprig of rosemary fell to the floor.

'Work,' she said, raising an arm. 'Come on. Spiros will let himself in.'

\*      \*      \*

'*Iris germanica*, Jane.'

We stood at the top of the phrygana, looking over swathes of the plant, its brown, toppling growth a witness to seven months without rain. 'The ancients used its aromatic oil to disguise body odour.' She knelt down to pull out dead leaves. 'All this stuff needs removing. Leaf tips need topping. I want them perky.' She pointed to a mature yucca and went to pat one of its swollen trunk bases. 'Elephants' feet. *Yucca elephantipes*. The botanical, Jane. Remember.' She stood up to light a cigarette then grabbed at the brown leaves hanging below the new growth. 'Take this out. Each and every—'

The rumble of engines and squealing machinery sounded from behind the Neanderthal's fence.

'Bloody man.' Joy waved a fist at his gates, picked up Winston and stomped back to the house, shouting over her shoulder. 'You know where the tool shed is.'

I stuffed iPod plugs into my ears, turned up the sound and got to work. By lunchtime my arms were covered in scratches from the sharp tips of the yucca leaves, their edges like serrated blades. After eating, I lay beneath an olive tree and gazed into its canopy. I half-closed my eyes and slowly lost all sense of perspective. With each flurry of wind the leaves on the olive's branches appeared to ripple and swirl like darting silver fish in the deep blue sea. In this rapt state, the shout close to my head was shocking.

'Jane! You're not on holiday!'

Joy bent over me, her eyes blind behind her red plastic sunglasses, a slab of blueberry lipstick over her tightened mouth. 'How can we communicate? We're five acres. I've been shouting for you for five minutes.' She yanked out my earplugs and pointed to the Neanderthal's fence. 'It's bad enough with that racket. I don't want you wearing them. Now, the drill is I go shopping. You tell me what food and drink you want. I'll leave your bag outside my front door with the receipt. Do you want treats?'

\*     \*     \*

The week dragged on. To stop myself thinking about home, I worked hard, finding some comfort in the physical exercise. At break times, I would take a mug of coffee and acquaint myself with the garden. It had a grand, somewhat ravished air, like a dilapidated stately home, its fixtures sparse and frayed, covered in a fine shroud of dust.

Despite Joy's order, I wore one earplug looped under my T-shirt, discreetly hidden. It wasn't as if she was around much to spot it anyway; she only

46

stopped occasionally to speak to me about shopping. Each day she went to the village to collect her mail from the post office and if I needed anything I made sure to hand her a written list, as the first expedition had resulted in her bringing back masses of Marmite, which I hated, and two boxes of halva, a semolina-based pudding that glued my teeth together. Then, unexpectedly, the bag arrived one day containing a bottle of ouzo together with a note scrawled in red ink: 'It will make you work harder.'

At some point each day, I would catch Joy peering at me from behind the trunks of olive trees or from inside the walled garden. Her feathered hat would bob above the stone parapet, occasionally stopping to rise slowly and reveal a pair of watching eyes. If I lifted a tentative hand in greeting the eyes and hat would quickly vanish. I would then redouble my efforts on a seemingly never-ending task, like Sisyphus waiting for the boulder to roll back down the hill only to push it back up again.

'It's like basic training in the Navy,' I told Zeus that evening as I frantically stirred chopped garlic around a scratched pan. Its main cooking ring was highly sensitive—food either burned to a crisp or barely cooked at all. 'Breaking you down to build you up. Assault courses, being shouted at. Trapped.' A breeze from the open window ruffled the lion's mane. A candle blew out. I looked at the metal bars in the dim light of the overhead light bulb. I'd once visited the penal island of Alcatraz while on holiday. In some ways its cells were preferable to mine. At least they had people to talk to.

Each morning I mentally prepared myself to face a nine-hour stint of hard labour, the crash and boom of machinery ever present. Joy, convinced the Neanderthal was building a swimming pool, would grab my shopping list and stomp around the garden, flapping her arms in disgust.

'Hot summers. Water shortages. What does he do? Chop down trees that saw Plato in nappies and put down lawns. Sprinklers on the go most of the year. He must have a borehole, Jane.'

On Friday morning I paused in my work and took out my earplug. The noise of machinery had stopped to be replaced by the soft purr of a car engine. A black Porsche Carrera had stopped on the track, the Neanderthal's gates slowly closing behind it. The driver stared at me through the open car window, his blond hair waxed and uplifted like the stiff peaks of a meringue. Classical music played from the car stereo.

'You the old bird's new gardener?' he shouted, and then smiled as if he already knew the answer.

I raised my hand, quickly dropping it as he sped off, dust-balls billowing down the track.

Before the gates closed on his pacing guard dogs, I peered inside at the terraced lawns, dotted with sprinklers and surrounded by pseudo-classical columns. The arm of a JCB digger poked out from behind the furthest corner of the house, a pile of rubble beneath it.

\*       \*       \*

That evening, I sat on Alcatraz's veranda sipping ouzo. For a brief moment, between the setting of the sun and the deepening of twilight, it was as if a

48

spray of golden dust had fallen from the heavens. Entranced, I watched the yellow blooms of sternbergia pulse like that of effervescent light bulbs, the rocks near to them glowing. Then, quickly, darkness unfolded its heavy cloth and all was rendered flat and black.

I tipped my chair back against the wall, pooled in the soft light from the hanging lanterns. The ache in my back and the cuts on my arms and hands had been a large sacrifice for a 'perky' phrygana. And I'd yet to start work on the hilltop. I tried to study a plant book, but instead reached for my personal diary and scrawled:

*I don't see anybody apart from my 'keeper', Joy. I miss everything, even Oxford Street on a wet Saturday afternoon. I've started talking to a stuffed lion and am wearing the same clothes every day. My fingernails are dirty. I'm going feral and* Strictly Come Dancing *starts soon.*

I chewed on the end of my pen, drawn to the airport, its lights twinkling in the distance. I let my mind wander back to the moment when Joy had first taken me around the garden. Standing over the compost beds, she'd thrown out an arm towards the Attiki Odos highway slicing through the olive and vine groves. 'They say it's progress.' She had pointed to where the telephone wires looped along the track to Charles's house. 'Put up last year. Bloody awful.' For a brief moment she'd looked vulnerable, slim as a cigarillo and as easy to break in two.

I shook my head and came back to reality. A pile

49

of dirty clothes and dishes needed to be washed. As I pummelled the clothes the wind picked up and slapped the pine branches against the windows. Goose bumps pricked my arms and the cold lather stung my scratched hands and wrists. After hand-wringing the clothes I hung them over a rope tied between two olive trees, then went inside to turn on the rattling boiler and prepare myself to shower. There was Joy's report to finish. Nine hundred species of salvia to learn. A plant ID test.

I picked up the cutting that Joy had given me to report on. Four large seed pods, separated by the most delicate of skins, nestled within a much larger pod. It was strange how a pot of the plant had turned up with my first food bag. The name of the genus and species on the label was smudged but partly legible. I ploughed through Joy's books to discover its full name—*Pancratium maritimum.*

The Greeks call it 'Lily of the Sea', its haunt the sandy shores of the Mediterranean. Archaeological digs had discovered paintings of it on Minoan walls in Crete and on houses preserved in volcanic ash at Thera. To the ancients, the Lily of the Sea had celebrated beauty, fulfilling their desire for symmetry and harmony.

There was a scrabbling at the door. I opened it to find Winston, teddy hanging from his jaw. He sat down and glared at me through his brown eye, the other weeping from its blue bloom.

'WIN–STON!' Joy's voice scythed through the wind, the two syllables landing like sledgehammers, pinning his ears back. He scampered away, teddy still clamped between his decrepit teeth.

I undressed and scurried over the cool stone floor to enter the tiny cubicle, stand in the plastic bowl and turn on the tap. A meagre trickle of water dripped from the shower rose. I removed it from its perch and beat it against my hand. Some rust fell away and a half-satisfying sprinkle emerged. I showered quickly in the tepid water. After drying and dressing I flicked through the glossy pages of the airport leaflet, the number of the British Airways ticket desk etched in my memory.

\*　　　\*　　　\*

Over the weekend, autumn whispered and tiptoed over the hilltop. Pirouettes of chilly wind danced through the trees and ruffled the feathers of surprised sparrows. Clouds with smudgy, grey undercarriages scraped the top of Mount Hymettos. There was a quiver of expectancy in the air, a shuffling, anxious wait.

My mood had dipped further with the change in weather. Saturday and Sunday had been a sluggish affair, only relieved by being able to watch DVDs on my laptop. On Sunday I had been so overcome with boredom and loneliness that I'd written in my diary: 'Giving it one more week, nobody should endure this.' I'd then left the garden, bent on walking to the village. But the walk along the dusty road packed with speeding traffic had me turning back in fear for my life. I'd returned with the intention of watching yet another episode of *Fawlty Towers*, but was distracted by finding a copy of Dylan Thomas's *Under Milk Wood* beneath the fridge. I'd read a few of its pages to Zeus,

51

acquainted myself with Captain Cat, when suddenly I'd felt my heart slip.

'Starless and Bible black'. A strip of panic curdled in my stomach. In my head was desolation. I put down the book then picked up my diary and wrote:

*Sunday, Bloody Sunday. Have got a devilish imp on one shoulder and an angel on the other, tearing me in two. He's screaming in my ear, 'Run away, go home. Leave while you can!' The angel's fluttering her wings and mute.*

Early Monday morning I woke to nothing but bleak thoughts. I went to the house to push my report underneath Joy's door then trudged up the hillside to work. Storm clouds burgeoned overhead. Thunder rumbled and lightning speared and flashed in the distance. I ripped out dead leaves, pushed barrows up and down the hill, joined Sisyphus in purgatory. Mount Hymettos, which lay menacingly heavy and black, seemed to draw nearer with the darkening sky.

I heard Winston yapping and saw Joy scrambling towards me up the hillside. I took the shopping list out of my pocket. The leaflet with the airline numbers fell out with it. I hastily picked it up and stuffed it back in my pocket as she arrived.

'Look!' She grabbed my list and raised her hands to the sky. A few fat raindrops fell and plopped on the cracked ground. 'Rain!' She grabbed my shoulders. 'Demetri just phoned. It's pelting it down in Kiphissia. Rain, Jane!' she cried out, laughing.

When she calmed down and left me I felt an intense anger. Why hadn't she said something complimentary about my work on the phrygana, or asked about my weekend? What kind of a deranged woman was she?

After she'd disappeared I went back inside Alcatraz to pick up my mobile, then I ran up to the hilltop and tapped in the number for British Airways. The connection was made but the phone bleeped forever. I switched off with a kick at the stone cistern then slumped against it and watched the storm clouds drift away. My head lowered, I limped back down the hillside.

'*Ya su*, Jane. Is great to see you.'

I looked up. There was Pavlos, all sparkling eyes and warmth, his arms extended. Then Joy appeared with Wizard on her shoulder. She carried a tray bearing three long glasses of ouzo, tinkling with ice.

'Tea break,' she shouted.

We sat down on boulders. Joy stared up at the now clear sky, in mourning for the rain. She then lowered her head and surveyed my work on the hilltop, her lips twitching into a small smile.

'Good job, Jane. Well done.'

She'd spoken in a businesslike voice, but I nearly wept, such was the warm rush that ran through me. Joy sipped her ouzo, then took out a tube of aloe vera cream from her pocket and handed it to me. 'Soothe your injuries. Plant ID test tomorrow, don't forget. Finish the hill by the end of this week and we can get on with planting. Rain will fall on Helikion soon.'

Wizard squawked, pushed off her arm and joined a gust of wind to soar towards the hilltop.

I decided I would give Helikion a month.

\* \* \*

'Should we wake her?'

'On Ohi Day? Yes!'

I sat up with a start. Demetri crouched in the doorway, while Vassili sat cross-legged beside Zeus, chuckling like a jolly Buddha. It was 10 o'clock the next morning.

'Joy is waiting, Jane.'

I'd slept through my alarm clock. 'Oh God!' I stared at them in horror. Joy was going to kill me. 'Am I in trouble?' They giggled, leaving me bewildered.

'It's Ohi Day, Jane,' Vassili said. 'Greek national holiday celebrating the balls of the dictator Metaxas. Balls made of steel, darlings.'

'Oh, thank God,' I gasped.

They went outside while I quickly dressed, then herded me back to the house. The sun shone between pillows of white clouds, the wind soft and cool.

Vassili grinned and punched the air with his fists, hopping around a spurge olive.

'*Ohi* means "no" in Greek,' Demetri said, reining in his long limbs to avoid the prickly pears. 'Metaxas warned Mussolini not to march his Fascist skinheads through Greece. Then he crushed them.'

Vassili urged me into the house. 'So Hitler invaded us. Flew a swastika over the Acropolis.' Both shuddered in mock horror then waved me inside.

'Three and a half years of miserable occupation.

54

An excuse for a party, *ne!*'

On the veranda Joy and Pavlos sat chatting on a spread of oriental cushions, a hookah and tall glasses of ouzo between them. A bird dropping splattered close to my feet.

'Wizard. Bad boy!' Joy glanced up at the rafters then gestured at the hookah. 'Jane, have a puff on this.' Joy held the pipe up to me and I stared at its covering of worn, purple velvet then at the mouthpiece, blueberry lipstick smudged around its rim. I hesitated then took the plunge. The bowl of liquid bubbled as I drew in the smoke from the molasses. I'd tried hookahs before but wasn't prepared for its bitter taste, which caused me to cough and splutter. For one weird moment I thought I'd been deceived. It was punishment after all. She was poisoning me for sleeping in and had used Vassili and Demetri as decoys.

'Quite a kick, isn't there? Special stuff. Spiros gets it for me. Knows someone who knows someone, if you know what I mean.'

Gradually my coughing subsided and I shook away my paranoia.

'Right. Let's talk about plants.'

She led me into the house and around her desk.

'Gree ce is the birthplace of medicine and botany, Jane. Aristotle. Theophrastus. Dioscorides. There are six thousand plant species in Greece, ten per cent of which are unique—found nowhere else on earth.' She opened a scrapbook and flicked through it. A pressed flower fell out from between its pages. 'Ah, that's *Conium maculatum.*' She leaned over her desk to rub the bronze inlay mask of Socrates. 'Hemlock. Poisoned him to death.' She picked up the flattened brown leaf, popped it back into the book and then put an olive leaf on the slide of the microscope. 'What do you see?'

'A bunch of tiny raised umbrellas. Or jellyfish . . . there's breathing pores. Er, stomata isn't it, used for the exchange of gases?' I waited for her reaction. There was none. Instead she picked up a book with Sellotaped binding and handed it to me. 'Hellmut Baumann. *Greek Wild Flowers and Plant Lore*. Cults. Myths. Medicine and the arts. Borrow it. Your world is going to be so much more than planting depths and learning when and how to prune, Jane.'

'I thought I was having a plant ID test,' I said tentatively, and followed Joy back to the veranda.

'Another time. I forgot it was Ohi Day. We don't work on Ohi Day. And tomorrow you're coming with me to the village.'

Wizard dropped from the rafters and landed on the stone seat with a gentle squawk. Joy stroked his throat and then sank down beside me. Crossing her legs and taking the hookah pipe from Vassili, she drew in a deep breath and fired out a thin stream of smoke. 'And there's no need to sign out books from the library now. You're on my list of trustworthies.'

\*     \*     \*

The next day wispy clouds gently scuffed across a blue sky, the sun bright and warm.

'The Greeks call this period the little summer of St Demetrios,' Joy said, bundling me to the Jeep. 'Careful, your door doesn't open sometimes. Lock's buggered.' She drove without her spectacles. 'I'm not distracted if I can't recognize

56

people.'

Memories of my first car journey with Joy came flooding back and I gripped the door handle. As we bounced slowly down the bumpy track Joy momentarily abandoned the steering wheel for a small atomizer to spray her neck and wrists. The Jeep again veered into Spanish broom, branches crashing over its metal sides. 'The rattle of *Spartium junceum*, Jane. The ancients used it to make sails. Dioscorides said its seeds drunk with melicrat doth purge upward with violence.'

With that she braked hard at the bottom of the driveway then let the Jeep roll to the edge of the road. Traffic hurtled from right and left. A truck with a huge trailer honked its horn as we ventured slowly over the tarmac. 'You have to show them you mean it. Anything coming?'

'Yes!' I screamed.

My head flew back as Joy flat-footed the throttle. The Jeep shot across the road and swerved in parallel with the Armco railing but only inches from it. A car overtook us, the driver shaking his fist at Joy.

'Somebody waving at me in that car. Do I know them? They do drive so fast nowadays,' she added. 'Can you pass my cigarettes?'

We sped past a hedge of bamboo and tall grasses. Huge plumes of dusty old seed heads swayed over the road. Graffiti-covered walls, closed gates and long driveways led up to other hilltops. On the opposite side of the road were sloping, open olive groves and a B&B that looked like tumbleweed ought to be blowing around it. Joy flung her arm across me and pointed at a clump of uninspiring leaves. 'Winter horta, Jane. Wild greens. Old and

57

young grub up the rosettes. The—'

I let out a yelp of horror. Tyres screeched. The Jeep shuddered to a stop. I opened my eyes to find Joy nodding at traffic lights on red.

'They're often wrong,' she said. 'You're as much in danger on green as red. But it makes it lively. Nobody falls asleep ... can you smell burning rubber?'

I was about to ask what she meant when there was a knock at my side window. A thin short man held out his hand with a pained smile, a few pointed teeth poking through red gums. One shirt sleeve hung limp beneath a withered arm. Joy delved into her basket for her purse. 'Give him this.'

The lights changed. Joy waited until I handed the man his gift. A chorus of horns hooted behind in protest. We turned into a road and passed a row of small shops. Outside were newspaper racks and inside, piled against windows, were jars of food and knitted dolls, their small heads poking out of large embroidered dresses.

We crawled around a small piazza. Tavernas, cafés and bars huddled underneath a church with a bell tower. Stray cats snoozed under tables, where old knotty men sat with worry beads wrapped around their knuckles, waiting their turn to toss dice into pitted backgammon boards. A young man plucked on a guitar in front of a tree festooned with bougainvillea.

'Bugger. Usually a space.' Joy drove out of the piazza and past a small police station where two policemen sat on plastic chairs. They turned their heads slowly and from behind mirrored sunglasses watched Joy pass by. One officer touched the arm of the other and made a comment, bringing a laugh out of him.

'Did they wave at me?' asked Joy. 'They usually do. They stop me at least once a month. It helps fill their quota. They tell me to wear my specs and that's another point in the bag for them. I've got off so many times it's not worth counting.' Five minutes later, we were back at the piazza. 'Ah! Got one, Jane.'

Joy turned the wheel and drove into a space. 'Oh dear.' She looked down through the window, noting the few inches clearance from the other vehicle. 'Now, specs here would have been useful. This is not going to be easy.'

She started to reverse but turned the wheel too soon, the front nearside wing threatening to scrape the side of the adjacent car.

'Stop,' I cried.

'Good. Keep talking.' Joy slowly went forward, then reversed but found the situation no better. She tried again. And again.

'I'll get out. I'll guide you.'

'No! I can't see you at the back.'

Traffic backed up behind us. An old man wearing carpet slippers hobbled over towards Joy shouting and miming the steering of a car wheel. A woman, with two small children, leaned on a balcony waving her instructions. The crowd grew. Joy's name was shouted out. Finally, the young man, minus guitar, pushed his way through the throng. 'Joy. I do it.' He took her keys with a smile, escorted her from the Jeep and then jumped inside. I was still in the passenger seat, slumped as far down as possible, wishing the crowd would go away.

The young man parked and looked down at me with a grin. '*Ya sas.* You must be another of Joy's victims.' I looked obliquely at him. His dark eyes had a twinkle in them.

'Don't worry. She's a great lady. You have a good time there, yes?'

'Hi, yes, just about,' I said, blushing. He was nice and good-looking. I slowly lifted myself upright to open the door. I made a mental note to slap on a bit of make-up next time I visited the village.

'They know me,' Joy said unnecessarily as we walked away to ragged applause.

We entered a winding street and went into a small, wood-panelled shop. Burlap sacks brimming with pistachio nuts and dried beans leaned against a counter full of cheese and olives. Joy marched behind it and grabbed two ouzo bottles. 'Forgot to tell Pavlos. Remind me, Jane. We need supplies.'

Tucked behind a fridge crammed with tubs of feta and yoghurt was a small tobacco counter, on its top a burning incense stick, a set of worry beads and a packet of opened mints.

Joy rapped her knuckles on the counter. The shopkeeper appeared, his big head darting forward like a turtle coming out of its shell. Behind him packets of cigarettes were haphazardly stacked in a display cabinet that reached to the ceiling.

'Ah! Joy. *Tee kanees?*' He brought out a litter picker from under the counter, checked its mechanism, then pointed the pincers at the top shelf. He slowly brought down three packs of Silk Cut and released them onto the counter. 'Booooom!' he cried, and flung his arms outwards, the picker knocking over a stack of boxed matches.

'He's trying to give up,' Joy whispered in

explanation.

After helping him pick up the matches and then paying for our goods, we walked down a cobbled alleyway that led onto a road crowded with market stalls.

I heard a shout and turned around to see the shopkeeper hurrying towards us, Joy's packets of Silk Cut and bottles of ouzo in his hands. She took them from him, apologizing for her forgetfulness.

*     *     *

'COME IN! NO BELLS OR KNOCKING, JANE! COME IN ANY TIME!'

Joy sat behind her desk, arms folded. Sunlight flashed off the sunken and chipped marble floor, brushed across her shoulders and fashioned her ear tips a devilish red. Blue veils of cigarette smoke drifted to the ceiling.

'Sit.' She pointed to the straight-backed chair opposite the desk where I was to take my plant ID test.

On the chair's seat was a gnawed stubby pencil and a sheet of lined A4 paper, a hastily scrawled note in its top corner: 'it's not the dog in the fight but how much fight is in the dog'. Ten plant cuttings were placed across the back of the desk. I glanced at Winston dozing on his stool. A village shoe poked from between his paws.

'Five minutes to state their genus and species.' Joy picked up a large stopwatch and pressed a button. She stood up and paced behind my chair. Flip-flops methodically slapped on marble.

Suddenly she dropped her head close to mine, causing me to jump in my seat. 'Don't just twirl them around, Jane. Inhale their scent. Are they sweet? Vile? Snap them, break them. Is the sap like coconut milk? Is it sticky? Are the leaves hairy? Smooth? How do they face each other on the stem? Are they lovers facing each other or do they take turns to climb up to its top? Or do they swirl around the stem like a whirling dervish?' Joy rocked the chair for emphasis and then put her lips to my ear, lowering her voice to a cracked whisper. 'Or does the flower slip from your grip like silk . . . or crumble to ash as would an insect's wing?' She raised her voice. 'A botanist is a detective, Jane.'

The minutes passed. 'Time's up.' Joy picked up a large ornate magnifying glass from the desk, took the paper from my hands, held it at arm's length and squinted. Nervously stroking Titan's head, I scanned the objects on top of Joy's desk: the Tiffany lamp, its stained glass shade depicting dragon flies, the rusty microscope, the stack of botanical magazines, a small statue of a Buddha with the metal cap off a champagne cork blu-tacked to its head, a Victoria and Albert Museum pocket diary, a photograph of a young attractive woman on its front cover. Judging by the hairstyle and clothes she wore it was taken in the fifties.

I looked at Joy and then at the model's face. The same hooded eyes. Nose. Pitch of the head. Defiant.

'Nineteen-sixty, Jane,' Joy murmured, her eye still examining my paper. 'Photographer was a lecherous old goat. Didn't model for long. Met my first husband at a wholly inappropriate party . . . had a baby or two.'

I surreptitiously looked around the room for any framed photographs of Joy's loved ones or holiday snaps, searching for any clue as to what might have made her. But there were none. Suddenly she slammed the magnifying glass down, screwed the paper into a ball and tossed it under the desk with a sigh of disapproval.

'Ten out of ten *if* you count the common names. Didn't ask for them.' I stood up to go, dejected.

'Only one botanical name correct.' Joy impatiently waved me to sit down. 'How did you know the name of *Sarcopoterium spinosum* but not the others?' She picked up a tangled mess of what looked like dead twigs.

'It grows around Jerusalem and is said to have been Christ's crown of thorns . . . oh, and I read that if boiled in urine it's a cure for black eyes,' I said, and shrugged. 'It caught my interest.'

'Pliny?' She stared intently at me. 'Your application stated that your aim was to apply for the Kew Diploma?'

I nodded.

She slammed her hands on the edge of the desk. 'Why do you think I've banged on about botanical names, Jane? You'll need them for Kew. Sometimes horticulture is a hard slog.' She reached behind the Tiffany lamp and handed me a paperback book, its yellowing pages cut unevenly at the edges. 'Fortunately for most of the time it isn't. Read that. You and I can't do rote. It's history,' she stressed. 'Poetry. Art. Medicine and poisons. That's what fires our blood.' While she talked I looked at the book's cover. A faded red wine stain covered an etching of a horned devil cavorting with an angel in a flowering shrub. I looked forward to reading it.

'Now. Make yourself comfortable. I've made us

63

some lentil soup. Good for digging. Vinegar, olive oil, onions, garlic. Lentils. Looks like frog spawn but tastes delicious.'

An hour later, after polishing off a large saucepan of soup between us, Joy plonked down a small teapot, its ceramic spout poking out of a yellow knitted cosy. A piece of material roughly sown around its hem had 'Mum' scrawled across it in indelible ink.

'PG Tips. Thought you'd like a taste of home.'

Wizard rocked on his swing, the metal squeak joining our satisfied slurps. Suddenly the crash and boom of machinery shook the windowpanes. Wizard screeched, flew out of his cage and whirled around the room like a banshee.

'Bloody Neanderthal!' Joy shouted, and shot up from her seat, knocking her cup over.

I remembered the man in the black Porsche. 'Joy,' I said conspiratorially, making her sit down, hoping she would quieten down and mull over the information I was about to give her. 'I met the Neanderthal coming out of his gates. I saw rubble and a JCB digger at the back of his—'

'So I was right.' She cut me off. 'He's digging out a pool, Jane. Come on. Show me.'

She nearly pulled my arm from its socket in a rush to get me out of the house and down the phrygana. It reminded me of the scene in *Rebecca* when she is propelled towards her intended suicide by a determined Mrs Danvers.

Once we reached the Neanderthal's property Joy paced up and down the fence trying to get a glimpse of the digger, staring fiercely, ignoring the guard dogs clawing at the bars. I jumped away from the snarling beasts and took the role of an

64

uncomfortable onlooker. 'Joy, the Neanderthal might come out. We should go,' I whined, always the one not to make a fuss. I just couldn't understand what purpose this was fulfilling. After all, many people in Attica had their own pools. But then I wasn't Joy, a woman who would peer through a fence protected by snarling beasts rather than finish a nice cup of tea.

Back at the house, Joy snapped back her marigolds and let loose over a meagre sink of dishwater. 'He's a criminal. Backhanders here, there and everywhere to hell!'

I was startled by her intensity. She must have seen my shock as she softened, took a breath and spoke deliberately.

'You could get into his garden, Jane. Take pictures. It won't be legal, whatever he's doing. Bound to be a borehole. Would you do that? Not for me, but the world?'

# 4

# Off-beat Smelling Salts

'CARRION FLOWER'

*Stapelia
variegata
Asclepiadaceae*

The next morning Joy greeted me with a fixed smile. 'Now then. Go to the terraces. Write down the names of all plants without marble signs. We need to paint them up. Come to the house afterwards.' She handed me a clipboard and pen. I was mystified. All the plants on the terraces had signs; most were cracked and the ink was faded, but still legible.

Three hours later, I found Joy at her desk, drinking tea and reading a botanical magazine. Jazz music played on the gramophone, competing with the sound of the Neanderthal's machinery. Wizard hung from the top shelf of the bookcase, the wooden cross clenched between his talons. I handed her the clipboard, saying that all the signs had been removed.

'I know. I took them out. Test of memory, Jane.' She studied my list. 'Genus ... species ... native habitat ... all there. Good, you've changed the family names. *Leguminosae* to *Fabaceae* ... *Cneoraceae* to *Rutaceae* ... et cetera, et cetera. A bore, I know, but we must try and keep up with the times.'

I slumped onto the sofa, grumbling about the name changes. It was confusing: I'd learn a name one minute, the next it would be something different.

'Beware the modern scientist, Jane,' said Joy, her eyes still on the clipboard. 'In the past a simple plant disguised in robes of silk could find itself placed in the flamboyant orchid family. Now they can identify it for what it really is and the taxonomist will move it to its rightful place.' She

69

stood up and pointed at the hard stool at the end of her desk. 'Which is where you should be.'

I got up and quickly went to the stool like a child. The desktop had been cleared of its usual clutter, making way for two pots of black ink, Chinese calligraphy brushes and new marble plaques, the latter ready for scribing. We quietly made our way through the list, slabs of fresh marble decorated with our diligent penmanship. Joy put down her brush when a windowpane vibrated in its frame, joining the rumbling crescendo of earthworks outside.

'Listen to that rubbish. Try and get *them* to build the Parthenon. Do you know that a stone joint was calculated to be exact to one thousandth of a millimetre? It's survived wars, earthquakes, Elgin's pilfering, pollution, Balanos's iron clamps . . .'

She tutted and went to open a bottle of red wine.

'Thank you, Joy,' I said as she handed me a glass. Her eyes held mine—was there just a faint hint of a smile?

Each night I'd found it harder to sleep. The remnants of my last depressive episode, a packet of sleeping pills, had run out. Now, I lay wide awake during much of the night, imagining burglars and sadists queuing up outside the door, ready to batter it down. It wouldn't take much, with the only obstacle a dinner fork and a stuffed lion to frighten them. To distract myself I tried reading postcards friends had sent to me. But that didn't work, so I scribbled in my diary instead:

*Sal's on a wine tour in California. Leslie's*
*met a new bloke and having drinks in Soho.*
*I'm jealous, wide awake and wishing I'd*

*never watched the* Blair Witch Project. *It's so remote out here. God knows what's out there . . . this is crazy . . . what am I doing?*

I must have fallen asleep at the desk. When I next opened my eyes, Spiros was standing beside the bookcase, Wizard on his arm. He went to put the macaw in his cage then lit a cigar, puffing out a stupendous smoke ring.

'I-got-pick-up-grandkids,' he said in stilted English.

'How many now, Spiros?' Joy said, smiling, knowing the answer.

'*Dodeka.*'

'Twelve—and still counting.' Joy gave a cackle.

Spiros raised his eyes, brought out his worry beads from his waistcoat pocket and went out with a sigh.

In a trice early evening was upon us and our work was complete. The wine bottle now empty, our work displayed a marked downturn in quality—ink blots not only on the plaques but also on our faces and hands. Apart from Cootie Williams playing on the gramophone, all was quiet; the Neanderthal's earthworks were over for the day. Ordered to by Joy, I opened another bottle of wine just as our neighbour Rachel stomped into the house, a white pashmina stretched around her vast bosom. 'Good, you're in. Charles has had an email from Tom in America.'

'Tom?' Joy said quizzically, reaching for her newly charged wine glass.

'You know. Marilyn's son.' Rachel tipped back an armchair and smoothed out the rug beneath it. 'Wouldn't mind a wine, Jane. Can see Joy's got her

71

hands full.' She strode to the sofa and sat down between Titan and Joy, its upholstery sinking to the floor and then bunching in the middle. Rachel looked at Wizard cradled in Joy's arm. 'The racket upset him, did it?'

'Hooked his talons between *Hamlet* and *Macbeth* and stayed there until Spiros coaxed him down.' Joy gently stroked Wizard's throat and told Rachel about the digger in the Neanderthal's garden.

'Corrupt as they come,' Rachel said, patting the combs and clips in her hair. I handed her a wine glass.

'Charles has had dealings with him, Jane. Anyway, chin-chin.' She took a large gulp and then her brow furrowed. 'Joy, Tom says he's coming over in the New Year. In the meantime, he wants double glazing put in. He remembers that awful winter we had—'

'What!' Joy shouted, rousing Wizard into a flutter. 'I told Marilyn before she died I don't want double glazing. If he wants to spend money, spend it on the garden.' She paused. 'When's he coming? Did he say?'

'January. He's graduated from Emmanuel, been in America since. Working out where to go next, I suppose.'

Joy stayed in a long silence and then spoke. 'Classics. So Greece would be an ideal place for him to live.'

\*       \*       \*

Early the next morning I was awoken by a sudden rat-a-tat at my door.

'Meet me in the nursery. Ten minutes.'

72

I heard Joy clump away in her wellingtons. Groggy and shivering, I switched on the heater, my breath steaming in the cold air.

The noise from the Neanderthal's machinery once again shattered the silence. With my pyjama-clad arm I wiped condensation from the window and peered outside. A layer of mist hung over the plain. I hurriedly dressed then charged out of the door—only to stop abruptly. A red shag-pile rug, duvet, a thick mattress, blankets, a small fan heater, a new shower rose plus a lamp with a bright orange shade blocked my passage onto the veranda. I stared at them, for a moment in wonder and then in the relief that came with realization. I took each item inside and, smiling, made two mugs of coffee.

On reaching the nursery I nearly dropped them in shock. There was Joy sitting cross-legged outside the potting shed, her head dramatically crowned in an Arabic headscarf. Swathes of patterned cloth swept around her shoulders, gold, ornate tassels dropping to her waist.

'Lawrence of Arabia garb,' she said, noting my open mouth. 'I always wear it in times of trouble. Keeps the brain warm. And so does coffee. Thank you, Jane.' She reached up to take the drink from me.

I was about to thank her for my 'comforts for the troops' when soil suddenly shot out from the lower branches of a nearby lentisc shrub. A few seconds later, Winston emerged to greet me, tail wagging. It was the first time he had welcomed me and I felt all the better for it.

'Thanks so much for the duvet and things,' I said.

'Pardon? Speak up! I've got cotton wool in my

ears. It's that bloody racket.'

I moved closer to Joy and was about to shout my thanks when she stood up and went into the shed. I followed to find her holding aloft a pot, brimming with small pink bulbs. '*Haemanthus coccineus*. Native to South Africa. Fascinating creature. In summer it produces two *huge* fleshy leaves. They die, then up poke thick green stems splattered with red dots. Delightfully sinister. Blood-red bracts and stamens.' She rooted in a bowl full of stones and seashells and picked up an ammonite.

'You've heard of the Fibonacci sequence? Thirteenth-century mathematical theory? Each figure is the sum of the preceding two. Found in leaves, shells.'

Suddenly there was a loud cracking sound like that of gunshot fire. I flinched and spilled coffee over my fleece.

Joy sighed and reached into her pocket. 'Hunting season, Jane. Small birds. Anything that moves. Here.' She handed me two cotton-wool balls.

Throughout the morning we potted up and planted out while Joy talked about books, the sound of earthworks and gunshot all around.

'*Lolita*. Read it a thousand times. Tragic, really. Terrible character. But deliciously erudite. Almost excuses his foul crime. I named one of my dogs Humbert. He's in the graveyard. Pass the ballota, will you? Needs a repot.'

By noon, the noise from the machinery had ceased and the sun had by now gathered enough strength to dry the dewy morning leaves and weave its way through the branch and bamboo awning. Joy took the cotton buds from her ears and went to tap the glass front of what looked like an old barometer, its tapered top strapped to the cane wall with a pair of old tights. 'It's ninety degrees, Jane.'

'Are you sure?' I joined her to look closely at its temperature gauge.

'No. It's a meat thermometer. Present from my first marriage. Snapped its spike off in the first chicken I laid my hands on. Has its uses, though. Let's pretend it is ninety degrees. Have a siesta, Jane. Meet me by the compost beds at three?' She unravelled the end of her headscarf, handed it to me then twirled around until her hair was released and sticking out with static electricity.

After lunch and a restorative nap, I found Joy clipping her fingernails over the first compost bed, Winston flopped at her feet. A broken eggshell wobbled on his head and bits of compost were attached to his fur.

'He fell in,' Joy said. 'Had to haul him out. The sight in his good eye's deteriorating. Follow me.' She had changed out of her gardening clothes and now wore a floral-patterned dress. Shredded twigs and a ball of dog hair from the compost heap had caught in the silver sequins dotted around its hem. Joy talked as we walked to the lower terrace.

'I had visitors at one. Ancient Italian ladies. Wore the highest heels. Anyway, along the way I spotted something quite marvellous.' She stopped to push the nail scissors through her chignon then bent down to hold up the dipping growth of a cistus. Thick, gnarly, succulent 'fingers' popped out of the soil beneath, some bent and crooked, others pointing upwards in a variety of colours— grey, red and green.

'*Stapelia variegata*. Usually sprouts up in the shade of another plant. Now, here's the best bit. Smell this.' Joy cupped a flower head with her hand and raised it towards my nose. 'Well, smell it.'

I gave a delicate sniff and immediately recoiled. Tentatively, I lowered my head once more. 'Phew! It stinks of rotting meat.' Grimacing, I lowered my nose again, quickly withdrew it and took a step backwards. 'That's terrible. Wakes you up, though. It's like off-beat smelling salts.'

Joy grinned and nodded. 'Common name is carrion flower. Such a rich temptation for the flies, its pollinators. But look.' She pointed to a clump of shrivelled 'fingers' that were without the benefit of the shade provided by the cistus. 'Only a few centimetres out in the sun, but the difference between life and death. That's the real horror.'

\*　　　\*　　　\*

Early the next morning, while waiting for Joy, I lay under an olive tree looking up into its tightly woven canopy. I picked a fallen olive leaf off the ground and studied it.

'The "umbrella" shapes that you saw under the microscope are scales.' I looked up to find Joy standing on the stone cistern.

'They trap moist air near the leaf's surface. It slows the rate of water loss. Partly why olives survive in the Med.' She lifted up a long wooden cane from the depths of the cistern. It had scratches etched into its length every ten centimetres. Yet only its tip was dark with the stain of water.

'Not good . . .'

76

A distant gunshot and shouts came from the other side of the hill. Joy tutted and carried on. 'Now. Olives. What did I tell you yesterday?'

'Six hundred or so species. In ancient times chopping one down was punishable by death. The Bible's two Testaments refer to olive oil one hundred and forty times. Kalamata olives are the best ... er ... You've never mastered the art of preserving them.'

'Yes, yes. But why are we here?' A bewildered expression crossed her face.

'Pruning. Olives. You told me to bring the tools. They're here.' The sun flashed down between clouds, causing me to blink. When I looked up again her face was in darkness. 'Pruning,' I emphasized. 'You told me to—'

'Of course I did. Sorry. Things on my mind.' Joy sat on the edge of the cistern and lit a cigarette. She pointed the cane at trees dotted around her. 'These have been neglected. I think Marilyn did them last.' With a slap on her knee, she raised her voice. 'No good for picking, anyhow. Olives fruit on young wood. They need sunlight to stimulate the buds. Talking of stimulus, Pavlos rang. He's popping around with our ouzo.' She dropped down onto a large boulder and hopped to the ground. 'Be careful on that ladder. Its third rung's buggered. Titan. Winston, *ela, ela!*' She strode off, gathering the dogs, one trouser leg caught in the top of a boot, the other hanging loose.

Two hours later, with the machinery noise back again, I proudly surveyed my first pruned olive tree then, after a few finishing snips, placed the ladder underneath the dusty canopy of its neighbour. I was halfway up when I nearly fell off

77

at the loud bang of a shotgun. Twigs, leaves and lead shot clattered onto my cap. I jumped down in alarm and leaned against the tree, furtively peering around its trunk, looking for the shooter.

'Are you all right?' Joy asked as she arrived with two mugs of tea.

'Somebody just took a pot shot at me,' I said, breathing heavily.

Joy stared up the hillside and then down to the Neanderthal's house. Nothing could be heard or seen, apart from a 'V' formation of birds regrouping after being disturbed by the gunshot.

'We'll go back for tea break,' she said quietly, her eyes darkening, still fixed in the direction of the Neanderthal's house.

Back at the house, Joy scuttled to the kitchen and reached into a cardboard box to bring out a bottle of ouzo. 'Thank God for Pavlos, Jane.' She poured out two long glasses, then banged an ice-cube tray on the worktop with such force that sparkling chips fired out of the open window and into the dogs' water bowls. She tipped the rest in the stone sink and battered them with a wooden mallet.

'For years we've kept the boundaries open. Yes, there's the goat fence, but people can easily climb over. It's how Marilyn wanted it. She sold land to friends. All doors were open then. We built the terraces together. Planted together. Of course lives change. Of course they do. The world moves on, even Charles and Rachel lock their doors now.' She dropped her head and narrowed her eyes. 'Then there's him. CCTV cameras, watered lawns, guard dogs, complete lack of consideration for the—' The shrill of the telephone took Joy away and I went onto the veranda with my drink.

Was Joy planting seeds in my mind to galvanize me into action? Thinking the Neanderthal had shot at me, I would seek retribution and climb over the fence, dodging the canine killers to find his illegal borehole and deliver him to the authorities. Perfect, if I was that kind of person—a 'Jane Bond'. But I wasn't.

Joy peered around the doorframe. 'Got to go, Jane. That was my dear friend in the village. Haven't seen her in a while. Suffers from arthritis. I was supposed to be there now.' She looked at her watch and waved a hand in the air. 'Written it down but forgot to check my diary. I'll be staying the night. Feed the animals, will you? Keep them in. No work this afternoon. Rest, and think of a way to stop that infidel next door. Oh—and help yourself to ouzo.'

*     *     *

Late that night, while tucked in bed reading, I heard the sharp snap of twigs outside. Orwell leaped from his bed of rugs and went to sniff at the door. A beam of torchlight swept across the window.

Oh God, Joy was right. The Neanderthal had shot at me and now he was intent on finishing the job. I grabbed the spade beside my bed and tiptoed into the cubicle. Through a gap in the bead curtain I watched in horror as the dinner fork moved in the lock. It slipped. The door slammed open, smashing my 'burglar alarm' of empty bottles. I screamed as shards of glass scattered over my feet.

Joy poked her head inside and stared at the

mess, then up at me. 'Oh dear. Did I frighten you?'

I exhaled a huge sigh, my heart still pounding, and pushed aside the bead curtains. 'Sorry, Joy. Thought it was the . . . the . . . a burglar.'

She peered into my eyes, looked at the spade in my hands, then spoke quickly. 'There's no need for it, Jane. We've never had any burglars. I told you that when you arrived.' She brought out a newspaper from her coat pocket and held it up for me to see, her eyes glinting.

'Had to come back. Couldn't wait to show you this. My friend saved it for me.'

I took the paper from her and read the article which had been neatly outlined in red ink: 'The surrounding coastal areas of Attica, up to seven miles inland, has been contaminated by saltwater, largely the result of illegal boreholes used to fill swimming pools and water gardens wastefully—the level of salts is well above EU standards in many places.'

'You see, Jane. We can't counterattack with guns. But we can get him with this. Do you follow?'

After she'd gone I wrote in my diary:

*Joy's turning into Captain Mainwaring from* Dad's Army. *I'm sure she thinks the Neanderthal shot at me. Even had me believing it for a minute! She's forgotten I'm a gardening intern. Instead I'm a member of the SAS involved in covert operations. What next? My suicide operation?*

I grinned to myself and made a further note: 'Life here was hard and miserable. Now it's hard and exciting.'

# 5
# Jar No. 10

'Bloody man!'

Joy downed her pickaxe and glared at the black Porsche Carrera as it cleared the apex of the approach and raced along the track to screech to a halt outside the Neanderthal's electronic gates. A thumping beat came from its stereo.

'I hate disco.' Joy strode towards the car, a muscle hammering in her cheek.

She had reached the rear end of the Porsche when it revved and sped through the opened gates, leaving her cloaked in dust. She stood perfectly still then, to my horror, made as if to walk through the closing gates.

I shouted out. She stepped back, the guard dogs snarling and pacing a few metres away from her. The gates closed and Joy slowly walked back, her face ashen.

\*       \*       \*

After lunch, I met Joy by the cistern, as ordered. Her basket was hooked over one arm and she held in her hand a black rectangular box.

'An electricity conductivity meter, Jane,' she said, holding up a probe leading from its base. 'It will tell us whether the idiot has a bore or not.' From her basket she brought out a calibrated test tube and handed it to me. 'One hundred millilitres is all we need.'

After measuring out the water we walked to the phrygana in silence. She stopped near the small stone wall bordering the track and brought out a paper cup, teaspoon and a trowel, duly jabbing the

83

latter into the ground. With a studious frown, she carefully put three teaspoons of subsoil into the paper cup, added the water from the test tube then stirred the mixture for thirty seconds.

'Right. Five minutes for it to settle.' She sat on a boulder, alternately staring at her watch and the Neanderthal's fence.

As soon as the time was up she quickly dipped the probe of the EC meter into the mixture. 'Measures how much electricity moves through a solution—the saltier it is, the more electricity moves through it, the higher the reading on the—' She looked at the dial with rising indignation. 'The bloody wretch. It's gone up by half a point. He's wrecking my garden!' She sat down and lit a cigarette then jabbed a hand at the ground. 'What's the salinity danger level?'

'Er . . . one?' I ventured.

'Four. You should know that. When it reaches that level it's harmful to most plants. Difficult for roots to take up water.' She raised an eyebrow at the Neanderthal's gates and mused. 'If only we could get in. Get some pictures, proof of the borehole.' Her voice rose in rasping increments. 'Anything that comes out of that imbecile's gate, log it in your brain. Note it down, even if it's a fly. Now tell me what you need from the village. I can't have us both off guard duty. Gather evidence, Jane.'

I swallowed a sigh. I wanted desperately to go with her to the village. It was a fillip to scrub up a bit, wave or chat to the man with the guitar, or watch the shopkeeper use his litter pickers to bring down packets of cigarettes—just to be with other people, really. Without human contact it was

84

difficult to retain my sense of humour and put the world of Helikion into context.

In the event Joy left for the village leaving me with a notebook and pen. On her return I was dismayed to find, yet again, she'd bought me pots of Marmite. I had told her I didn't like the stuff and had buckets of it stuffed inside cupboards. As I put away the new jars I wondered if she was testing me in some strange way or whether she had some sort of fetish about buying Marmite. I let out a short laugh at the thought. It would have been even funnier had I been on the outside looking in.

On my second day as a spy I was lurking close to the Neanderthal's fence when I heard the swish and crackle of the Jeep driven fast. It swerved towards me, Joy's face hard set behind the wheel, then came to a shuddering stop. She put her head out of the window.

'I've hired a hit man. We'll blame it on the huntsman. I'll get you some lunch. Do you believe in ghosts?'

I stared at Joy, my mind spinning.

\*     \*     \*

An hour later I was greeted with a glass of chilled white wine and a bowl of Greek salad. As I polished off the last of the feta cheese I wanted to ask Joy about the 'ghost', but was wary of what her answer might be. She was busy peering at my notebook and I decided to wait for my opportunity.

She read aloud. 'Eight a.m. Machinery starts. Five minutes past. Ford Escort goes in. Two dodgy men inside.' She glanced at me and frowned.

'*Dodgy* men! This isn't *Miss Marple*, Jane.' I suppressed a smile and dunked a wedge of bread into a bowl of olive oil.

'On Escort's back seat,' Joy carried on, 'large cardboard box. Guitar case. Twenty minutes past three. Escort leaves. One *dodgy* man missing. Nothing on back seat. Guard dogs chained to house on long leads.' Her eyebrows knitted together. 'Why is that? He usually leaves them free. Maybe they ate the missing dodgy man. What was the Ford's registration?'

'I forgot.' I took a long drink, my stomach contracting at Joy's heavy expression.

'Jane. For God's sake, we need vehicle numbers. How else are we going to get hold of those two men? How will we find out what's going on?'

'Joy, what did you mean by "Do you believe in ghosts"?'

She looked at me solemnly and raised a finger, then went to pin the papers on the noticeboard and turned around abruptly.

'Right. Follow me.' She marched towards the front door and then turned left down a small passage, at the end of which was a locked door. Rosary beads were wrapped around a crucifix hanging above it. She inserted the key in the lock and, looking at me, turned it slowly and deliberately.

I went into a tiny room that had a low slanting roof and smelt of mothballs. A jar of dead flowers sat on the ledge of a solitary window. In the corners of the room were stacked cardboard boxes, papers spewing out of their splitting sides. Folded chairs and rusting sun loungers were squeezed alongside a wooden crate brimming with

86

paperback books. A long black military coat hung from a metal hook on the wall, the grey skein of a spider's cobweb clinging to its angular collar. I stepped forward to peer at a sheet of yellowing paper tacked alongside. It was a drawing in crayon of the house, outside which stood Lowry-style 'stick men'.

'Young Tom's masterpiece,' Joy said. 'Marilyn put it there after she heard about the girl's suicide.'

'Suicide?' I stared at Joy in alarm.

'Yes. A young girl apparently. Overdose. A sad tale. Marilyn thought the innocence of a child's drawing would contain her spirit. She used to hear noises from in here. Nothing's happened on my watch. Thought you might be on her frequency.' A hint of a smile played on her lips. 'Do you read Edgar Poe?'

'I did. *The Fall of the House of Usher.*'

'Scary.'

'Yes.'

'Right.' Joy's tone became brisk. 'Ghosts done.'

She stopped outside in the passageway. 'The reason why I took you in there was because it's the only thing I can think of that might stop people buying this place. If any visitor came, sent by the new owner, and, let's say, stopped you in the garden, you would be able to tell them, wouldn't you? About the ghost?' Her eyes softened, almost in appeal.

'Have you made it up, then?' It came out suddenly, surprising myself.

Joy, smiling, placed her forefinger alongside her nose and spoke slowly and intently. 'You would tell them, wouldn't you?'

'Yes, I'd tell them,' I said.

'Good. Now go back in there and grab a couple of sun loungers. Put them on the threshing floor. I'll be with you in a minute.'

I watched her go back to the living room. It suddenly hit me. She was desperate. Her preoccupation with the Neanderthal. Her changeable moods. He could have become her target in order to release her pent-up fears and frustration, something to take her mind away from her worry over the future of the garden. I'd been so self-involved that I hadn't suspected it before. Joy wasn't paranoid, after all. She was simply scared of losing her garden and had made up the ghost story. Or had she?

I went back into the room to pick up a pair of loungers, their metal frames scratching my legs, and took them outside to a flat circular area overlooking the phrygana. Flowerbeds full of overhanging shrubs, wallflowers and cacti encircled it. Come spring it would be covered in camomile. Rather than name it a 'camomile lawn'—this smacked too much of the upper class for her liking—Joy called it a 'threshing floor', a more robust term that harked back to a time when man was at one with the land. Joy came out and settled on the lounger at my side. She adjusted her binoculars, peering through them.

'Rachel said she saw a hoopoe last evening. I think her sight's deserting her. Wrong time of year. They've long since gone. Still, I'm too old to be a cynic. We shall sit here until we spot one. Now. How do you focus these things?'

While the sun slowly dropped in a pink and blue streaked sky, we talked about the garden and took turns to look through the binoculars. Lulled by the soft light and the rustling leaves of the olive trees, I relaxed into a stupor. Joy carried on talking regardless.

'Aren't the olives beautiful in this light? Look at the two robins, dancing away.'

She jabbed me on the arm. 'Jane. Look!' I bolted upright and looked to where she was pointing. A flat-bed truck carrying cement mixers and rubble trundled out of the Neanderthal's gates. It was soon followed by a yellow JCB digger. Joy put down the binoculars and stood up. 'I'm going to ask them what that idiot has built.'

'Be careful.'

I faltered, giving up as she deftly hopped over a clump of cacti. I watched her trotting quickly down the phrygana, winding her way around the olive trees. She reached the track just as the JCB vanished over the steep drop of the drive.

I picked up the binoculars and focused on Joy. She was bent to her knees, gasping for breath. After a minute, she got to her feet, lit a cigarette and slowly made her way into the house. When she emerged it was with two large glasses of ouzo. She meandered carefully towards me, manoeuvring around the shrubs, dipping under the long, slim branches of a Jerusalem thorn tree.

She arrived with both glasses full to the brim. She'd spilled not a drop. 'Perfection in all things ...' she handed me a glass, '... is not a necessity, but striving for it is.' On that note she sat down on the lounger and let out a long sigh.

\*     \*     \*

Helikion was finally free from the noise of machinery, the JCB never to return. As the days went by, Wizard returned to his normal 'devil' state, and Joy focused her thoughts on the work to be done.

'November: "The lonely season in lonely lands when fled are half the birds".'

'Robert Bridges,' I said confidently.

'Well done. You learned it at school. So did I. But not here. Not in Greece. Hope you're up to November.' She stared down over the acres. 'It's a busy one. Pruning, transplanting, planting. And there's olives to pick. I've lost interns at this stage, you know.'

I thought of the boy who had left after only an hour.

'From now on, Jane,' she said brusquely, 'you're to meet me every evening for a walkabout and tutorial.'

'Every evening?' I said, then, in a flash, regretted my note of alarm.

'Not Sunday.' Joy wrinkled her mouth, dissatisfied with my reply.

\*     \*     \*

As day slipped into dusk, I reluctantly went to the terraces for my first 'walkabout'. It wasn't that I found Joy's teaching dull; on the contrary, she had a wonderful turn of phrase, firing my imagination with oddball facts and tales, making me want to learn more about the plants. But I could never truly relax during the day and had always found comfort in the fact that I could escape *to* Alcatraz in the evening.

I found her sitting under the bough of a small myrtle tree. 'Sorry, I'm late, I didn't know where or when—'

Joy raised her hand to silence me. 'The myrtle was sacred to Aphrodite, Jane. Symbolizes beauty, youth.' She picked off a leaf, rubbed it against her cheek then crushed it in her hand and let the pieces fall to the ground. 'As Shakespeare wrote, "Golden lads and girls all must, As chimney sweepers, come to dust".' She shook her head quickly and tutted—a now familiar affectation, it was as if she were chastising herself—then she reached to the ground and grabbed two glasses of ouzo. I gratefully took hold of one.

'To Kew, Jane. I'm going to get you shipshape if it's the last thing I do. But don't be late again. You'll get me drunk.'

'You didn't give me a time.'

Joy shushed me and marched along the lower terrace, pointing at the spread of *Oxalis pes-caprae*, its leaves shaped like the club in a deck of cards. It strained upwards to rub against the twisting leaves of paper-white narcissus, poked through the paddles of prickly pears and crawled from out of the most infinitesimal of cracks.

'*Oxalis pes-caprae* is not a weed,' Joy announced, looking at it with disdain. 'It's an invasive, arrogant bully. Alexander the Great would have been proud of it. Not its fault, though,' she said firmly. 'It was perfectly happy growing in South Africa then some idiot thought it would make a wonderful ornamental plant and brought it to Europe. Eighteenth century, I think.' She carefully pulled out an oxalis and looked at the small bulbils attached to the roots. 'Stops the germination of

91

other seeds. Look.' She gently shook it and most of the bulbils fell to the earth. 'Each one of those will sprout new tentacles. And you can be sure there'll be some left in the ground. Impossible to get rid of. We can only exercise damage control.'

Joy leaned down for her glass, found it empty and so took mine from me, taking a quick sip before handing it back. 'Never be defeated, Jane. As Winston Churchill said, attitude is a little thing that makes a big difference. When weeding let your mind roam. Take the great Christopher Lloyd's advice: develop the plot of your next novel, think up the perfect repartee to unreasonable relatives.' She paused, then dropped her voice to a croaky growl. 'Or gardening curators.'

I brushed against the leaves of a rue shrub and grimaced, holding my nose. 'Ugh, I hate its smell! Like cat pee.' Joy barked out a short laugh and went to the tool shed. On her return she told me to close my eyes. As I did so she clipped a clothes peg on my nose.

'Ouch!' I cried, opening my eyes.

'Don't be a ninny, Jane. Learn to love rue. The ancients considered it the "herb of grace". A cure-all. It's an antidote against snake bite and it calms those of us who enjoy a good old erotic dream.'

As the shadows lengthened into giants, Joy took me to the hilltop then down the rocky path and back to the terraces, the phrygana and the Neanderthal's gates visible in the distance.

'Why does he plant stuff that isn't native to a Med climate, Jane? We're bursting with flora. Plenty of show-offs around.'

She stopped to gaze at a Cape honeysuckle, the dwindling sunlight dappling its nonchalantly

92

hanging flowers, some illuminated to a flaming red, others in shadow and dark orange. Joy's voice lowered, in harmony with the descending darkness. 'Homesickness is not only felt by people, Jane. If a plant's put in an unsuitable place it will pine away if not given constant attention.' She glanced at me. 'Like you? Are you homesick?' Seeing my hesitation she grabbed my arm. 'Now, what would the admiral say when you were at sea in the Navy?'

'I never went to sea. I was shore based. At a place called HMS *Dryad*. Where Eisenhower planned D-Day.'

'Your parents must have been proud of you. It certainly impressed me. What did you do in the Navy?'

I felt a resumption of guilt. In my miserable nine months' service I had completed six weeks' basic training, made a few overhead projector slides, cleaned out a couple of rooms for an admiral's visit and wheedled myself out of the service. Not much to write home about.

'I learned to strip an SA80 gun and put it back together blindfold. I came second on the shooting range.' That was true. It was my favourite part of training and my parents were impressed with that, I told her.

She put her head back and laughed, then rooted in the pockets of her culottes to bring out a bar of chocolate. She broke it in half and handed me the larger portion. 'That's my cure for homesickness.' She looked up towards the looping telephone wires and then out over the patchwork plain to the highway and airport, her wrinkled face showing a hint of melancholy.

'You didn't like the garden at first, did you?' The

question shot sideways from her mouth as she lit a cigarette. I remembered Joy's whirlwind tour the morning after the worm hunt. I hadn't exactly been forthcoming about the garden.

'Sorry, I was tired after—'

Joy put a hand out. 'We all need time,' she said, and paused for a moment. 'Time and experience. Time to change our way of looking. Do you fancy a hookah?'

I wanted nothing more than to watch the DVDs that my parents had sent me, but Joy's expression was so beguiling that I didn't have the heart to refuse. 'Yes. Thanks,' I said, trying to sound bright.

Under the light of oil lamps, huddled under blankets, we took turns puffing on the pipe, Joy happy to ramble on until finally she wound down, content to listen to the sounds of the garden and the rumblings of Winston and Titan.

I was ready to make my excuses and leave when Charles strode through the doorway of the veranda. Each evening he dutifully delivered a weather report from the internet.

'Bonnie and Clyde,' he chuckled, pointing at first Joy's straw hat and then mine. I had bought a similar hat from the weekly market, which Joy had duly decorated with one of Wizard's scarlet feathers.

He handed Joy the report. 'Get your wellies out.'

Joy scanned the graph. 'Thunderstorms, Jane. Within twenty-four hours!'

Charles ruefully smiled, then handed her another piece of paper. 'And there's this. Another email from Tom. His travel plans and a date to put in the double glazing.' Joy started to read and then suddenly held her breath.

94

'What is it, Joy?' Charles frowned at her. 'About selling Helikion as a last resort?'

Joy was sitting rigid in her chair. Her face had grown pale. With a great effort she blinked hard, tightening her mouth. 'I'll man the barricades. Charles, you've got a shotgun. Jane, you're a good shot.'

'Don't worry yourself, Joy,' Charles said sanguinely, putting a hand on her shoulder. 'He's sent it without thinking. It won't come to that. You know it won't. The garden's too important and it would perish without you.'

I looked at Joy in concern. She sat so still and her face had become so white that I thought she might faint.

# 6

# The Bone China Set

Narcissus
serotinus
Bulbous perennial

I awoke to a feeling of foreboding. The forecast of thunderstorms had also added a warning of the possibility of near hurricane-force winds sweeping upwards from the coastal plain into the hills. Joy had ignored that part of the report, so obsessed was she with the promise of rain.

My first job of each morning was to cross off the previous day on the small calendar stuck to the fridge. A month had passed. It was now the second week of November. I meditated on my mental state as I did every morning. I was neither happy nor unhappy, but somewhere suspended between the two. During the daytime I was a notch higher on the scale, even peaking at odd moments of bliss.

The glimpse of an opening bud, a fleeting scent lost on a breath of wind, the sound of birdsong and rustling leaves—these pleasures I would recall in my lonely cell as Wordsworth did of nature's delights, 'emotion recollected in tranquillity'. They served the same purpose as the retained airline pamphlet in giving me some reassurance if all else failed.

'I mustn't run away,' I said to Zeus, the statement I always repeated on leaving Alcatraz. But last night, after witnessing Joy's reaction to Tom's email, I feared what the day would hold.

Usually I would find Joy seated at the kitchen table, reading and drinking coffee. Briskly, she would ask me to sit down and, after lighting a cigarette, give me my list of jobs. This morning I entered the house to find smoke billowing from the kitchen's entrance. I coughed and spluttered my way to find her poking a knife into the toaster.

'Joy!'

I rapidly unplugged its lead from the wall, then switched on the overhead fan and rushed to open the veranda doors. I watched her sit down to slap honey on the cremated toast. Then she reached out for the ubiquitous packet, raising her eyebrows at my expression.

'Jane? Are you sure you're all right?'

'Yes.' In that polluted atmosphere it was the most natural thing for her to do—light a cigarette.

\* \* \*

On the journey to the village, Joy drove with her eyes fixed to the road, which was always a bonus. But then the stare became hypnotic, a big minus.

'Joy, watch out!'

'What?'

She came out of her trance in time to slow down for a bend. Once safely round she bent down to hunt for an English radio station.

'The lorry, Joy!'

To the accompaniment of blaring horns, she sat upright and took command.

'Infernal noise. That's when I miss England,' she barked. 'Road discipline here's gone to pot.'

I closed my eyes and took a deep breath, relieved that we were approaching the village. Then I gasped on hearing a news bulletin.

'What's wrong? Did I hit something?'

'No. Didn't you hear that? They said there are only a hundred and forty-eight donkeys left in Greece. The rest have fallen off mountains. Can you believe it?'

'Smoke and mirrors, Jane,' she said. 'Smoke and mirrors,' her voice fading to a murmur. I heard her say something about Tom's email and 'reading between the lines' then grabbed the side of my seat as she slung the Jeep in front of an oncoming van and into the first available parking space.

While Joy hunted for her shopping list, I waited on the narrow pavement. Two old ladies, dressed in black, sat knitting behind a wrought-iron gate. They raised their heads and nodded at Joy as she joined me.

'Oh, isn't he gorgeous,' Joy rasped, distracted at the sight of a piebald kitten dozing in the boxed pit of an orange tree. She bent down and stroked the kitten, causing it to yawn and stretch then sit upright to scratch a paw around its ears. A metal tag fastened to its collar jingled. It was in the form of a key.

'Oh shit!' Joy's shout caused me to take a step backwards. The kitten leapt up in alarm and the old ladies clutched their rattan seats. She was back at the Jeep in an instant.

'Bollocks!'

She turned round to wave chaotically at the two ladies before hurrying back to grab my arm. 'It's in there. Come on.'

'What's in there?'

'Come on. Hurry.'

I followed, breathless and bewildered, as she trotted down the street, around orange trees, past concrete tubs of oleander, through an alleyway, past a graffiti-daubed wall, a lone patisserie and a skeleton of a building with steel rods poking out in twisted sculptural forms.

'Where are we?' I asked, catching up with her.

'Joy, what's happening?'

'Pavlos's friend, Jane,' she said, intensifying my wonderment. Finally, we reached a cobbled side street where a man, wearing blue overalls, stood outside a garage cooking slabs of meat on a rusting barbecue. A young tousle-haired boy sat at his feet tossing pebbles at an empty Coca-Cola bottle, both surrounded by tyre racks and pots of dusty yuccas. The other shops were boarded up, their signs faded and splintered by the sun.

'Remember, Jane, angels and knights come in all shapes and sizes. Demis!' Joy raised her arms at the mechanic.

'Joy!' The mechanic put down his spatula to lift his arms in greeting. They spoke rapidly in Greek. The mechanic then talked to the boy, who dashed into the garage and came out a minute later driving a white golf cart loaded with toolboxes.

'Jane, get in,' Joy commanded.

'But Joy, what's happening?'

She frowned at me. 'The key. It's in the Jeep. Don't you ever listen? We're locked out.'

I squeezed next to her on the back seat of the golf cart.

'Oh, I see now.' I gave a nervous laugh, biting back a profanity. 'Never mind, these things happen,' I added, nearly in tears of frustration.

One moment I'm her helper, the next made to feel like an unruly kindergarten kid. And, at that thought, I became one, crossed my arms and sulked. She'd said nothing to me about 'being locked out'. But then I glanced at her, accepting that it was her unreliable memory that was at fault. Nevertheless, I remained peeved. To my irritation she was now frowning at the potted plants, as if they offended her. But it was in a sympathetic voice that she spoke.

'Those poor yuccas. I told him to repot them and wipe their leaves down. Don't people ever listen.' She shook her head. 'How can the poor things photosynthesize with all that dust?'

The mechanic took the place of the boy and drove us away. It was a bumpy and uncomfortable ride, but we soon arrived back at the Jeep. Leaving him to deal with the lock, Joy marched me to the post office and hurried to a row of tall metal cabinets, while I joined the queue to buy stamps. Standing on tiptoe she opened a box and dragged out her mail, which included a brown package. As she joined me in the queue she glanced at the sender's name and address on its back.

'Another one from your parents. How nice,' she said quietly, and with a note of sadness handed me the package. 'I write to my two children—one in Canada, the other in Ireland. They will insist on sending emails to Charles. Not the same as a written note ...' She double-checked the handwriting on the letters, sighed, then nodded at my package.

'Let me guess. It's a book.'

'Yes. Alan Bennett's *The Uncommon Reader*. I asked them to send it.'

'The one with the Queen? It's good that you read. Books support us, keep us from becoming a burden to ourselves. There are books which take rank in our lives with parents, lovers and passionate experiences.' She touched me on my shoulder. 'A quote from Emerson, Jane. *Society and Solitude*. I've got a very good book you'll like.'

'Thanks, Joy. That's really nice of you.' My head

cleared itself of worry. No matter how much Joy annoyed me, she would always surprise me with some comment to show her insight into human nature, or offer a rare few words of praise—just enough to keep me from running home. But I wondered whether she planned it that way, or if I was someone she liked to manipulate. No. I decided that I had seen true sincerity in her eyes at times, even humility, and neither expression gave credence to that silly notion. I tried to order myself not to get upset the next time. I was served at the counter and we went outside.

'Now then, how about a glass of ouzo?' She directed me towards a small taverna. Outside, on the dusty pavement, stood an empty metal table. 'Adelphos owns it. He's a friend of mine. His father was in the resistance against the Nazis. Blew up tons of ammunition on its way to Rommel in North Africa. Splendid chap. No, not ouzo. Let's celebrate. Champagne?'

I was amazed. I'd no idea what we were celebrating, but after the morning's events I was intent on enjoying it, whatever.

*　　　*　　　*

That night, as I lay in bed, a gale swept down the valley and raced up the hillside to whack Alcatraz head on, moaning through cracks and crevices, slamming shutters and rattling windows. Then, at the peak of its ferocity, the storm abated and for a moment there was an uneasy peace. As if nature could not tolerate such a vacuum a peal of thunder suddenly reverberated around the hillsides and banged overhead. Orwell leapt off his blankets and onto my bed, ears flapping in all directions.

A flash of lightning illuminated Zeus's glass eyes. Fat raindrops clattered on the rooftop. Then the gale returned, having gathered reinforcements. Unable to sleep, I was about to put on the kettle when, in another flash of lightning, I saw the brown stain on the electrical socket and abandoned the idea. Instead, I poured an ouzo then peered through the shutters, making out split and ripped branches, with twigs and leaves tumbling in the wind.

Sheets of black rain swept over the swaying pendulums of the cypresses. Vegetation whipped like seaweed in high seas. Each flash of lightning suffused the garden with an eerie light of blue and green.

Came the dawn and the rain still fell. I was rinsing out my breakfast bowl when Joy suddenly bounded through a curtain of water dripping from the awning. She dumped a pair of wellington boots and a poncho under the wooden chair and swept back her loose hair, sprinkling droplets on the floor.

'Thirty-two millimetres and still falling.' She clapped her hands in delight. 'Three hundred and forty-nine total last year.' She looked back into the rain, her eyes keen and vivid. 'We need over four hundred. I can't bear another winter drought.'

She jumped from the veranda into a puddle and pointed at the chair. 'Put your wellies on. We need to put the watering cans out, buckets, anything you can find.'

After checking the water butts for any blockages, we stood on the hillside and looked down in dismay at the widespread web of rivulets and canals tumbling into each other, while scouring the terracotta earth. Joy's initial euphoria was now reduced to an angry frown.

'All this run-off. It's not going in.'

She shook a fist at the black heavens before making her way downhill. Suddenly, the network of canals to our left merged into a charging torrent. Within seconds a bank not more than ten metres away collapsed, exposing the roots of a young pear tree.

'Sod it!' I was first to the pear tree, packing the fallen earth and small rocks back against the roots with my bare hands.

'Don't swear, Jane. I'll do that. Get a larger rock to hold it fast.'

Muddy and drenched, I managed to roll a small boulder into place as overhead thunder and forked lightning forced us back to the house for shelter. Small branches, leaves, geraniums and their cracked or shattered pots swept across the drive. Pools of water collected among gazanias that lined the small stone wall of the track.

'You pray for rain and that's how the gods repay you. Go home, Jane. Get out of those wet things.'

After changing, I went back to the house, the rain now fading into a drizzle. Joy kept muttering about the iniquity of it all. 'It's like giving a starving child a mountain of bread. He'll be dead from overeating.' She shook her head in bitter disappointment, then glanced at me, a flash of guilt crossing her face. There was no eye contact when she said, in a defeated voice, 'Go back, Jane. Have the morning off. Let all this water go.'

I walked back to Alcatraz, stopping to stare at Mount Hymettos. It was covered with new thunderclouds. Sheets of shadow and glaring sunlight raced across its bulk, while a rainbow curved over its flat back, dipping into the hidden bowl of Athens.

I entered my cell to find Orwell poking a paw at what looked like tiny, black, coiled strings. Intrigued, I picked one up, only to drop it back to the floor as it squirmed in reaction. Curiously, touching it with bare hands had released a strong smell of disinfectant. I gathered the millipedes up on a sheet of paper and went outside to put them in the garden.

After lunch, Joy appeared with Titan and Winston on leads.

'I'm taking these two for a mudlarks' constitutional. Start clearing up the mess now. Oh, I forgot to tell you. Tom's windows. Workmen are supposed to start putting them in this afternoon. The garden volunteers are here as well. But they always bring homemade cakes. I'll get stuff ready for them, then join you. OK?'

A minute later I heard a bellowing cry of pain followed by Titan's barking and Winston's shrill yaps. I scrambled up the hillside to find Joy lying by the bike sculpture, the dogs' leads tangled around her ankles. She had a hand to her head. A trickle of blood seeped between her fingers.

'Oh dear,' she mumbled, and managed to sit upright with Titan gently licking her face.

'Oh, Joy.' I bent down to unravel the leads. I knew that a blow to the head was potentially dangerous, even if the victim was conscious. I was deeply worried. Joy managed to raise a small, apologetic smile.

'Not your fault. Could have been me,' I said

firmly, trying to reassure her. I helped her to stand upright. She teetered a moment, steadied herself and slowly, clinging to me, managed to drag herself back to the house. For the first time in our relationship I was in charge. All her grand gestures and impassioned tirades had only served to make me feel powerless, but now I actually felt good, selfishly pleased in a way that the accident had happened.

I switched to thinking about her children. I had made the decision to ask Charles to tell them what had happened by email and then they could call Helikion, but then I shook off the idea. If they couldn't be bothered to write letters to Joy they might not be bothered to pick up the telephone. After applying antiseptic to the wound I wrapped a bandage around her head and then called Pavlos to tell him the news. Joy insisted on talking to him.

'*Ohi. Ohi.* No doctors, Pavlos. I'm fine. Just a bump . . . that doctor's a quack. See you soon, be careful on that moped thing. Mud on drive.'

I handed Joy a tumbler of brandy. She swished it around and, bleary-eyed, took a sip. 'How lovely. Should fall down more often.' She held her head. 'Hurts.' Her eyes flashed wide, illuminated by an urgent thought. 'We must check the rain monitor, Jane. Fill in the chart. Measuring tube on the stick.'

I dashed out to the nursery. At the back of the potting shed was a wooden pole stuck in the ground, a calibrated tube tied to its top with a length of transparent fishing line. It was full of water. Then I rushed back to find the tumbler empty and Joy dozing on the sofa, her legs splayed over a slumbering Titan. As I quietly opened and closed the drawers of Joy's desk, looking for the rain chart, Pavlos came in out of breath, carrying his helmet. He raised his eyes when he saw the large, untidy and bloodstained dressing on Joy's head.

'*Oh Martys moy o Theos. Ti kanate!*' He kneeled beside the sofa and held her hand.

'Pavlos,' Joy murmured. 'Only a scratch. No fuss.'

'How's feeling?'

She raised an eye and offered a slow smile. 'Better seeing you, you big lump.'

'You didn't say it this bad. I'm calling doctor now.'

'*Ohi*, I'm fine. Stay here.' She clutched his hand, her knuckles whitening.

'Doctor, Joy. Jane and I not happy if no doctor.'

'No, we're not,' I added. 'What if you collapse?'

Joy flapped a hand. 'All right. Get on with it.'

Pavlos winked at me and walked to the telephone.

'And anyways, Joy. If you had refused to see doctor, I would have stopped bringing your supply of ouzo. So all done for the best, *ne*?'

She grunted and, as if to regain her authority, reprimanded us both. 'Jane. The rain chart's on the bottom shelf of the library. Only rummage through my drawers if it's an emergency. Pavlos, don't talk so loud.'

An hour later, the doctor arrived, a tall, middle-aged man wearing a creaky leather jacket and a pair of large horn-rimmed glasses. He sniffed in disdain at the amateurish dressing that I'd applied.

'Joy. Do you know who I am?' He spoke in perfect English.

109

'If I don't, you're not here,' she replied.

He laughed out loud. 'That is the most non-concussed reply ever!'

Five minutes later, following detailed tests of her vision and answers to questions, he replaced my dressing with something more professional, then informed her that she had mild concussion, that the injury didn't require stitches but at her age she should not be working on steep hillsides. She had to stay in bed for three days. He then left, Winston and Titan sniffing at his heels.

Joy was outraged. 'At my age!' She flinched at her own loud voice and croaked. 'I don't trust anybody with a squeaky jacket.'

'Come on. You need rest.' Pavlos gently lifted Joy from the sofa, her arms wrapped around his neck, and carried her to the bedroom. Winston, Titan and even Wizard trudged behind, making tiny scratching sounds on the marble floor.

It was arranged that Pavlos would stay in the 'ghost room' for the duration of Joy's enforced recuperation. As I helped him tidy the room and put sheets on the mattress, I thought it was as good a time as any to ask him about the ghost. I was eager to know whether it was as I suspected, an invention of Joy's designed to put off would-be buyers of Helikion.

'Pavlos? Is there a ghost here? I'm not great with ghouls and stuff.'

He chuckled but gave no reply.

'Pavlos?' I gave his beard a gentle tug.

He laughed, shaking his head. 'I've never seen or heard anything.'

He swiped a hand down the bed sheets and switched off the light. 'My friend told me about

Joy locking you out of Jeep,' he said, matter-of-factly, striding down the passage. 'Don't worries. I have talks with her.' He went into Joy's bedroom.

I hovered outside, pretending to look at the books in the library. Perhaps Pavlos had lied to me about the ghost. Maybe he thought it might scare me enough to make me desert Helikion. I heard whisperings then Joy's voice.

'Garden volunteers here soon, Pavlos. Get the table ready. Coffee. Tea. Bone china set, not the usual rubbish.'

'Rest, Joy.'

Pavlos came out and looked to the alcove.

A slim, short woman was standing in the doorway, wearing a cycling helmet at a jaunty angle. She wiped her forehead before greeting Pavlos, raising both hands. '*Kalimera*, Pavlos.'

I detected a faint smell of whisky in the air.

'Jane. This is Hilda.' Pavlos laughed, blanketing her small frame with a big hug.

We exchanged a quick smile.

'Where Joy?' Hilda asked.

'Joy bangs her head. She rests in bed,' said Pavlos.

'Oh!' Hilda exclaimed, her eyes swamped with concern.

'Go in. She wants to see you.' Pavlos watched Hilda enter Joy's room and whispered to me. 'Hilda is Joy's cleaner. Albanian. Nice woman, comes once a month. Has problems in her life though. Joy can't bear to sack her. Not the best cleaner. Ends up cleanings after *her* sometimes.'

Hilda soon rejoined us. She brought out a broom from a cupboard painted with sunshine and gecko motifs then set to chasing dust-balls around the

Minoan statues. I was helping Pavlos prepare the table when Joy opened her bedroom door to let Titan and Winston out. Holding a hand to her head, she spoke quietly. 'Take the dogs for a walk, Jane. They need a constitutional. Tell them to have one for me.'

Sunlight and the soft tinkle of water droplets accompanied our walk. The ground appeared to swell and ebb, exhaling a rich aroma of awakened earth. The olive trees appeared darker, plusher, their rich foliage played upon by the mellow shadows of the pines.

The dogs kept their snouts to the damp ground. On our return from the hillside, Titan suddenly yanked me towards the tall yucca opposite the house. A small newborn bird lay on the ground, its thin translucent skin revealing a rapidly pumping heart. I pulled the dogs away and rushed back to the house to find Pavlos.

On hearing the news, he gathered a tin, stuffed it with cotton wool and sprinted out of the house, muttering to himself in Greek. *'Oh! Kaki ligo ena . . .* all right, little one . . .' He gently picked the bird up and placed it in the nest of wool.

Inside the house we looked anxiously at its tiny body, uncertain what to do. End its misery, or try and keep it alive?

The cowbell clanged outside. There was a pause and then in walked three middle-aged women, two with swept-back apricot-coloured hair, the other pale and covered with freckles, each laden with cake tins and Tupperware boxes. A chorus of *'Kalimera'* rang out. Pavlos quickly introduced us, his forehead creased with a frown as he held out the tin containing the stricken bird.

'Oh my,' the pale lady said in an American accent, screwing up her nose so hard that her freckles almost disappeared. 'That's a strike out if ever I've seen one.'

A powdery old lady shuffled through the doorway, tapping a walking stick. Two more ladies, topped with Burberry headscarves, followed behind, each taking quick steps to stand either side of the old lady in case she lost her balance. They spoke in English.

'That's it, Mother.'

'Mind the dogs.'

The old lady painfully raised her stooped head and gazed at Pavlos for a few seconds, then pointed her stick at him.

'Lovely to see you ... er ... er ... young man. Where's Joy?' she said, shakily.

'Pavlos, bring in the dogs and ladies.' Joy's voice, though frail, was penetrating.

Pavlos pointed to the bedroom and picked up the tin. 'Come on, everyone. Joy had little accident. Bumps her head.'

Joy sat imperiously in a king-sized bed, Wizard perched on its gothic headboard. Clenching a purple shawl around her shoulders she raised a hand of greeting to the dogs. Titan leapt on to the bed, his tail thumping. Winston hopped on a stack of large hard-backed books and from there jumped onto the mass of coloured cushions that kept Joy propped upright.

'Oh dear! What happened to your head, Joy?' the two headscarves cried in unison as they herded the powdery lady to sit in a wing-backed chair. The old lady offered a papery hand to Joy. 'Nice to

113

have a rest.'

'Bea, it's been so long. Wasn't it marvellous, the rain?' Joy adjusted the strap of the pink sleep mask resting on her forehead. 'I'm only here because of the wretched doctor.'

Wizard cackled and threatened the tin in Pavlos's hand. Joy said dreamily, 'What's all the fuss about?'

Pavlos opened the tin to show her the ailing bird.

'Oh, the poor thing.' Joy screwed up her eyes. 'Ring Spiros. He'll know what to do.'

While they discussed the bird's fate, I looked at paintings crammed on the walls. They reminded me of Jean-Michel Basquiat's work. Graffiti-like sketches of plants, parts of flowers, arrows and figures, even articles from botanical magazines glued into their design. Below them a range of framed photographs jostled for space on top of a simple sideboard. Four of them caught my eye. The first depicted a Greek wedding in which the bride—obviously Joy—beamed with happiness. The man, ruggedly handsome, echoed her expression, his eyes sparkling with adoration. The second picture showed the same man, now slightly more rotund and with a beard, rolling around the floor with a lion cub, 'Christos & Zeus' handwritten across a yellowing corner. In the third photograph Pavlos and Christos sat outside a taverna, each holding a spread of playing cards and smiling at the camera. The fourth showed a younger Joy and two children, a boy and girl, each wearing rain ponchos and playing on a windswept beach. A man stood apart from them, looking sternly out to a choppy sea.

I was distracted by a universal groan and sigh.

114

'Bird's dead, Jane. Hearts stopped.' Pavlos looked sadly at me.

A weatherworn-looking man and a youth came into the room. Both wore baggy dungarees and apologetic expressions. The older man raised his furry eyebrows at Joy then brought out a folded piece of paper. Pavlos took it from him, opened it up and read its message with a heavy sigh.

'Ah, *ne*, it's windows, Joy. Tom's windows. Lorry coming shortly. Joy?'

A loud snore came from the bed. Pavlos left the room carrying the tin. 'Jane, get a pickaxe. Meet me at pet cemetery. Come on, everyone.'

I went to the tool shed to collect the pickaxe and then pursued the mourners up the hillside. At the cemetery, Hilda, duster draped out of her back pocket, stared at a marble headstone bearing the roughly etched legend, 'Humbert 1990–2002'.

Pavlos gestured at the window men. 'Jane. This is Angelo and Anthi, father and son. Supports Panathinaikos footballs team. But they OK.' He smiled wryly, then walked to a young cypress tree. 'Let's plant littles one here.'

Pavlos watched me dig the hole, then carefully placed the tin inside and packed soil around it. He stood back to let the group pile stones on the tiny grave. Hilda placed a flat stone at the back, so it looked like a headstone, and then joined the group to walk down the hillside, the murmur of our voices mingling with the rustle of windswept leaves.

'Do you do this for all dead animals?' I asked Pavlos.

'No. I do it for you. You brought it in house. You wanted it saved. Precious.' He gave me a warm smile. 'English very sentimental. David Attenborough. Have you got pet, Jane?'

'A cat,' I said, a wave of homesickness rushing through me.

'Cats kill birds.' There was a pause then Pavlos laughed, but stopped as he saw a lorry lumber into view between the olive and cypress tress.

'Tom's windows. Joy will be pleased,' he muttered to me dryly, lighting a cigarette.

As we rounded the corner of the house, two men jumped out of the lorry. The driver had the shape of a body builder. The passenger was half his size and wore a battered Stetson above a pinched face. Angelo greeted them and they smiled sheepishly, pointing at an Aleppo pine. The lorry had struck a large branch that had once dipped dreamily over the track. It now hung vertically to the ground, a jagged white split where it had parted company with the trunk.

Angelo glared daggers at the two men and snapped something in Greek. The driver gesticulated at the volunteers' cars parked by the Neanderthal's fence. He held his hands a few centimetres apart to emphasize how small a space it was between the vehicles and the pine tree. Pavlos puffed his cheeks out. 'This day can't get much worse.'

He accepted their apologies and then clapped his hands together. 'OK. We can sort. Jane, you saw branch off. Chops it up for log pile.' He then addressed the twittering volunteers. 'Clear up the rain mess, ladies. I'll have tea ready in an hour. Earl's Grey. Anyone who wants to join me for something stronger, shout now.'

116

Later in the evening, when everybody had left, Pavlos took a bowl of chicken soup and a mug of hot chocolate to Joy's room. He returned with it still in his hand. 'You like this? Joy wants warm milk with whisky instead. Sounds disgusting.'

I offered to make it and ten minutes later took the drink into her room.

'I'm not in hospital. There's such a thing as knocking, Jane,' Joy muttered.

She broke off to take a sip of the milk and whisky. 'Ah. Delicious. Now, do you want to go and prepare for your *Salvia* plant ID test or stay in here for *Jackanory* time?' She nodded at Pavlos, who sat on the wing-backed chair, a large hardback book on his lap. 'What are you going to read to me?'

'It's Greek mythology, Joy-bells. Just keeping you up with latest news.'

Joy smiled faintly, sighed and closed her eyes. But then she opened them again to look at me. 'Jane, don't waste time watching me. Do something useful.'

I stood up in relief, deciding that studying would be a better option than waiting for Joy to fall asleep. Hoping she would be impressed, I collected a stack of plant books and sat where she could see me, a large glass of red wine at my side. She wouldn't begrudge it me, I thought. In fact she often said that 'a glass of a fine wine while studying can grease the oils. Too much, though, and the words will slip through one ear and out the other.'

Later, Pavlos tiptoed out of the room and closed the door on Joy's deep snoring.

'Ears of a hawk,' he said. 'She heard branch snap. Wants to see Angelo first thing. May gods help him.'

*       *       *

The next morning, Angelo and the driver arrived to give Pavlos a bottle of champagne in apology for the severed pine branch. 'Stetson' followed, carrying a tray piled with polystyrene plates holding cakes and baklava sealed beneath wrappings of cellophane.

'It's Angelo's name day, Jane,' said Pavlos. 'Their saint's feast day. Like birthday. It's tradition to give people sweets. Now to gives him bad news.'

Pavlos sent Angelo into Joy's bedroom with cakes and a pot of tea. He watched him shuffle through the door. 'Like lamb to slaughters, Jane.'

Joy's voice was heard, sharply rising and then falling quickly. There was a silence and then Angelo could be heard uttering his apology in a stutter. Joy said something in a pointed retort. Finally Angelo emerged, chuckling nervously. He spoke to Pavlos in Greek. '*Tha prepei na einai o Prothypoyrgos.*'

Pavlos laughed. 'He says Joy should be Prime Minister. Do better jobs than Karamanlis!'

I went out to the garden, my first job being to prepare a tub of potting compost—Joy's recipe of sieved cotton waste, terracotta earth and a dash of perlite. Then I potted up tender seedlings that had sprouted from beneath a tree spurge.

I rejoined Pavlos and the workmen for lunch on the veranda. Cakes, sweets, olives, bread, cheese, cans of beer and ouzo were laid out on a dust sheet. After Angelo and his workmen had left we listened to the scratched tones of Billie Holiday drifting from out of Joy's bedroom. The still, warm afternoon slowly gave way to a breezy and chilly night. Pavlos made a log fire and we huddled around it, playing backgammon while sipping champagne. Gusts of wind whistled through the cracks of the plywood boarding tacked to the windowframes.

'Seen or heard a ghost yet?' I said, tossing dice into the board, trying to distract Pavlos and maybe curtail his winning streak.

He looked up at the print of Bosch's triptych of Paradise and Hell. Flickering candlelight illuminated the wing of Hell. He was about to say something, but then Joy shuffled out of her room, a large, white blanket wrapped around her like a chrysalis.

'I have a plan,' she croaked, ominously.

# 7

# Scrabble Wars

Two days later, Joy emerged from her room dressed in a purple velveteen tracksuit, her hair tied back in a loose ponytail and the bandage removed. She sniffed the air. 'What a gorgeous smell.' Her eye fell on the table. 'Pavlos!' she exclaimed. 'You dearest man. *Koulourakia portokaliou.*'

'That's cookies to the Yanks, buns to you, Jane,' said Pavlos, giving me a wink.

He passed round a plate of the warm cakes, declaring it was time for him to leave, and then wagged a finger at Joy. 'Remember what I said about Tom's email and what you always tell me? "Nothing's either good or bad, but thinking makes it so"?'

'Yes, Pavlos,' said Joy. 'Shakespeare's a fair exchange for your tales of the gods, and thanks for everything, especially the buns. Now off you go. Jane and I have a dragon to slay.'

Dragon? I inwardly groaned. I'd only come in the house to give Joy my lunchtime report on progress in the garden. Well, that was my cover story. My real purpose had been to spend time with Pavlos. He was fun, warm-hearted and his presence compensated for the uncomfortable moments I spent with Joy. I wanted him to stay and hear her 'plan'. I could already see myself dressed in a balaclava and camouflage jacket, face blacked up, ready to penetrate the Neanderthal's lair, a violent and painful death awaiting me. It didn't appeal.

'Ah, Jane. Goodbyes.' He enveloped me in a hug of farewell.

'Come back soon,' I said, wanting to shed a tear. Instead I grinned up at him and gave a tug at his beard. He broke away, laughing, then gave Joy a quick kiss and left, reminding her to watch her step on the hillside.

Joy waved him off and, always the one to have the last word, shouted at him to 'put your helmet on before the wind changes.' Then she returned to survey the new windows. 'Well, Tom's got his double glazing. I can hardly believe that motley crew managed it. Good for them.'

She burst into activity, first scurrying to unpin a newspaper cutting from the pin board, then to grab a bun and put on her straw hat, wincing as it caught her wound. Orders came out with machine-gun staccato: 'Jane? Have you removed the dead ptilostemon? Did you plant the clerodendrum? Moved the arbutus? And I must get you to lay a pathway through the herb garden.' She went out in a whirlwind, her words spilling into the air. 'Oh, and collect ant soil. It's perfect for seedlings. And take the dogs. Don't forget the dogs.'

A minute later she stormed back in. 'What on earth happened to that pine branch, Jane?'

I stared at her. 'You remember. It was the lorry that hit it.'

'What lorry?' She glared at me. 'Ah, yes. I remember. Oh, by the way, I want you to build a path through the herb garden. And don't forget the dogs.'

She had made no mention of her plan. I hoped it would stay that way.

\*　　　\*　　　\*

At dusk, I was on the lower terrace picking up an oxalis that I'd tossed towards a bucket and missed, when suddenly Joy's voice cut through a blaze of chrysanthemums above me. '*Oxalis pes-caprae* may be a weed, but it deserves your respect. An undertaker wouldn't throw your dead mother about!'

I looked up to see Joy's head bobbing above the flowers, frowning down at me. 'Leave them for now. Follow me. Bring a sword. Or a twelve-bore. Preferably an SA80.' With a sinking heart, I followed her down the phrygana to stop at the Neanderthal's fence of spiked iron bars.

'I've copied the *Athens News* piece about the illegal boreholes.' Joy carried a roll of sticky tape and a pair of scissors in one hand, copies of the article in the other. She handed me a few of them. 'I've put some up around the village. Leave him in no doubt. I'll do the gate. You do the fence. Our first salvo across his bows. Give him a jolt, eh?' So this was her plan.

I quickly put both hands through the fence in order to tape the leaflets into position. All I could see on the other side was shrubbery.

'Where are they?' I whispered. 'The dogs.'

'They'll bark,' came the fierce whisper. 'You'll have warning. This is only the start, Jane. He'll make a move and then it's action. We'll flush him and his bloody borehole out, have no fear.'

Oh Lord. It was getting worse. Joy stepped back, having completed her work, and with a few quick sidesteps looked up at the CCTV camera, raised her arms high above her head, twirled on the spot and finished with an aggressive two-fingered flourish.

'That's for you, Mister Borehole!'

Later, I sat on the stone cistern at the hilltop and called my mother, telling her that I was very concerned about Joy and that I might have to come home.

'I think that bump on her head has tipped her over the edge. She gave the V-sign at her neighbour's closed-circuit camera.' All my mother did was laugh and tell me that Zak, my six-year-old nephew, was outside playing football with my brothers, Andy and Martin. 'And Roz is watching *The X Factor* with me,' she added.

'That's nice.' This was bloody awful. I was nearly in tears again. Then I lost contact, mercifully. Rather than ring back I called a friend who was working in LA. The reception was perfect. I told her about Joy's latest escapade.

'Wow, she sounds great.'

'What?'

'They'd love her out here.'

'What's wrong with everybody?'

\*      \*      \*

I awoke in the darkness, sensing danger. There was a shuffling sound.

'Aaagh!' Something had touched me on the shoulder. I jerked upright in terror.

'It's only me, Jane,' came the whisper.

'What?' I unglued my eyes to see a spectral shape hovering over me in the gloom. It was Joy. I recoiled, gasping in relief, then looked at the glowing hands of my alarm clock.

'Joy, it's three-thirty in the morning. What's going—?'

'Shush, Jane. Meet me on the phrygana. There's something you must see.' She disappeared.

I fell back on the pillow, breathing heavily. I was right. The concussion had destroyed whatever frail linkage had kept her memory and rational mind together. After a pause, I roused myself quickly to dress, grabbed my mobile in case I needed to call the police or ambulance, then went outside.

A full moon had transformed the garden into a colourless, bleak landscape. A thick mist hung around its upper reaches.

'Here!' I heard Joy hiss at me.

She was at the side of a pine tree with Winston and Titan, beckoning me to follow her down the track. Stopping near the Neanderthal's gate, she pointed at a patch of blooming crocuses and the arching stems of a teucrium shrub, both covered in bits of paper. I picked up a piece and recognized it as part of a copy of the news article. Those that we had taped to the Neanderthal's fence and gates had been torn into pieces.

'The true actions of a Neanderthal, Jane.' Joy broke off to put her hand to her mouth. She handed me the dogs' leads and rushed towards the terraces. I followed as quickly as I could, but was slowed down by a reluctant Titan and an arthritic Winston.

I found Joy flitting here and there, checking everything was in order. Then she set off up the hillside towards the nursery. When I caught up with her she was standing in the nursery clutching her chest and staring down at the numerous potted plants. She spoke in a tight and contained voice. 'Our neighbour has swapped labels around and crushed cigarette ends into my potting compost.

127

Now, what else has the delightful man in store for us?'

She went out to labour towards the hilltop, her figure soon disappearing into the mist. When I joined her near the cistern she had an empty beer bottle in her hand. 'Nocturnal drinker to boot. Oh no!' She quickly handed me the bottle and went to stare at a mound of freshly dug earth. Two holes had been dug in the ground.

'He's stolen my urgineas.' She shook her head in disbelief.

I sniffed at the open neck of the bottle, detecting what I imagined to be a faint smell of perfume mixed with that of stale beer. Perhaps there was lipstick around its rim. Impossible to see in the moonlight.

'Do you really think he came up here, Joy?' I said.

'What? Of course. Who else could it be?'

'I did hear a car sounding close by earlier on. In fact, it woke me up.'

'Nonsense. Greeks don't do this sort of thing. I refuse to get a security fence. A garden shouldn't be like Fort Knox.'

She stretched herself, taking a deep breath. 'That speech, you know, in those dark days, was needed. "We shall defend our island, whatever the cost may be. We shall fight on the beaches, we shall fight on the landing grounds." '

Joy looked severely at my smiling face.

'You may laugh, Jane, but sometimes you need a call to arms. That's what we got in nineteen-forty. It quickens the blood. Far better than that twit who came back from Munich holding a piece of paper. "This morning I had another talk with Herr Hitler,

128

and blah, blah, here is the paper which bears his name upon it. Peace in our time." '

She stomped back downhill. 'You can't make peace with a bloody vandal.' She carried on talking although I was out of earshot, courtesy of a struggling Winston.

I'd no doubt that the news cuttings had been torn up by the Neanderthal in a fit of anger, but couldn't believe that he'd taken the trouble to climb up the hillside in the middle of the night just to drink beer and swap a couple of labels around. He may have been a water thief, but her conviction that all our ills could be attributed to him was a tad harsh.

Joy halted her descent and waited for me to rejoin her. 'He also said that failure isn't fatal, it's the *courage* to continue that counts. That's why I named that little one after Churchill.'

She pointed at Winston. 'He'd been beaten, was covered in sores, and had been blinded in one eye. But he's a warrior, Jane. That's what we've got to be.'

I looked at the old lady and suddenly felt humbled. Her spouting Churchill's call to arms, calling upon the nation's fighting spirit, would have amused me had I not been involved with her. But she meant it. She would have been brave in war. I could imagine her working for the wartime spymasters, parachuted into France, captured and tortured by the Gestapo and not giving anything away. And what would I have been doing?

Well, at least I hadn't run away—yet. But I would have gone, had my present situation existed a year ago. That thought in itself, that I'd taken a positive step forward, gave me a faint pleasure.

But then I became troubled and confused. I was never a faded flower at school. As the only girl playing in the primary school's football team, I was known for my aggressive tackling. I competed hard at all sports. Why had I lost my self-confidence? I had no answer.

'Jane,' I told myself, 'just get on with it. One day at a time.'

Joy's last Churchillian quote had stuck in my mind. 'Failure isn't fatal. It's the courage to continue that counts.'

We arrived back at the fence. Joy grabbed the bars in both hands and shouted at the house. 'You in there! Come out!'

I joined her at the bars. 'Chicken!' I shouted.

In the dead of night, our voices seemed to echo around the hillsides. Titan grumbled and Winston sniffed at my feet as we waited for a reaction. But, apart from the hoot of an owl and the rustle of leaves, the only other sound was a distant rumble of thunder.

'Notice, Jane? No dogs.' Joy cupped her hands to her mouth. 'You in there!'

Nothing, no sound of human or animal movement. I raised a hand. 'Joy, if the dogs aren't there, maybe he's not there either. We could get a ladder. I'll go over the fence, look for the borehole. It won't be . . .'

Oh God. My new-found zeal had gone. Joy was nodding slowly, chewing upon my suggestion as if about to give her consent. What was I doing? I wasn't ready to scale the barricades just yet. I was a student of horticulture and should have been tucked up in bed.

Joy stared at the line of sharp arrowheads along

the fence top. 'We could find some way of getting you over without impaling you, I suppose.'

I felt sick.

'But I don't think your parents would be happy if you went home in a coffin. If we can prove the dogs aren't there, it's a different matter.'

Oh, blessed relief. She was not entirely mad.

She turned away from the fence. 'Let the dogs off the lead. There's no danger.'

I let Titan and Winston slip away towards the house. As we parted ways Joy gave me a brief pat on the arm. I walked slowly back to Alcatraz, wondering whether it was a gesture of apology for dragging me outside at half past three in the morning. Or was it more in the way of an acknowledgement, that she had taken my offer to find the borehole as an act of comradeship?

\*　　　\*　　　\*

A second low-pressure system had moved in and stabilized itself over the Aegean. Fortunately this 'low' promised only the lightest of winds. As I turned up for work, rain fell steadily from a plodding line of grey and dismal clouds.

Joy was tapping the barometer as I shuffled in, my eyes bleary from lack of sleep.

'Less than a thousand. And still falling.' She noted down the reading in a brown leather book that she kept on the hookah table.

'Oh, that's great, Joy,' I said, trying not to sound too grumpy.

She turned to me, businesslike. 'Right. Now I know you worked all day through hell and high water on Hyde Park but you're the only intern I've got so I'm not letting you get wet through and catch your death of cold. I'm not fetching and carrying for a sick gardener so we'll do some study instead.'

She seemed to have forgotten about our night-time excursion. Her eyes were bright and she looked sprightly, in complete contrast to my dishevelled state. I hoped it would stay that way. But, no sooner had I felt my mind ease on the matter of guerrilla warfare than I was plunged into another challenge. There I was, stationed at the dining table surrounded by books, magazines, plant and seed samples, my memory of them about to be examined like that of a London taxi driver doing the Knowledge. Study was to be followed by questions, then more study and more interrogation.

*　　*　　*

The rain was still falling at lunchtime on the following day when Joy declared an extended break from my studies. I took the opportunity to catch up on lost sleep. At 5 p.m. I was called back for a half-hour question and answer session, my afternoon nap having served to improve my recall, which seemed to satisfy Joy.

Two days later and the rain still fell. I left Alcatraz early to get some fresh air and quickly survey the garden. Although the yuccas' drooping heads had risen and the opuntia paddles had fleshed out to look like fat pin cushions, all the succulents and cacti appeared sad and incongruous in such a drizzly, British-like rain, as if yearning to be inside a warm glasshouse.

As I entered the house, Joy looked up from her desk and nodded at the table. The mass of material I'd been dealing with had now been pushed to one side and replaced with piles of small brown envelopes full of collected seed heads, plus a coarse sieve, a pair of tweezers and Joy's ornate magnifying glass.

'Clean and sort that lot out. See what you make of it.' She went into the kitchen to make tea.

I sat down and picked up an envelope, its contents recorded in a black slanting scrawl:

'*Caesalpinia gilliesi*: (deciduous shrub/tree) Third terrace: Common name: Bird of Paradise. Drought resistant four months. Named after Andreas Cesalpino. His book *De Plantis Libri* 1583 based taxonomy on the study of sexual organs of flowers. Theologians denounced it.'

Joy had added a coda—'Idiots!'

The next envelope had a description of myrtle then, beneath it, written in red ink and capital letters: 'Eating myrtle leaves gives one the ability to detect witches.'

I smiled to myself and glanced at Joy who was bent over her desk, cigarette smoke curling around her. She was feverishly scribbling away with an old quill pen. Occasionally she would stop to shake it and wait for ink to fall from its long nib. Wizard suddenly screeched from the rafters, giving us both a start.

'Be quiet, you foul creature,' Joy hollered, then lowered her spectacles a notch to stare over them at me. I looked back hesitantly, wondering what I'd done wrong.

'Jane.' She gestured at me. 'Come on. Never waste time unless you're on a railway station.'

'Oh sorry.' I hastily took an envelope and poured its dusty seed heads into the sieve, gently shaking it over a plate. Coarser pieces of dried vegetation were trapped by a piece of gauze. Then I picked up a pair of tweezers and set to removing small black seeds from the remaining detritus, the final remains of a once exotic flower.

I sighed quietly to myself. How I longed to be outside working in the garden where, for most of the time, I was left all to myself. After ten minutes of seed sorting I drifted into a daydream, wishing I was back at Alcatraz, watching DVDs on my laptop. *Fawlty Towers* was my favourite. I'd watched the twelve episodes at least six times over and they never failed to make me laugh. I thought of myself as the long-suffering Spanish waiter, Mañuel.

I glanced again at Joy and a smile came to my face, imagining her and Basil Fawlty together as hotelier and wife. A comment she made brought me back to reality. She was looking out from the veranda to the walled garden. 'Isn't it beautiful,' she murmured, 'the pitter-patter? Just like rain in England.'

In the late afternoon we stood together, glasses of ouzo in our hands. The promise of improved weather lay over the distant coastal plain where a thin strip of blue sky slowly grew in size. Close by, Mount Hymettos was almost invisible, still cloaked in thick mist and rain-bearing cloud.

Joy pursed her lips and looked ahead as she spoke. 'So, how are things going, Jane?'

The tersely spoken question caught me by surprise. Did she mean generally or in particular? About how I felt in myself or my studying? Joy saved me having to reply.

'You've never told me anything about your parents. What does your father do?'

'He's a writer. Television drama, mainly.'

'Hmm. I never see any drama. Not for years. This place is dramatic enough—especially the weather,' she added ironically.

'I've got two brothers; one's a potter and artist,' I said, thinking of the unusual paintings in Joy's bedroom and the many art books crammed in the library's shelves.

She didn't flicker an eyelid, so I switched tack to her favourite topic, rain.

'When I left home we'd had a summer that was the second wettest ever. I was glad to get away.'

'Is that why you came here?'

'No, no. Of course not,' I said quickly. 'Just thought I'd mention it.'

I need not have worried. Joy wasn't accusing me of being a flibbertigibbet—I was desperate to shed that label—and chatted on, regardless.

'One thing's certain. We'd die without rain.' She jabbed a finger at the garden. 'Plants out there don't take anything for granted.' She swilled her glass around, chinking the ice cubes. 'Nor should you. Bear in mind, you're not as clever as the Resurrection Plant.' With a mischievous sideways smile she watched for my reaction.

'Er . . . resurrection?'

'You see. Hardly anybody knows and yet it could be the key to save the world. It has a secret, Jane.' Her voice sank to almost a whisper. 'An amazing secret. What does the word mean? What do you think happens to it, the Resurrection Plant?'

'Does it die and come alive again?'

135

'Yes. So what nearly kills it?

'Heat?'

'What happens in heat? What do you get?'

'Drought.'

'I'll have you in Kew yet. OK. So what resurrects it?'

'Water.'

'Exactly.' Joy drank the remaining ouzo and replenished her glass from the bottle standing on the wall. 'It's called *Xerophyta viscosa*. Grows in mountainous rocks in South Africa. Survives extreme heat, months of drought, with only a tiny fraction of its normal water content. When the rains finally fall it becomes Lazarus and resurrects itself. Back to normal in only three days. Scientists are trying to discover how its genes work and somehow engineer it into corn seeds. Think of the millions of lives saved wherever there's drought. Especially if it's true that the world is going to run short of food from global warming. That one plant could be priceless. It's nature that will save this planet, Jane, not civilization. This garden is at the forefront of the battle, here in this little European backwater.' She stared at the leaden sky, not moving a muscle, passion and excitement palpable in her sparkling eyes and short breaths.

And then, suddenly and as unpredictable as ever, her body language and expression changed. She was back to her brisk and severe mode.

'Now then,' she said sternly. 'I have a real challenge for you tonight.'

My stomach fell. 'Tonight?'

'Yes. Come back after supper. Best time for it.'

I inwardly cursed the rain. All I wanted was to wake up in the morning and go out to work the warm earth under the sun.

*      *      *

When I returned that evening Joy handed me a glass of ouzo before sitting me down at the table. The envelopes had vanished. In their place was a flat cardboard box, its front face down. It was tatty, scratched and torn in places. The colours that ran along its sides had faded. It would hold many packets of seeds. There would be dozens of Latin names springing out of it, beyond my tired brain.

My heart heavy, I watched Joy turn over the box in order to open it. She lifted the lid. I stared into the box.

'Best out of three,' she said.

There lay the hinged board and a jumble of yellowing plastic tiles, each with a letter of the alphabet etched into it.

'Oh great,' I said in relief. 'I've not played Scrabble for ages.'

My relief was to be short-lived. I enjoyed the first game, kept going by the adrenalin rush of winning—or being allowed to win? The game lasted almost two hours. But then came a second, which I lost. Glancing at the clock—it was 10.30 p.m.—I assumed that was the end.

'It's a draw. Thanks, Joy.' I made to stand. 'I'd better be—'

'Hold on.' Joy raised her hand. 'We have to play a decider. We're down to the wire. Or aren't you up to it?' She gave me a tough smile.

I looked into the eyes of a woman over seventy years old, a heavy smoker, a hard drinker but an equally hard worker. What freak of nature was it

137

that gave her such limitless energy? She reminded me of Dora Black, Bertrand Russell's second wife. My father had met her doing research and had given me a signed copy of her autobiography as well as her photograph. Not only did the two women look alike, but his description of Dora matched my assessment of Joy—both tough, resolute, hard working and campaigners in altruistic commitment.

I sat down again, dejected.

'Your turn to pick.' Joy sat back and lit a cigarette.

I slowly pulled out seven letters. It had been meant as 'a real challenge' after all. Half an hour later, finding it a struggle to add points to my total, I blinked at a word that Joy had misspelled.

'Well?' Joy waited.

I hesitated. She had spelled a word incorrectly. It was no good, I couldn't let it go. I may have been a deserter of jobs, but I hated losing at sports or games.

'Joy,' I spoke tentatively. 'The u is missing in Quoin.'

I held my breath as Joy picked up the dictionary to check the word. I knew I was right and was expecting her to throw it on the floor in annoyance.

'Hmm. You're right.' She closed the book. 'You look tired. Do you want to finish?'

'If you don't mind, Joy, I would, yes.'

I'd won; I was ahead on points and could leave with my head held high.

'Fine,' said Joy. 'But you realize I'm the winner by your default? We'll play another night.'

I almost laughed out loud at her audacity, but

instead I merely shook my head and watched her take out a folded sheet of paper from the box and place it in front of me. On it was drawn multiple columns in ink, headed 'Christos' and 'Joy', their score totals below.

'He was a great one for games. And gambling. Sometimes it worked. Often it didn't.' She stared at me through a haze of smoke.

'Do you believe in fate, Jane?'

In my anxiety to leave I gave her an answer which I'd remembered from a TV programme. 'Well,' I said, perhaps a tad too tersely, 'I suppose if I did, then every wrong decision I made would be easier to deal with.'

'That's a very clever answer, Jane. Is that yours, or somebody else who said that?'

My mind scrambled to think of an answer, but it was her searching smile that defeated me. 'Somebody else, on TV,' I said lamely.

Joy showed no triumph, nor satisfaction, from my confession. She merely shrugged and flicked her cigarette over the ashtray. 'In Greek mythology, the Fates were three sisters, all daughters of Night. The overseer of our destinies.' She paused, narrowed her eyes, and then drained her glass of ouzo, putting the glass down firmly on the table. 'So, the next question is, do you believe in God?'

I gave an honest answer. 'I don't think St Peter's waiting at the pearly gates or that there's an old bearded man sitting on a cloud, but I believe in a great intelligence behind all creation. I suppose that is God.'

Joy paused, mulling over her thoughts. 'Ask why a loving God allows us to feel guilt if fate has already mapped out our lives, made our decisions for us?' She got up. 'But that's not the Christian position, is it? We've got free will. It's heaven or hell depending on the life we lead. I think what we do here is good. So you can sleep the sleep of the innocent, Jane. Off you go . . . Oh, by the way . . .'

I stopped and turned round. Joy stood outside the house holding up a finger.

'I think we said a euro a game. You owe me one.'

*     *     *

The next morning, having slept a dreamless sleep, I awoke to sunshine slanting through the shutters. I was about to wash my hands and face when I heard Joy shout through the door.

'Choose ten rosemaries from the nursery and bring them to the phrygana.'

After dressing, I opened Alcatraz's door to find a clear blue sky. I lifted my head to the sun's warm rays.

'One of my better days, Zeus,' I said, patting him on the back before I left.

At the nursery I selected the healthiest-looking rosemaries then trundled my wheelbarrow downhill to the phrygana. Joy, who was weeding, stood up to stretch an aching back as I approached.

'Well done.' She took the rosemaries from me and pulled off a sprig, inhaling its scent and sighing with pleasure.

While I decided where to position the pots of rosemary, Joy sat on a boulder and watched me, occasionally making notes on a clipboard. 'Don't forget the sand. Mix that with the original soil

140

from the planting hole. Sharp drainage is what they need. And why?'

'It allows the water to penetrate below the plant's root ball. Encourages the roots to grow downwards. Vital for when the drought hits.'

Joy nodded and looked to the sky. 'Just look at that.' Thick dark grey cloud was backing over the hills towards us.

'Autumn's not my favourite season, Jane. The loss of light. How do you feel about it? Do you ever get depressed?' Her tone was businesslike.

I flushed. I wasn't comfortable talking about my depression. Everybody back home seemed determined to 'out' themselves in the media, from cricketers to spin doctors. It wasn't something to be ashamed about, they said, even the most successful people suffer from it. It was an illness brought about by a 'chemical imbalance' in the brain. That was where I stopped listening. Mine had everything to do with being challenged and was brought on by self-pity, a corroding introspection. I didn't want to speak about it. I was enjoying the sun while it lasted, so I decided that attack was the best form of defence.

'Why, do you suffer from it, Joy?'

'No. Just mood swings, what everybody gets.' She paused, watching me. 'I think I've seen you looking sad.'

'I have, yes, with darker nights. Lots of people do. I had a special light to help me.'

'I know. A kind of sun lamp. It lifts the spirits. But you didn't bring it with you, did you?' Joy looked at me deliberately.

She wasn't going to drop the subject easily.

'No. I'm mostly over it now. My parents think it's

because I was kept shut in the house too long as a baby. I needed to be outside; as soon as I was in the garden I would crawl to the flowerbeds and eat mud. They were always pulling me out by my nappy pins.'

Joy laughed. 'Jane, doesn't gardening help a lot? It does me.'

'Oh yes!' I replied with enthusiasm. I told her that gardening should be on prescription, that I found working with plants a cathartic and humbling experience, since they suffer from winds, fierce rainstorms and blazing sun, are uprooted to be replaced by cement driveways, emaciated by pollution, yet still set down roots, providing flowers of beauty and the very oxygen we breathe. And not a single complaint from them. I was almost breathless when I'd finished.

Joy shook her head at my outburst and said softly, 'You know what, Jane? You have a vocation.' There was a pause. 'Never stop learning. As well as understanding the soil, *watch* the plants. Watch how they tick, how they live. Their very essence must course through your blood. Patience, and an ability to understand a plant's needs makes the gardener.' She raised a finger. 'You've got green fingers because you're a mud baby. Did you know that three people in a hundred have substances like plant growth hormones in their sweat? Maybe we should have you tested. Now, sit down when you've done. Enjoy the garden.' She continued to make notes.

I closed my eyes in pleasure. In one of those rare moments Joy had taken me out of the darkness of confusion into the bright sunlight of optimism. Happily, I finished laying out the rosemaries and

142

went to sit near Joy, content to listen to the whispering leaves of the olive trees and the tweeting of redstarts and finches.

As she bent to her clipboard I managed a sideways look at it. She hadn't been writing notes at all, but sketching the scene in front of her. I could make out the young olive trees and tall cypresses, the arching shrubs, succulents and the paddles of the prickly pears. Even the seedlings bubbling among the rocks, crocuses and colchicums. And then there was me, bending over the wheelbarrow, picking out a pot of rosemary.

Suddenly Joy caught me looking and instinctively tipped the clipboard towards her chest.

'I only draw to keep a record, Jane,' she said severely.

'Sorry. I couldn't help looking.' My heart fell. The reproof, hard on the heels of her insight and understanding, hurt badly.

Joy lowered the clipboard again, but at an angle which made it difficult for me to see. But I'd observed the confident, vibrant strokes, some so delicate as to hardly touch the page, caressing the paper to form a vivid picture.

She reached for a packet of cigarettes and was fumbling with the cellophane wrapping. 'Damn thing—got a touch of arthritis.'

'Here, let me.' I took the packet from her and slipped off the plastic. At that moment I had a flash of memory and, hoping to regain contact, dared to speak.

'Joy, those paintings in your bedroom. Did you do them?'

She cut in brusquely. 'I think you should get the sand and start planting.'

I left dismayed and demoralized. When I came back she had disappeared, leaving a pickaxe impaled in the ground.

# 8
# Volcano Sunrise

By midday, it was warmer still, with a light wind ruffling the trees. Normally, in such pleasant conditions I would eat outside, but Joy's sharp rebuff had sent me scurrying back into Alcatraz. I ate lunch sitting on the bed, trying to read, but could only stare at the words, my mind fixed on what had happened. I put the book down and picked up my pen to write in my diary:

*I don't get it. Joy said she's seen me looking sad. She must think I'm vulnerable. So why be angry at me just for asking about paintings? It's weird.*

'What would you have done?' I asked Zeus. 'Eaten her, no doubt.'

I got up to make a cup of tea, glanced through the window and stopped dead. She was sitting outside. I hesitated. Was she there to apologize? If so, why hadn't she knocked at the door? Unsure what to do, I sat down to wait and automatically picked up my book and then put it down again having doggedly read the same sentence three times.

I took another peep through the window. She sat staring out towards the plain. It was clear that she was waiting for me to exit. I had no option. I hesitated, took a deep breath and pushed open the door.

'Hello, Joy,' I said, as if surprised to find her there. There was a plastic bag at her side.

She spoke formally, but softly. 'I brought you some things you'll need when you come to the house later.'

'Oh, thanks, Joy.'

'It's getting colder. And darker. Things for a bath. Come over when you're ready. The lamp's for walking back in the dark, obviously.'

She stood up. 'I'm going out now. Finish the rosemaries, then take Winston for his walk. I'll leave a towel out for you.'

She set off back to the house. I watched her upright, taut figure pass the wheelbarrow full of straggly herbs, then disappear. I closed my eyes tightly and tried to remember the exact dialogue that had ended with my question about the paintings and her reproof. It led to no insight, none whatsoever. I sat down to delve inside the bag and found a loofah, a bar of olive soap, a potholer's lamp and a pair of fur-lined boots. Whatever her problem was, she had clearly brought these things in the way of an apology, as it would have been much simpler to have handed them to me when I returned to the house.

Whatever, there was the prospect of a hot bath. I hadn't had one since I'd arrived at Helikion. The chance of being able to lie in hot soapy water in candlelight was a pleasure not to be missed. I could read my book as I lay there, enjoy a glass of wine. But then I remembered something Joy had told me, 'Baths are for loungers, Jane. A shower is for workers.'

I could almost imagine that she'd made her offer to test my resilience. She lived like an ascetic—no doubt she would thrive in Alcatraz herself—and therefore expected others to do the same.

It set me thinking. A hot bath might weaken my resolve. I might, lying there in relative luxury,

148

decide to go home. I'd come this far on my adventure, and living the Spartan life had actually helped me to cope.

'It's a no-go, Zeus,' I said, and went out to plant the rosemaries with renewed determination. I'd arrived at Helikion determined to finish the year's trial for my sake, to rid myself of a butterfly mentality, to make something of my life. There was work to be done.

Weeds were spreading their tentacles in the most awkward of places, poking up between the sharp barbs of the perennial plants, the devil to fork out. But, of all the tasks, it was the forthcoming olive harvest which called for intensive labour, a time when the hanging drupes on the olive trees gradually change from a light green to a berry-black—the Greeks call this stage *drypetides*, the perfect time for collection.

The previous day Joy had targeted this work to begin at the start of the next stretch of good weather and had asked her perennial band of volunteers to search the forecasts, as would she. 'Clear the week and clear the decks' was her rallying cry. Having planted and watered the last of the rosemaries on the phrygana, I went into the house to collect Winston. After I'd torn him away from teddy we made our slow journey up the hillside. I popped him over the wire goat fence and onto a trail that led along the crest of the hill. Wild shrubs and twisted old olive trees studded its sides.

Far below me stood Spiros and Eleni's stone-built house. A faint wisp of smoke came from its chimney, the bittersweet smell of burning logs carried up to me on a blustery, cold wind. I let Winston off his lead and followed him as he

149

limped along the rough path. After a few minutes we reached a dead and hollow tree trunk, our 'turn around' marker. Time to go back.

As I turned, the wind suddenly increased in strength, pricking tears from my eyes. With an arm shielding my face, I stumbled along the rocky ground, calling Winston to follow. His trick was to pop out from a particular shrub, his snout covered in dust. I'd already passed this spot when there came a loud screech, followed by a scuffling noise and the sound of broken twigs. I froze and scanned the hillside. The only movement came from the windblown scrub.

'Winston? Winston?'

There was no sign of him. I ran along the hilltop, bending low as I went, peering into the undergrowth. At the end of the line I dropped downhill ten metres and turned to make a parallel return search. 'WINSTON!'

I stopped, caught by sudden fear as I remembered Joy's warning on my first day. Her earthly comforts, she'd informed me severely, were led by her pets. Winston had a special place in her heart.

I panicked, screaming out Winston's name again and again, haphazardly dashing around and through the bushes, lifting undergrowth, all the time ignoring the tears to my clothes and scratches on my arms and face. The screech I'd heard could mean he'd been the victim of a hunter. It was the season for trapping. It was common knowledge that some hunters were not particular about trapping animals that were protected by law.

I stopped, short of breath, my hands on my knees, sweating and listening hard, but the fierce updraught, roaring through the trees and vegetation, would mask any dog's bark unless unless it came from close by. Tears of distress mingled with those produced by the wind. I dropped to my knees, sobbing. It could have been a fox. The slow-moving Winston would not have stood a chance.

I stayed on the hillside, shouting and roaming, for another half-hour, then gave up. I hoped and prayed that Winston would have found his own way downhill. I looked at my watch. Since Joy rarely went out and returned within two hours, I reckoned I had another half-hour's grace. I hopped over the goat fence and began the descent, my coat unbuttoned and blowing wide open in complete disregard of the wind.

\*     \*     \*

Wizard sat perched on top of the sofa. Occasionally he would gently nudge my head with his beak while I stared transfixed at a small tear in a Persian rug. I'd not moved in forty minutes of waiting. I caught my breath as I heard the front door open and close, followed by the sound of Joy's tip-tap tread on the marble floor.

I stood up as Titan heaved himself from the sofa and padded across the room to greet her. She appeared and patted his head. 'Been a good boy?' She looked up. On seeing me she knew that something was wrong.

'Joy. I—'

She looked quickly round. 'Where's Winston?'

'He disappeared,' I blurted out. 'He vanished as I turned round to come back.'

151

Joy stared at me. 'He won't walk far, not with his arthritis. It will get dark in an hour. I suggest you take your potholer's head-lamp and go back to look for him.' She went back to take off her coat.

'I looked for ages,' I said in a stressed voice. 'I heard a screech. Could it have been a fox?'

'No. A fox won't go for a dog. Maybe a cat, but not a dog.' She came towards me, her eyes narrowing at the mess I must have looked. She shook her head and came closer still to reach out and remove a small twig from my hair.

'Look at you.'

Encouraged by her calmness, I said, 'Joy, are you sure about a fox not—'

'Yes,' she cut in with acid certainty. 'Absolutely. Especially a bruiser like Winston.'

She disappeared into the kitchen and returned with a bottle of TCP and some cotton wool. 'Hold your head still.' She gently dabbed my face. 'Here. You can do your hands and arms.' Leaving me with the antiseptic and cotton wool she went to a side table and poured out a small tumbler of brandy.

'Now then. I want you to drink this, then go back and get your wash things. There's a red towel waiting for you in the bathroom. You need a bath.'

Minutes later I stood in the cubicle at Alcatraz as whacks of wind shook and rumbled the shutters. I stared into the cracked mirror at my scratched and mud-stained face. Red-rimmed eyes and tangled hair stared back. I wanted Winston back. I'd grown to love his ugly face and strange ways. For Joy the feeling I had must have been a hundred times worse. I opened a cupboard door and had got hold of a bottle of shampoo when I heard Joy's voice.

'Jane! Are you coming to the house? I've got

something you must see. Come as soon as you can.'

I gathered my wash things and hurried over to the house to find Joy sitting at the dining table opposite a small man whose face was partly hidden by a flat cap. He sported wild sideburns and a large drooping moustache. He clutched a glass of ouzo with his right hand, the index finger of which was missing.

Then I saw Winston. He was sitting next to Titan. I let out a cry and rushed to him. He raised his good eye, then blinked slowly as I put my arms around him. His claws were ragged and bloody, but otherwise he seemed intact. The man said something in Greek that brought a laugh from Joy.

'But how . . . where . . . where was he? I looked everywhere.' I turned my head in confused appeal.

'Jane, this is Nikiforo. He found Winston. He's a very good friend and goat herder, among other things.' She added something in Greek to Nikiforo, who stood up and with a shy smile snatched off his crumpled cap, allowing a mop of black hair to leap out as if on springs. He came to shake my hand.

Joy spoke to him again in Greek, then spoke to me. 'This is how he found Winston.'

She gestured for Nikiforo to illustrate what had happened. He put up his arms, the right hand adjacent to his right cheek, the other hand cupped as if supporting something two feet away. He then closed his left eye and with the other stared down the length of what was now clearly meant to represent a gun.

Suddenly, he froze and stared into a corner of the room, dropping his arms. He went to the

153

corner, bent down and put his arms around an imaginary object and stood up cradling it and giving me a big beam.

'What was he doing?' Joy looked at me.

'Was he hunting when he found Winston?'

'Yes. And guess what he was hunting? Foxes. He lives on the other side of the hill. They kill his chickens.'

'But what happened to Winston?' I said.

'We don't know. When Nikiforo found him he was just lying down under a bush. The vet's coming. Now you go and have your bath.'

Suddenly, from outside, there was the sound of a plant pot breaking. Nikiforo put up his arms in realization, babbled something and dashed outside, followed by Joy. She stopped dead, making me almost fall into her back. She was staring in horror at a herd of goats chewing the leaves in the flowerbeds. Nikiforo, cap in hand, was chasing around, trying to herd them together, at the same time shouting out his apologies.

Joy was frantic. 'My gazanias. Stop them!'

A shaggy-haired goat had stopped eating and walked towards Joy, staring at her with a demonic yellow-eyed glare.

'He looks angry, Joy,' I said cautiously.

The goat bent its head as if about to charge but Joy merely put up the palm of her hand in a gentle movement and then, eyes cast down, walked slowly backwards. After a moment the goat hesitated and then turned away.

'Animals are all the same,' Joy said tersely. 'Well, not all, but goats especially like slowness and gentleness. If you treat them like that they'll behave like that.'

As if hearing what she'd said, Nikiforo changed his tactics. He produced a bamboo pipe and began to blow monotonous notes while walking downhill to where a large white van stood, its rear doors wide open, its rusting chrome handles held together by nothing stronger than a piece of bent metal.

As soon as he drew near Nikiforo put away his pipe and turned to grab the first goat that came to hand, lifting it expertly into the van. Once the last goat had been loaded, he shut the doors and twisted the piece of metal into a more practical shape, before dropping it into place.

He turned and said something to Joy. She responded with a stern look and to my amazement backed away, both hands raised and shaking in an act of absolute refusal. Nikiforo moved towards her gesticulating, annoyed. Then, with a shake of the head, he climbed into his cab. Joy watched him drive away, his arm waving goodbye out of the window, then turned to walk back to the house.

I was forced to ask, 'What was all that about Joy?'

'About what?'

'You looked angry and he was upset.'

'Oh that. He wanted to pay for the broken pot. I wouldn't let him. The nerve of it.'

She gave a short chuckle then ushered me inside the house. 'Go on. Get that bath, for goodness' sake.'

\*       \*       \*

As I luxuriated in the hot bath I no longer felt concern that it might weaken my resolve. Too much had happened between Joy visiting me at Alcatraz and the drama of Winston's disappearance and reappearance. Joy had shown her warmth, for what it was. I decided that if it happened again I would simply wait for the recommencement of our normal relationship. At least I hoped that's how I would react.

The vet came to examine Winston. When I returned to the living room Joy was cooking a meal. I listened anxiously as she gave me his report. 'Dodgy ticker. On two pills a day now. Got to cut his walks down. Jane, do you know what connects Winston with today, November seventeenth?'

I shook my head.

'I only told you this morning. Students demonstrated against the Greek junta. Their tanks smashed through the gates of the polytechnic and killed at least twenty of them. I did tell you.'

She'd not told me.

'It's Winston's biorhythms. Like his namesake, he hates injustice.' She laid a second place at the table and told me to get myself a glass of ouzo.

I paused before speaking. 'Joy? Are you inviting me . . . ?'

'What do you think? It's a veggie. Eggplants and zucchini. And olive oil for your health and strength. You've had a rough time. Got to get you fit for the olive harvest.' She looked at me sympathetically. 'Now you're not to worry about Winston. You did your best. It could have happened with anyone. And I need at least another game of Scrabble if just to get euros out of you. It's expensive running the garden.' She gave me a wry smile. 'Oh, you still owe me a euro.'

156

Having eaten and played a game of Scrabble, which Joy won, I returned to Alcatraz much happier than when I'd left it. I thought of what my next move would have been had not Nikiforo gone out to shoot foxes. Joy's talk of 'fate' being the 'overseer of our destinies' struck a chord.

*     *     *

The next week, along the way to the village we passed cars with bags and baskets of olives in half-open boots, straining at the ropes holding them inside.

'Look, Jane.' Joy flung her arm across my body and pointed to an olive grove. 'We'll soon be doing that, picking up sunshine. Nothing gives me greater pleasure.'

'Watch out!' I shouted, as an oncoming car swerved away from the Jeep.

'You *are* a nervous little flower. You ought to see Greeks at roundabouts. New thing around here. Great fun. Like the dodgems.'

We slowed down at the back of a traffic queue, adjacent to another olive grove. Joy pointed at a group of pickers, mostly men, thrashing at the olive branches with long sticks, forcing showers of drupes to fall on groundsheets. Women and young children were gathered round, picking up the fruit and dropping them in burlap sacks, baskets and plastic bags.

Joy reached for her atomizer. 'That's us soon. Troops are on alert.' Motorists in the queue had started to blow their horns impatiently. Joy decided to pass the time by giving me a lecture. I was a captive audience in the Jeep.

'At the time of Pericles olive oil made Athens rich. The city was given a monopoly to export it. It's very good for the skin. I use it. Keeps it soft. You must try it. And . . .'

Joy talked on. The traffic began to move. As we neared the village my favourite olive tree came to mind. It stood at the corner of the track leading to Charles and Rachel's house. Before our walkabouts, I'd often climb its wide and gnarled trunk to lie in a natural curve between two branches. With the sun out and in a blustery wind, its leaves would flash silver and gold, exquisite tints that I could not see on other trees—'sparkling jewels', Joy called them. At lunchtime I would recline in the tree to read a book and munch on snacks. I would frequently glance out over the plain and in the odd moment of homesickness imagine I was in one of the planes climbing out of the airport. Mostly, though, I'd be happy to be alone, without the interference and hassle of the modern world.

And, at dusk with a fiery violet and red sky, of all the trees at Helikion, my olive tree had the blackest of silhouettes.

My safety belt dug into my chest, jerking me back to reality. Joy had slammed on the brakes before a red light.

'It's at red, you see,' she said crossly. 'Any other time it's yellow.'

She gave a heavy sigh and looked at me. 'By the way, I've got something interesting for tomorrow morning. It needs an early start.'

Then she sat back and smiled—I thought rather smugly.

'Meet me at the lower terrace at six fifty-nine

a.m.'

I frowned at her. 'Six fifty-nine. Why not seven o'clock?'

'Six fifty-nine. You were in the Navy. Let's synchronize watches.' She looked at her wristwatch.

'Not while you're driving!'

'No. Quite right, Jane. We'll do it tonight.'

I sighed and sank deeper into my seat. Her order was not entirely a surprise as she had an odd attitude to punctuality. Once I'd arrived at a meeting place fifteen minutes early. To my immense surprise instead of being applauded I had received an admonishment. I was never given any reason.

I returned to the subject as we walked to the village shop. But Joy, inexplicably, would have none of it. 'Dead on time is six fifty-nine. It doesn't mean being early. On the other hand, if you're late by a minute . . .' She paused to raise a finger, giving me a twisted smile, 'I'll make you *dead* on time.'

How weird. She was always relaxed about lunch and tea breaks. As long as the work was done and the tools were cleared away, I could take as long as I liked. So what was going on? Joy was a continuing mystery.

\*　　　\*　　　\*

Getting out of bed at 6.30 a.m. in Alcatraz on a chilly morning had no attraction or mystery. With the first splash of cold water on my face I came alive to the possibility that Joy's eccentricities were multiplying as well as becoming increasingly

159

bizarre. I'd scoured my mind for a reason why she should order me out an hour before my normal working day began. There was nothing in the garden that required attention from either of us at that time in the morning.

I stepped outside at 6.56 a.m. The previous evening I'd timed the walk to the meeting point as taking approximately three minutes. I could always adjust my speed of descent because she would be visible, even in the half-light.

Yes, there she was, her dark outline sitting on the stone wall below. As I reached halfway distance I could make out two mugs of steaming coffee at her side. l looked at my watch—6.58 a.m. I was on schedule. Now I could make out the two prostrate rosemaries I'd planted out, stretching along the wall behind her, their dark-green needles hanging over its vertical drop.

I approached, kicking the gravel to announce my arrival. She looked towards me then stared at her watch. 'Bang on cue. Drink your coffee.' I sat beside her and stared at the murky plain.

'You know, Jane, when I first arrived, the airport, highway, none of those hideous advertising boards were around.'

I clutched my mug of coffee and took a sip, wondering what on earth I was doing sitting on a cold stone wall at seven o'clock in the morning. Joy suddenly tensed and pointed at one of the mountains in the distance. 'Look at that, nothing else. Keep your eyes on the mountain.'

I fixed my gaze. Nothing. Wait—there was a dim orange glow around its jagged outline.

Joy looked at her watch. 'Ten, nine, eight, seven, six, five . . .'

The mountain suddenly erupted, shooting flames of fire and lava high into the sky. The entire plain in the foreground was obliterated, pitched into total blackness.

'Oh my God,' I breathed, my mouth open.

'Don't look at me. Keep watching!'

Amazingly, the eruption spread around the mountainside, enveloping it in a gigantic ball of fire. It was the sun. As its crescent rose slowly into view I stared in wonder.

'You've just witnessed your first volcano sunrise. Performance art, created by sun and mountain. You were lucky. I mean, we were lucky.' She stood up. 'You can see why the ancients had their gods. Man needs some form of explanation.'

I sat stunned, not in the aftermath of one of nature's great spectacles, but from my sudden and marvellous liberation from deep anxiety. Joy was sane, for the moment at least.

Then I frowned suddenly. 'Joy? Why did I have to meet you exactly one minute before?'

'Because I know you. You'd have been here at least ten minutes early if I'd told you what to expect. It gave you nine minutes more in bed. I need you rested as much as possible.' I lowered my head and smiled to myself.

*       *       *

Joy insisted on cooking me breakfast, scrambled egg and tomatoes with a sprinkling of feta cheese. We'd finished eating when the cowbell clanged and clanked, the first of the volunteers arriving for the olive picking. Joy answered the door.

'Nikiforo. *Ela*, come in. You remember Jane.'

161

The little man entered, carrying a brown paper bag. On seeing me he raised a hand in greeting. He was almost unrecognizable from two days ago. His shock of hair was gelled flat and he'd trimmed his sideburns. He patted down a stubborn curl and smiled at me then dipped into the bag and brought out a handful of green leaves. 'Horta.'

Joy clapped her hands. 'How wonderful. Wild greens for elevenses, Jane.' She thanked Nikiforo then looked anxiously on as he threw teddy across the room for Winston to chase. Joy stopped him with a hand on his shoulder and, pointing at Winston, talked sadly in Greek. Nikiforo's face fell as he digested the news about his heart.

Joy looked at me. 'I told him why I've hidden my village shoes. Can't have Winston popping off *in flagrante delicto.*'

Concerned, she watched Winston settle on his Zulu warrior stool and then spoke again in Greek. Nikiforo laughed and took up a position to point directly at me. He pretended to pick up something and, holding it aloft at an angle, began to shake the imaginary object with sharp, snappy movements then jabbed his finger up in the air.

'What's he doing, Jane?'

I laughed. 'No idea, Joy.'

'He was asking if you wanted to pick olives.'

'Oh, of course,' I said. 'Do the pickers play charades a lot?'

'Yes. Nikiforo's in training. He's practising on you. Christos was a great one for charades.'

\*     \*     \*

We were washing up when Charles and Rachel

162

arrived.

'Mind where you're putting that, Charles.' Rachel stumbled in, wearing knee and elbow pads.

Charles followed, carrying a long-handled plastic rake and a large groundsheet. He placed them on the marble floor. 'Nikiforo, hello, old chap.'

Nikiforo stood up, bowed and then shook Charles's hand. Vassili and Demetri were the next to arrive, carrying a large hamper bulging with food and bottles of wine.

'Greek champagne!' cried Vassili, showing me two bottles, which he placed on the table, each displaying a picture of an old bearded Greek on its label. 'For your bumped head, Joy.'

Joy laughed, then Pavlos arrived, wearing blue overalls and carrying an accordion. 'Music for laters.'

'Wonderful. My darlings, let's begin now.' Vassili spread out his arms and sang a Greek folk song out of tune, abruptly stopping at the sight of Joy's face. 'Forgive me, your ladies,' he said, chuckling. Champagne was poured. Everyone stood in a circle and toasted the olive.

'*Stin Elia!* To the olive!'

It was savoured at first, then drunk quickly as Joy briefly outlined her plan of campaign. She finished with a rallying cry. 'Everyone to the phrygana! Jane, Pavlos, bring the stepladders.'

She marched out of the house followed by her troops. Ten minutes later we stood in the middle of a circle of fruit-laden olive trees.

'Each team has three volunteers on the ladders,' said Joy. 'The rest will be pickers on the ground.'

'Could I be hamper and coffee duty?' Vassili said with a hesitant smile.

163

Joy glared at him and spoke slowly. 'For the benefit of those of you who haven't done this before . . .' She nodded at Vassili and then at me. 'Be careful on the ladders. I don't want anyone suffering a broken ankle as Charles did a few years ago.'

Charles wiggled his foot. 'Good as new. Metal pins in there.'

Rachel grinned. 'He's always the terrorist at every airport metal detector.' She looked around at the sound of a straining car engine. A mini arrived and parked next to the Neanderthal's fence. The American volunteer, Angela, hopped out to escort her passenger, a tall lady with a stooped back.

'Sorry, Joy,' Angela huffed. 'Twins playing up again.'

'Not at all, Angela. Bang on time. Now then, Mary, you sure you're up to this?'

Mary, the tall lady, opened up a paper bag she'd been carrying. 'Of course—got my protection.' She drew out a pair of surgical gloves and a face mask.

Joy saw my look and sidled up to me. 'Mary adores plants,' she whispered, 'but she's allergic. So plays safe.' She turned away and raised her voice.

'Now, everybody, please listen.'

The chimes of a mobile phone sounded. Everyone patted their pockets and looked at each other. Joy put her hand on her hips. 'Nikiforo.' He grinned sheepishly, brought out his mobile and turned it off.

'Thank you. Now I'll pick the teams. Mary, Demetri, Angela and Nikiforo are team one. Charles, Rachel, Pavlos and Jane, team two.

Ladder and ground jobs to be rotated every half-hour. And Vassili, please get rocks to put on the dust sheets. The wind may lift them up otherwise. Now, remember, whichever team has the heaviest load wins a prize which Vassili has brought with him. I hope.'

Vassili smiled smugly and proudly pointed to the hamper. 'Lovely presents.'

'Right.' Joy looked at her watch. 'The record is one hundred and twenty-six kilos from two years ago. Good luck—and let's begin.'

The trees were assaulted by ladder. As Charles reached the top rung he said it reminded him of D-Day when the American Rangers flung up their ladders to scale a cliff. Climbing to the highest point, he gave the tree an enormous whack with his rake.

'Charles?' said Joy, looking up. 'I know there's a debate about whacking versus hand-picking and I know that you've won the prize the last three years but the olives don't exactly enjoy being smashed about. Nor does the tree especially. A little less sadism, please.'

'Who got the prize three years ago?' Charles panted, stopping to wipe his face.

'I've got a Neanderthal for a neighbour and another one up a ladder,' Joy muttered wearily, then raised her voice. 'Carry on, Charles. There's no proof I'm right.'

'The olive is a strong tree, Jane,' said Pavlos, scrabbling on the groundsheet collecting the fallen olives.

'True, Pavlos,' said Joy, overhearing him. 'But does it benefit the quality of the oil? Do we bash oranges or apples? No, it would ruin them. Why

165

should olives be any different?'

When the top half of the tree was cleared Charles and Rachel descended to the ground to pick from the lower branches. The other team were five minutes behind. Joy looked at her watch. 'Half an hour gone. Right, everybody, changeover time.'

The drill was that after a thirty-minute stint, the 'hogs' on the ground would swap tasks with the 'rakers' on the ladders. And so the morning progressed. After each tree had been stripped of its drupes, we would move the groundsheet and ladders to the next tree and start all over again. As the sun grew in strength, with it came a gradual removal of layers of clothing. It could have been spring.

Joy called lunch break and I accompanied her and Vassili to the house. We returned with bags containing bread, olives, feta cheese and a cold box holding bottles of lemonade.

'Hard stuff later,' Vassili said, his face beaming.

We tucked in. I listened to Demetri and Angela's conversation about the presidential election in America with interest—I was out of the loop where news was concerned—when Joy demanded silence with a sudden gesture.

'Listen. He's back.'

The roar of a sports car shooting up the drive in low gear changed to a growl as it approached the Neanderthal's gates. The driver of the black Porsche Carrera, his eyes hidden by a pair of black wraparound sunglasses, turned his head towards us.

'So, the devil's back.' Joy made to stand. 'I think I'll go and—'

'No, Joy.' Pavlos gripped her arm and watched the Porsche glide through the gates before releasing her.

She took a deep breath and stared at the ground, composing herself.

'It's your turn on the ladder, Jane,' Charles said quietly, breaking the silence. He rubbed his back and handed me the long-handled plastic rake.

'Yes,' said Joy with a tight smile. 'Back to work.'

'I have ideas, Joy,' Pavlos blurted out, his brown eyes lit with inspiration.

He pointed at the Neanderthal's gates. 'Saw on TV programmes. We could put a video camera on a remote-control aeroplane. Fly over his garden and film the boreholes.' He jumped up and ran forward, spreading his arms wide to imitate a plane.

We laughed, while Joy lit a cigarette and nodded sagely. She flicked an olive twig off her arm. 'Pavlos, do you know someone with this kind of equipment? Because it would be very expensive.'

Pavlos replied by pulling down his face and casually lowering his chin before tossing his head back. It was the characteristic expression of a Greek answering 'no'.

'Pity,' said Joy.

Mary pulled down her face mask, pointed at Angela and quickly said, 'The twins have got one,' before covering her mouth again.

'Oh yes,' Angela said. 'Little tykes drive me mad with it.' She screwed up her forehead. 'Flew it into next door's geraniums yesterday. Yep, borrow it, feel free to lose it.'

Pavlos rumbled with laughter and put his arm round Joy's shoulder. 'We shall call it ...' He

paused and lowered his voice to a dramatic bass:
'Operations of the Watershed.'

'Operation Neanderthal,' Vassili said, pulling a
macabre face.

'Operation Churchill,' Charles murmured from a
prone position on the groundsheet, his head
resting on Titan's back.

Joy looked to the Neanderthal's fence then
swiftly turned to pick up a rake and quickly
dragged it along a hanging branch weighed down
heavily with drupes.

*       *       *

At five o'clock, Joy called an end to the day's work.
Sweaty and tired, we carried the bags of olives to
the garage. Charles, Pavlos and Nikiforo managed
to carry one each, Joy warning Charles not to
strain his back.

We gathered outside the garage, where each bag
was weighed on a set of dirty bathroom scales, the
weight and name of the team of pickers recorded
by Joy in a pocket book.

'Thank you, each and every one,' Joy said when
all was finished. She did a quick mental
calculation.

'You have broken the record for a first day.
Ninety kilos.'

Cheers rang round the garage.

'Now. The prize to the best team, with sixty-one
kilos, goes to ... Jane, Pavlos, Charles and
Rachel.'

Charles raised his hands over his head, clenching
his fists like a victorious boxer. Rachel put an arm
around my shoulder, smiling affectionately at him.

'Such an exhibitionist, Jane. It's those pins in his leg.'

Vassili opened his hamper. Inside were party hats, cakes, pink sherbet lollies and bottles of champagne. Since the prize would be shared by all, they were left in the hamper ahead of the celebration. Joy lit a cigarette. 'Right. Now take it in turn to use the bathroom and get that muck off you. Did you bring towels? Jane? Pavlos? Would you get chairs and a table from the ghost room. You know where the key is.'

*     *     *

It was 6 p.m. We sat around the oldest olive tree on the phrygana, close to the 'threshing floor'. Robins hopped on and off branches as Vassili and Demetri emptied the hamper's contents onto the table.

'Plenty of champers. A bottle each,' Demetri joked, peering at us over his half-moon spectacles.

'Music, we need music,' Joy said, and went to fetch her wind-up gramophone.

She walked across the 'threshing floor' to cross under a pine tree, then stopped suddenly in the dappled light beneath it.

'Jane, everyone. The first winter iris is out!' She beckoned us over.

Champagne glasses in hand, we went to join her, looking down at a dense clump of grass-like leaves. A solitary lavender flower gently swayed in the breeze, the sun's rays dancing upon its petals in a shimmering light. I bent down to poke around the leaves.

'Jane's looking for buds,' Joy said. 'I had a

scientist from Washington. He wanted data on their breaking out. I've been sending it for five years now. This one's out early.'

'Messenger of the gods,' Pavlos said softly, squatting down to study the flower. 'Iris in mythology. She transported souls of mortals to the underworld, leavings a rainbow in her wakes.'

'Not a bad thing to leave behind,' Charles said robustly, and lifted his glass. 'A toast to Iris.'

We raised our glasses.

'To olives,' Vassili said, smacking his lips.

'To Winston,' I said, looking at Joy.

'To his finest hour,' she replied, smiling at me.

The feast began, conversation muted at first. After a few minutes Pavlos donned his accordion and—between eating and drinking—played Greek folk music. That, and the comfortable ease of friendly companionship, soon lulled me into a doze.

I woke up to a slight chill in the air. Long shadows and stripes of fading light decorated the phrygana. Joy noticed me shivering and rubbing my arms.

She stood up and observed, 'It's getting cold.' She pointed at Pavlos. 'Time to dance.'

After a pause he struck an introductory chord, then launched into the staccato rhythm of a well-known Greek dance. Mary and Angela clapped and hummed along. Vassili and Nikiforo faced each other, placed their hands behind their backs and began to move their feet slowly and lightly in keen awareness of their pride and comradeship. The rhythm picked up and Vassili suddenly broke away, staggering into a mock collapse, gasping for breath. Nikiforo kept dancing.

'Go on, Jane, join him,' urged Joy. 'Play "Syrtaki" for Jane, Pavlos. She'll know it.'

I drained my champagne glass and stood up, ready for the challenge. Pavlos played a few notes at which Nikiforo smiled in acknowledgment. He stood next to me, his arms outstretched. Demetri came to position my arms gently over his. 'Hands rest on shoulders. That's right. Now follow his steps.'

The music began in an ultra-slow rhythm, giving me plenty of time in which to observe Nikiforo's movements. Finally, I had the basic pattern, first left foot forward, then tapping the ball of the right foot next to the left heel and swinging the leg forward to kick slightly at the end. Then Nikiforo introduced me to the art of squatting and kicking. Soon sweating, I began to perform with confidence until Pavlos let out a loud and joyous shout. Grinning and tapping his foot, he ratcheted up the beat, squeezing and pulling his accordion for dear life.

With the group shouting their praise and encouragement, I let myself go. As the music reached a crescendo, I was lost in a fit of giggles, unable to keep up with Nikiforo. I reeled away as Nikiforo drew applause as he kicked, squatted and sidestepped to a rousing finale. Still out of breath, I was congratulated by Charles. 'Terrific, Jane. As good as the Greeks. You'll be smashing plates and smoking like a trooper next.'

Nikiforo patted me on the back. Angela and Demetri stood up to dance as Pavlos began to play again, this time at a slower tempo. I went to sit next to Joy. Her hand was ruffling Winston's ears.

'You lent me the book,' I puffed. 'The music, it's

from the film. *Zorba the Greek.*'

Joy poured out a fresh glass of champagne, handed it to me and sat upright.

'If you want to be happy for a day, get drunk,' she affirmed. 'Happy for a week, kill a pig. For a month, get married. For life, be a gardener who reads. It's an old Chinese proverb, Jane, tinkered with by an old English gardener.'

She turned to watch the dancers, tapping her fingers on the side of her leg. I sipped more champagne and looked down the phrygana at the remaining olives on their trees, gleaming in the dying rays of the sun. I gazed upon the sprouting leaves of the spring bulbs, at the golden terracotta soil, and at that moment would not have wished to have been anywhere else on earth.

# 9

# The Odd Couple

ODD
couple
waiting
for olive
oil at
pressing
plant

Olive picking for the following day was cancelled owing to the sudden weakening of a ridge of high pressure. Instead of the anticipated fair weather we had heavy showers. Fortunately the run-off was not as severe as we'd experienced during the first storm and the garden hardly suffered—unlike me.

The weather befitted my mood. The happy gaggle of olive pickers had gone, taking with them their music, dancing and laughter, flown to their chatty families and friends, at liberty to go anywhere, to pass their days in the way people enjoy most—with other people.

Jealous of their freedom, waking with a sore head and churning stomach, I tried to assuage my ire by kicking Zeus. It only made me feel guilty and so I gave him an apology. I spent the day in the garage carrying out Joy's instruction of separating the large, juicy black olives from the smaller green drupes. It was a simple job well suited to a hangover. Joy brought me a mug of tea and helped for a while, then dived back into the house, saying she'd left a pan bubbling on the stove.

The rain continued to fall, so I moved from garage to living room. There were always seeds to clean and sort. Joy was forever delving into drawers and bringing out old envelopes full of dusty plant material. She'd pop husks and leaves onto the microscope slide and have me up and down like a yo-yo, consulting botanical tomes and cross-referencing information.

As I sat at the table opposite Joy I realized that I'd completely forgotten my worries over her behaviour. Yesterday, apart from her agitated reaction to the arrival of the Neanderthal, she'd been calm, funny and on top form.

But then something happened which brought back my concern. Joy stopped working, put a finger to her chin and frowned.

'Have I told you, Jane, in the New and Old Testaments of the Bible olive oil is referred to one hundred and forty times and the olive tree one hundred times?'

'Yes,' I answered. 'You have.'

She laughed. 'Doesn't that mean we're doing God's work? Yes, olive oil has quite a history. In the New and Old Testaments it's mentioned a hundred and forty times.'

I looked quizzically at her, but she was oblivious, shutting one eye to peer at a plate of tiny seeds through her magnifying glass. Had she repeated it in confirmation or had she forgotten she'd just said it?

She began asking questions about my childhood. They were the same questions as yesterday.

Tired, the hangover lingering, all I wanted to do was join Titan stretched out on the sofa. I told her I had a headache and quick as a flash she darted into her desk and brought out a tablet, then fetched a glass of water, plonking it down in front of me.

'Thank you, Joy,' I said gratefully, popping the Nurofen in my mouth and swallowing it with a sip of water. Then I took a silent inward breath. Had she forgotten that I'd related my childhood through into adulthood, even into my relationships, which I am either hopeless at or unlucky with, my last one a particularly sad tale?

She'd been intrigued by my story of the guitar-playing Moroccan who, after a two-year relationship, decided it was time to stop playing music, start practising his faith and give up drinking and so, as the natural consequence thereof, me.

My concern for her was tinged with resentment in that I'd replied to all her questions, but whenever I asked about her family and past she would cut me dead with a sharp command intended to change the subject. It was a diversionary tactic like the one she'd used recently when I'd asked about the paintings in her room.

I went back to Alcatraz to write in my diary:

*Now I know the real meaning of 'stir crazy'. Couldn't cope with Joy today. I wish somebody would put her in* Big Brother. *I'd even watch the live streaming if I knew I could get to know the 'real' Joy. I've asked about her first marriage and when she ran the zoo with her second husband, Christos. I've also asked about her brief modelling career. But got nothing. Why? What's she hiding?*

Thinking of all the hurdles I'd faced and crossed since arriving at Helikion, I scrawled across the page the wartime command taken from a Second World War poster, a call for resilience to a nation under attack: '*Keep Calm and Carry On.*'

\* \* \*

Because the volunteers were no longer available

for the final olive picking, Joy declared that, come the first dry day, she and I would bring in the rest of the harvest. She was sure we could face the challenge. 'I'll be the underdog, you be top dog, Jane,' she said.

Each time we walked out of the house, I'd glance at a small framed picture, which hung above the front door. It was of a man in a log pit covered in sawdust while his mate sawed away merrily on top. It was rather apt since, during the day, I was up the ladder with Joy below, seemingly content to suffer the leaves, twigs and dust that I showered upon her.

When I laid the groundsheet for the second tree, the wind blew up and I had to fetch extra stones to weigh it down. It was at this moment that Joy ended her lengthy denouncement of the Neanderthal, after which no jury would have sentenced him to anything less than hanging, drawing and quartering. That led to the whole business of water conservation. Interesting as it was at the first hearing, it was now just something to which I listened without paying attention. It was like listening to one of Joy's scratched vinyl records, the needle stuck on repeat.

I wondered if all the British interns who had terminated their year early had done so out of an inability to cope with Joy rather than privation in Alcatraz. Having thought about it, I guessed both—equally—had played their part.

I looked down to see her energetically working on the groundsheet. If olive oil kept you young, as Joy claimed, then the proof lay in the sight of her scrabbling below.

Suddenly she stopped and held a limp, arthritic

hand to her chest in pain. As she caught my stare, she flashed a quick smile as if all was well and resumed her gathering. At that moment of bravery I felt a lump in my throat. Her repetitive questions and failing memory were not her fault and—though it would be difficult—I resolved to try and do my best not to become upset by anything she did or said.

I thought about the stress she must be suffering as she waited on the fate of her beloved garden. No doubt some of this had been vented in the emotions she displayed whenever she talked about—or saw—the Neanderthal. His elusive borehole gave her a target to which she clung in the hope of forgetting her misfortunes.

I despised myself. Given all her problems, I should admire her the more.

*     *     *

The wind eased as dusk fell upon the garden. We were tackling the last olive tree to be picked at Helikion. The steepness of the hillside and the rocky ground made it a precarious challenge. I was balanced on the top step of the ladder, reaching for the last and highest hanging shoot, while Joy was steadying its legs.

I pushed out the long-handled rake, at the same time removing my foot from the top step to place it in a joint between the main trunk and a branch. Using it as leverage, I reached for the shoot. I felt the step give way. In alarm I clutched the nearest branch, searching for a foothold. I quickly found one and looked down.

Realizing that she'd let go of the steps, Joy

179

dropped the box of matches and unlit cigarette she was holding, quickly grabbed the ladder and secured it in position.

'Sorry, Jane.'

Tentatively, I put my foot down on the top step and tested its balance. Breathing heavily, I came down the ladder. 'Close shave,' I chuckled, nervously. 'Don't know what happened there. I should have kept hold.'

Joy, for once, was lost for words. In lighting a cigarette she may have forgotten I was up the ladder. In our mutual embarrassment there was an awkward hiatus. It was broken by a shout from the direction of the track. It was a man, waving a piece of paper.

It's Charles,' I said. 'He's got something. I'll go.'

'No. It might be to do with you. Clear up. Finish for the day. Olive pressing tomorrow.'

I watched her walk away, and made a mental note to ask her what she'd meant by saying it might be to do with me.

*        *        *

Early the next morning, I made my way to the house, zipping up my puffa jacket and tightening my scarf. The morning was crisp. Dewdrops glistened on plump leaves, while a flock of starlings wheeled over the house. A dark pink miasma cloaked the black bulk of Mount Hymettos, promising a sunny day.

On reaching the gravelled drive I smelled cigarette smoke.

'Joy?' I looked around for her.

There was a pinprick of red light between the

huge leaves of a 'century plant', followed by a white plume of smoke. Her head popped out. She looked around quickly and walked towards me, her feet crunching on the gravel. 'Doing a recce,' she said. 'I heard a van or something about six, looked out, saw it go in the Neanderthal's. We had them in the war, you know. Fifth columnists we called them. Infiltrators and saboteurs. Anyway, come on, there'll be a queue at the pressing. Don't want to be too late.' She hurried me into the house.

Joy fed the dogs and applied her blueberry lipstick at the dining table, while I sat next to Titan on the sofa, drinking coffee. The pressing, she said, would be interesting for the type of people who turned up, as well as the process itself. 'What do you expect to see, Jane?'

'I'm not sure, Joy,' I said, not wanting to sound foolish. I'd studied one of Joy's old books on olive pressing—a raggedy thing, its spine broken—and from its pages had developed a romantic vision of the pressing plant and our coming day. There would be a jolly farmer and his wife wearing leather aprons, a large shed with straw on the ground, perhaps a donkey tethered to a post, and a stream of golden light falling on grinding stones, olive oil dripping to the floor.

I looked at Joy gazing into the mirror, smudging the lipstick with her little finger.

For a moment she was still, her head tilted upright so the loose skin on her neck was stretched and hardly wrinkled. She'd applied shadow and mascara on her eyelashes, and used a delicate layer of blusher, highlighting her cheekbones. For a brief moment I saw the attractive woman who had graced the photograph in the V&A diary.

Once ready, she grabbed Winston, attached his lead and led me from the house, suddenly stopping to whisper in my face. 'Time for things ... *spiritual.*'

When we reached the Jeep I was astonished. All the olive bags were stacked in the back. 'Joy? Did you load this on your own?'

'Yes, why? Only took me a few minutes before breakfast.'

'Why didn't you ask me to do it?' I recalled the look of pain on her face the previous day.

'What? I can carry a ten-ton weight if need be,' she said with a bright, challenging smile.

I squeezed into the front seat, sharing it with Winston. Then I looked back.

'Joy? The bags. You won't be able to see through your rear mirror.'

'Who needs to be looking back? There's too much of it. It's what's facing you that matters.' She fired up the engine.

I closed my eyes as we reached the bottom of the driveway. Her habit of lurching across the road among speeding traffic always had my heart racing. I would usually slam my feet against an imaginary brake and grip the car seat until my knuckles whitened. Today, I tried to relax and imagined that I was a bird, flying over the trees of Kew, the gentle rise and fall of the Palm House in the background. I would let the Three Daughters of Night, the overseers of my destiny, decide my fate.

'I've told you about Homer,' Joy said, steering the Jeep into a straight line bound for the village. 'What did I say about his description of olive oil?'

'He called it liquid gold,' I said, opening my eyes now that Joy had the Jeep on an even keel. 'In *The*

*Odyssey.'*

'Now, what are the olive fruit's main constituents, Jane?' Joy put her foot down just as a van was overtaking us.

'Slow down!' I shrieked, as it came level, horn blaring.

Joy loudly tutted and slapped the wheel with her hand. 'Water, sugars, proteins, anthocyanins, oleuropein.' She answered her own question, then took her foot off the pedal to allow the van to swerve in front of us, narrowly missing an oncoming car.

I relaxed my grip on the car seat and Joy handed me a piece of paper.

'Haven't been to the plant in a while. Last year's harvest was terrible and there was a bad frost two years ago. Without a good prune they can be like apple trees: one year good, the next a bumper crop—in fact, so many you can't give them away.'

I looked at the piece of paper. It was a map, hand drawn. From the bottom left-hand corner of the page, two pencilled parallel lines led from a square labelled Helikion and snaked towards the top right-hand corner where there was a thickly outlined circle labelled 'Community pressing plant', plus a scribbled note:

*Jane. Memorize this.*
  *Extra Virgin Olive Oil—Roughly 5 kilos of olives make 1 kilo of olive oil. Completely natural and nutritious (no refining or blending with refined oil permitted).*
  *To qualify as 'Extra Virgin' a producer's oil must pass many tests. The IOOC— International Olive Oil Council—is a UN-*

*chartered body that regulates olive oil*
*throughout most of the world, but not the*
*United States. The principal determinant for*
*passing:*
*1. An oil must have no more than 1 gram*
*per 100 grams of oleic acid, a free fatty acid*
*that occurs naturally in the fruit.*

After ten minutes or so, Joy pulled off the road and crawled along a track bordered by hedgerows draped in old man's beard, cobwebbed tangles of seed heads glistening in the sunlight.

'Is this the right way? Course, you don't learn to read maps in the Navy, do you? Just point the boat in the right direction.' She gave a coarse laugh.

'No, we did learn map-reading in the Navy. In basic training we had to spend a weekend on Dartmoor. Got wet and frozen stiff.'

Joy gave me a look. 'But you put up with it.'

'Had to.'

'No, you didn't. You could have quit. If you found it too tough.'

I sensed the import of what she said. There was a pause before she spoke again.

'You're not a quitter, are you, Jane?'

I hesitated. This would be the perfect time to tell her about my 'time' in the Navy. I decided to take the plunge. I felt convinced that she had taken me on because of my 'four years' service' in uniform and I didn't want to perpetuate the myth any longer.

'Er . . . Joy, I have something to confess.'

'Oh?' She looked at me.

I spoke steadily, trying to keep my nerve. 'I left the Navy after nine months. I didn't go AWOL or

184

anything. I wouldn't have done that. It just wasn't for me and I . . . well, I got depressed by it and they discharged me. So I lied on my CV.'

Joy stared at the road ahead, her mouth clenched. I held my breath in anguish. She spoke, crunching the gears. 'Sometimes, you know, it's braver to leave things behind than stay. Some people take longer than others to discover themselves.'

I could have burst out in song, it was such a relief.

'Thanks, Joy. I'm sorry.'

'I've done worse things than lie on a CV, Jane.' She said it so quietly I had to listen carefully above the noise of the engine. It was as though she was talking to herself. I waited in taut suspense and with not a little excitement.

She spoke again, this time clearly. 'And I didn't accept you because of your time in the Navy, anyway.'

'Didn't you?'

'No. I liked the fact you'd done many things. I also liked your email address, it showed more of an imagination than the other applicants; it showed you had an appetite for gardening.'

I looked out of the window and smiled wryly. All that worry for nothing. And typical Joy—a puzzle never to be worked out.

Round a bend the road suddenly widened to reveal a flat area of land and a square concrete building in its centre. A blue metal chute came out through one of its walls, spewing out a brown dry material into a large metal skip. There wasn't a jolly farmer to be seen and it was nothing like a shed in an idyllic field.

'The community pressing plant,' Joy announced. 'That stuff coming out of the chute, that's what's left over from the pressing. Great for gardeners, enriches the soil and you can make soap out of it. How's that for a low carbon footprint.'

We joined the traffic queue. The truck in front had a large plastic bathtub strapped to its back. Two tousle-haired children sat in it, grinning at us, clinging on as the truck jerked forward and stopped.

Twenty minutes later we found ourselves in the car park. Beyond was a small block of low-level apartments, with satellite dishes festooned over its peeling walls. Washing hung from balcony railings. An old man sat smoking a pipe, sleepily watching the vehicles below.

There were no marked parking places. Every driver was on his or her own, slinging their vehicle into the nearest gap.

Joy was one of the lucky ones, poised to grab the place of a vehicle leaving. As soon as it was clear she drove the Jeep into the space with a whoop of delight. 'Confidence, Jane. Without it we get nowhere!'

As we left the Jeep I was drawn to a small crowd, some defying the chilly morning in T-shirts, others wrapped in hats and scarves. They were watching bags of olives being weighed, having been taken from a tiny red Fiat 500. A burly ponytailed man, wearing dungarees hemmed at the ankles by cycle clips, seemed to be in charge. He made a note of the weight of each bag as it was dumped onto the scales. Afterwards, the owner emptied it into a hopper adjacent to the wall of the plant.

Ponytail man looked at Joy and asked her to take

186

her place in the queue next to a fat man wearing a pair of round purple sunglasses. He heard Joy beckon me to join her.

'Ah, English?' the man said to Joy, his jowls wobbling. He took off his sunglasses, frowned at her, then jabbed at his chest. 'I Tunisian. There we pick olives still in ancient way. We grabs goat. Saws off last three inches of horns. We put horns over fingers. We claws at tree. Olives fall to feets.'

Joy looked at me sternly, daring me to laugh, then whispered. 'You know, they do just that.'

'Really?' I said. I was tempted to giggle, then realized she meant it.

While the Tunisian engaged Joy in conversation, I went to look inside the hopper. Black and green olives swirled inside the stainless-steel bowl, a vortex gradually being sucked down into a black hole. From there they emerged shiny and clean, minus any bits of twig or leaf that had been attached to them.

They then dropped onto a ribbed conveyor belt, moving along like jumping beans before disappearing into the plant through a square aperture in the wall. Joy sidled up to me and whispered, 'The fat man's trying to make money on the side.' She put a finger to her nose, meaning 'keep it quiet'. 'He tried to sell me a first pressing. Must think because I'm English I'm stupid.' Then she nudged my arm. 'Look. He's on to the odd couple now.'

A man and woman were conversing with the fat man in an increasingly frantic manner. The woman hopped from foot to foot, wearing mule slippers to which Winston had taken a fancy. The man had an enormous chin and looked like Popeye.

187

'There's no first or second pressing now, you know,' Joy said. 'That went out with the screws and hydraulic presses. Now it's a continuous press. If anyone claims otherwise, that's fraud.'

With an apology, Joy collected Winston from the woman's feet and tied him to a hook on a wall of the car park, then gestured for me to follow her into the plant.

'Are we allowed?' I said, hesitating in the entrance.

'Jane,' said Joy dryly, 'this is Greece. They're not barmy about all this 'Elf and Safely' as they are in England. Of course we can go in.'

I was laughing as we entered the plant, no bigger than the open-plan room at Helikion. Huge pipes wrapped in silver foil ran along whitewashed walls, leading to a small office at the back of the plant, its glass window part-covered by blinds and a poster of a basketball team. Occupying most of the floor space and illuminated by strip lighting were three grille-topped stainless-steel containers. Each was numbered with a large red sticker. Below this was a computer printout of the weight of oil as well as each producer's share of the total inside the machine.

Another man, wearing similar red dungarees as Ponytail, lifted a red barrel onto a large pair of scales that stood sentry at the side of the office door.

'Be careful.' Joy pointed to the floor. Exposed metal grinders furiously spun in pockets of darkness. 'That's why he wears clips. Could chew your toes off.'

I trod carefully past the perilous holes and peered through one of the grilles. A horizontal

188

centrifuge spun furiously, grinding the olives into a mash.

'Pressing the olives,' Joy said, 'releases the oil globules. Hot water liquefies the solids into a kind of paste, helping to separate the globules from it. See the temperature gauge? If it gets hotter than eighty degrees Fahrenheit it would destabilize the oil. If that happens it can't be called extra virgin or "first pressed" or any kind of pressed. That's why it's called "cold pressed".'

I said I was 'im-pressed'. It brought a smile from Joy.

Ponytail, sipping from a can of Mythos beer, appeared and began tapping a series of dials on the side of one of the machines.

Joy's voice sank to a conspiratorial whisper. 'Would you trust a man drinking at work? All this machinery?'

'I'd imagine under European law it's banned, isn't it?'

'Of course it is. Extremely dangerous. But I told you, this is Greece, Jane.' She added, proudly, 'Here, they trust you to make your own mistakes.'

She directed me towards another machine and spoke in hushed tones that befitted the fact that a number of people were grouped round it, their backs to us and heads bowed as if in prayer. She gestured at the machine's vertical centrifuge, whirling at high speed, pushing water, black and greasy, out of one pipe, the golden oil into another. 'The final process, Jane. The separation between darkness and light.'

I stared at the group, their heads still bowed. Their attention seemed to be focused on an old burlap sack. However, standing on tiptoe, I realized it wasn't the sack they were worshipping, but a man who knelt on the floor, holding a large tin placed beneath a spigot. Waiting.

Slowly, so slowly, a tiny drop of oil gathered around the tap's rim. There was a hushed silence, then an intake of breath. The drop clung to the spigot, grew in size and then, to the anguish of the expectant audience, hung there. Then it fell, releasing a collective sigh from the onlookers. They quickly fell silent again. Nothing more was happening. The tension grew.

Suddenly a rush of golden oil poured from the tap to loud applause.

We went back outside to find it was our turn. After five attempts, and accompanied by plenty of encouraging shouts, Joy managed to reverse the Jeep successfully to the hopper.

After their weighing, I eagerly poured Helikion's olives into the hopper's mouth for their first tub wash. We followed them at every stage, through to filtering. I made copious notes ready for interrogation on the homeward journey.

At the end of the pressing Joy handed me a large, clean olive oil tin. I knelt down, holding it under the spigot, surprised to find that my hands shook a little. Joy's lessons on the history, tradition and importance of olive growing made this moment for me something more than a satisfying ritual. It was an atavistic pleasure. For thousands of years mankind had nurtured the olive tree, harvested its fruit and, whether by ancient stone presses or horizontal centrifuges, waited in reverence, as I was doing, for the oil to flow. Now I had joined that select group of people.

I slowly opened the tap, my mouth dry in

anticipation. A drop splashed off the rim of the tin's opening. I quickly pushed it up against the spigot just as another fell. Then came the cascade.

I heard Joy laugh. 'You're rich, Jane.'

Watching the 'liquid gold' fall, I believed that I was.

Then came a big letdown as the man in the office checked us out with only two tins of oil, one only half-filled, ten and a half kilos in all. It seemed scant reward for so much effort.

Joy saw my disappointment. 'It's the quality that matters, not the quantity. Look at wine, how many grapes it takes to make a bottle. It's the same thing, the distillation of the sun.'

As we drove away I noticed the Tunisian fat man returning to his car without any tins and counting paper money. With a quick lick of his index finger he expertly flicked up the edges of the notes then stuffed them into his pocket with a satisfied grin.

'What he committed was not just fraud but heresy,' Joy said, reaching for a cigarette. 'First pressing, my arse.'

On the way home I put my head back and allowed my mind to roam. On arrival in Greece I'd expected azure-blue skies and the promise of a rustic Mediterranean, where young and old sat outside tavernas on rattan chairs, time an unknown concept. Apart from the blue skies, that hadn't been my experience so far. It was like any other place in the Western world nowadays—busy.

But I hadn't toured Greece. I hadn't been to the Oracle at Delphi, the amphitheatre at Epidaurus, the Temple of Apollo, the medieval city at Rhodes or the Acropolis in Athens, even. Then there were the Greek islands. One day, I promised myself, I

191

would visit them all.

That night I wrote in my diary:

*Feel like I got a 'get out of jail free' card today. Joy was OK about Navy stuff! I've no other get free card, though. But won't be leaving Alcatraz just yet. An odd thing keeps happening. Sometimes I feel Zeus is watching me. It has to be my imagination but if I look quickly at him, he looks quickly away.*

It was the following morning and I'd reported for work.

'Does it stink of aniseed?' Joy brought a crate of empty ouzo bottles into the living room and asked me to smell one.

I put my nose to a bottle. 'No. Fresh as a daisy.'

'Good. I cleaned them ready. I'm decanting the oil into them.'

I restrained a smile. In Joy's world, this made perfect sense—Homer's 'liquid gold' stored in empty ouzo bottles. She put on a pair of marigolds and snapped them back. 'Oil should be kept in tinted glass bottles kept in a cool, dark cupboard. Now why is that?'

'To stop light oxidizing the oil. It would go rancid otherwise. To stop that happening in large containers of oil you would spray inert gas into them, which displaces the oxygen. You can buy them in the supermarket, Joy. You could use it to preserve wine in opened bottles as well.'

Joy pretended to be indignant. 'I would never open a wine bottle if it wasn't going to be drunk within two or three hours at the most, Jane. Now, if you know so much, tell me, what antioxidants are there in the oil that help to prevent cancer?

192

'Er, flavenoid poly-something?'

'Flavenoid polyphenols,' she said. 'There are other reasons why oil goes off. Olives picked too late may have fewer antioxidants and a shorter shelf life. The longer the time before the olives are pressed, the more oxidation there is. They must get to the press within forty-eight hours of picking.'

She took a plastic funnel from a hook and placed it in one of the empty ouzo bottles. 'Ours took far too long. Not enough volunteers. Anyway, let's see.' She carefully poured the oil into an ouzo bottle and handed it me. I twisted its cork back in place and was about to place it to one side when she put out a hand. 'Keep it. It's yours.' There was no sentiment in her voice or expression. It could have been an apple she was giving me.

I took the bottle, wanting to cry and laugh at the same time. This would probably never happen again in my lifetime. I'd picked the olives, witnessed their pressing and now I had their oil.

'Thank you, Joy.' I stared at the bottle. 'That's wonderful.' I made a sudden decision. 'Will you taste it for me?'

'Certainly not. No, I won't.' Joy looked offended. My stomach fell.

'It's yours. You must do it.' Joy produced a dry expression at my sheepish smile. 'Go on. I'll teach you to be an olive oil connoisseur.'

I went into the kitchen and came out with bread and a wooden bowl. Joy took the bottle and, with the cork protruding from its neck, managed to pull it out without too much effort. She poured oil into the bowl, then dipped a hunk of bread in it. 'You too, Jane. You do the same.'

193

I obeyed.

'Right. Raise your hand. A toast. *Palaio krasi, neo petrelaio.* Old wine, new oil, Jane.' She waved her arms. 'No! Stop.'

I froze with the bread and oil halfway to my mouth.

'You can't do a tasting by swallowing it first. You must smell it first. Go on, smell it. Best to use the bowl. Don't do a long one. Do sniffs, one after the other. Like this.' She held up her nose and made little sniffing noises.

I followed her example.

'Anything in it you detect? A plant, flower?'

'I think . . . I think it's a nutty kind of smell.'

Joy paused. 'Good. Now taste it.'

I dunked a piece of bread in the bowl and delicately placed it between my lips. She watched avidly. 'Try and get your nasal cavity working. Is there a taste that's not nuts?' She looked at me in rising expectancy and—surprisingly—with a trace of nervousness. 'What can you taste, Jane?'

'There's a kind of lemon—I think,' I added hastily.

Joy's eyes flickered and lowered for a moment. Then she looked at me again. 'Now before you swallow, watch out for a final taste at the back of the mouth as it goes down—a kick.'

As I did her bidding she put a hand to her face, watching me on tenterhooks.

I swallowed the oil and paused, then opened my mouth in an attempt to expose the nasal passage to the aroma. 'I think I've got it—but it's only a guess, Joy.'

'Guess then.' Her voice was muffled by her hand.

'Er . . . I'd say it's a peppery kind of taste.'

194

Joy quickly rose and went to her room. 'Back in a minute.'

Used to her sudden and impetuous digressions, I thought nothing more of it and walked to the veranda doors to look out over the walled garden. I thought of the olive trees, their bounty destined for a parade of Joy's ouzo bottles.

To each gnarled trunk I'd given a personality; like the scrawl of a signature, their characters were revealed in twisting and turning branches, the shape and texture of a knot, or even a wound. In homage to Alcatraz I'd named a tree 'Scarface', its trunk slashed by a bolt of lightning. And there was my favourite olive, my 'hammock' tree. I looked upon them as my staunch, reliable friends.

Joy returned after a few minutes. She carried an old ledger, smudged and worn with time. 'Sit down, Jane. I've got something I want you to read. This is a record of every olive harvest we've had here. Started before me by Marilyn, of course. Oh, by the way, I've got some news you might like. I'll tell you in a minute.'

I was intrigued, but with Joy had learned a certain amount of patience. Joy stared at the ledger, frowning. 'Now, where was I?'

'The harvest.'

'Oh yes, the harvest. I started here in the early nineties, the trees well established by then. But this may interest you.' She found the page she wanted, pushing the ledger towards me. 'Read the entry for ninety-one.' Her finger pointed to the line.

My eyes ran along the headed columns.

'Read it aloud, Jane.'

I took in the looping, slanting handwriting.

'November the twenty-sixth. Hillside trees: Not picked after frost. Phrygana trees: Picked—a few unaffected by frost. Weight, a hundred and ten kilos. Volunteers: Nine. Tasters: Christos: His comments: Smell: Nutty. Taste . . .'

I broke off to glance at Joy. She was in repose, her hands on her knees, her eyes with a faraway look. I carried on reading, but lowered my voice. 'Taste: Lemon. Kick: . . .' I gave a long pause. 'Pepper.' Joy remained in silence and then took the ledger back to read the entry once more. She closed it slowly.

'Nuts, lemon and pepper. No one else has tasted any of our trees the same, except Christos—and you.'

She smiled sadly, then stood up quickly, tightening her face as if squeezing out any weakness. 'Jane, you're a very good taster.' She dunked her bread and held it high, letting her voice ring out.

'*Palaio krasi, neo petrelaio!*'

\*     \*     \*

It was the next morning, and I had barely started to dig out a planting hole on the hillside when I saw Joy approaching, Wizard hooked on her arm.

'Jane. I meant to tell you. There's a horticultural student coming to stay. That was Charles's news yesterday. She's from Dublin. Wants to take part in a working Greek garden. You can get drunk with her. You'd like that.'

I laughed. 'That's great, Joy.' I contained my excitement. Somebody of my own age. Then I hesitated. 'But how long for? Where's she staying?'

'She'll be in the ghost room. Don't say anything about that while she's here. I'm sorry but it's only a two-week stay. But it will add a bit of interest, liven things up a bit.'

I watched Joy walk back to the house and turned back to my work with enthusiasm.

# 10

# The Goldfish Was Called Trotsky

Trotsky

December arrived and the sun, albeit lower in the sky, continued to shine. But in the early morning and in the depths of night there was a marked drop in temperature. At these times Alcatraz took on the role of an icebox. I was reduced to wearing socks pulled over my pyjama legs, a sweater over my top and sometimes a woolly hat. The alarm clock would rattle and shake at 6 a.m. and I would race out of bed to switch on the two small heaters, then dive back under the duvet, waiting until it was warm enough to brave the cubicle. But even with the heaters working flat out it was still cold, courtesy of a northeaster that blew, seemingly, forever.

One night I awoke to a frightening commotion with leaves hissing, branches creaking and heaving. Shutters clattered furiously and a pine branch, which would normally tap the toilet window in a big wind, thumped against it like some foul creature bent on revenge.

The following morning I went outside, the wind strong enough to take away my breath momentarily, but I stumbled on towards the house. As I reached the threshing floor I glanced up to see a bird halted in mid-flight by the blast. It spread its wings and lifted its head to take the free express elevator. At the top of its ride, it tucked in its wings, falcon-like, and dive-bombed the garden, at the last moment pulling out close to the ground. Then, like a stealth fighter on a low-level run, it skimmed over my head, tacking from side to side and headed for the hilltop.

Once I reached the house, Joy told me to go

back. 'Day off, Jane. Work at the weekend. The plants will need you after this little lot.' On colder days, Joy wore her Arabic headscarf and a red knitted cardigan with buttons as big as gobstoppers. In the house, she placed pots of hand cream at convenient points, for use when her chapped hands became too sore for normal work. Oddly, I even saw a tub in Wizard's cage, but decided not to ask why. Joy being Joy, some things were better off left unquestioned.

*     *     *

With the days shortening, Joy brought our walkabouts forward, which meant I was working an hour less a day. I thanked her for it, although the extra hour of leisure time only served to encourage thoughts of Christmas at home—pubs full of well-wishers, the build-up to the *Strictly Come Dancing* final, Mum transforming the family home in Derbyshire into Santa's grotto, ensuring that mince pies and boxes of chocolates were laid out in every downstairs room.

I asked Joy if she had any decorations that I could borrow to brighten up the outhouse.

'No, Jane. We don't like all that razzmatazz. We enjoy Christmas Eve, Christmas Day and Boxing Day. We don't do it until then. Sorry, but that's the way of it.'

It was ironic. Each year I wanted to escape the early advertising bombardments, the crowds and the naff decorations. Now, trapped in my cold monastic cell, I would have gladly listened to a continuous loop of 'Jingle Bells' all day long.

In an effort to distract myself I made my own

decorations, cutting stars out of cardboard, colouring them in with red pen and hanging them together with gardening string. Flushed with the *Blue Peter* spirit, I used a toilet roll and silver cooking foil to make a crown for Zeus. As soon as I placed it on his mane it altered his expression from curious to irritable. It felt like a defeat of sorts.

But making the decorations helped to distract me from a state of maudlin reflection. I had thought of going home for a few days, but quickly realized that I would probably never return. Joy I could live with now, but could I put up with Alcatraz in winter? Whatever, the horticultural student, Sian, would be arriving shortly and I was looking forward so much to meeting her. I'd leave any thoughts of my future until after she'd gone. I just wanted some fun and a friend to eat and chat with.

\*      \*      \*

On the morning of Sian's arrival, I was eager to know if I would be joining Joy in greeting her at the airport, but was unsure how to broach the subject. I entered the house to find her in the kitchen, preparing a welcome meal for our student.

'I can dish this up as soon as I bring her back from the airport,' she said, her cheeks rosy with cooking. 'It's called Bekri Meze. Diced beef marinated in wine, cloves, cinnamon, olive oil and bay leaves.' She poured a generous helping of wine into the concoction. 'Commonly known as drunkard's snack. ' I looked in the saucepan on the pretence of being drawn to the enticing aromas, but really to see how much she was making.

'You've got big helpings there, Joy,' I said in hope, my stomach rumbling. A trip to the airport and then a meal to get to know Sian would be nice—something different from my usual routine.

'The Irish are big eaters. Oh, and she did say she liked Guinness. Must get some on the way to the airport. I know a place where they sell it.'

'Joy,' I said, impulsively, 'am I coming with—' I broke off suddenly.

'What did you say?'

'Nothing.' Since our visit to the olive oil pressing plant Joy had been relatively equable and I didn't want to upset the status quo. Instinct told me that she would be offended if I'd imagined I'd been left out and annoyed if I was so stupid as to ask. I went out, with an inward sigh, to do my chores, the first being to clean out the Jeep. I found it ironic that Joy, who cared little for appearances, should be concerned with making a good impression on a student who was only coming to work and observe the garden for a short time.

After I'd finished, Joy checked the Jeep over with a keen eye then informed me that she would be leaving for the airport at 5.30 p.m. prompt.

'Do you want me to do anything while you're out?'

Joy stared at me. 'Yes,' she said. 'I told you. You're coming with me to the airport.'

She hadn't, but I wasn't going to argue. The thought of going there lifted my spirits. I looked forward to the bustle of the airport with its electronic signboards, marble concourses and shops. I could buy an English magazine, browse in the music store, and indulge in one of my favourite activities—people watching.

* * *

I arrived at the Jeep at precisely 5.30 p.m. The only light in my vicinity came from the oil lanterns hanging outside the alcove. Then suddenly torchlight beamed at me, forcing me to shield my eyes. It was Joy, wearing a potholer's light on her forehead. She stopped to peer upwards at the house roof. 'I can't see. Did you remove that virgin's-bower, Jane? I can't remember you doing it.'

'Yes, I did.' Earlier in the day I'd cut away the twisted and overgrown stems of the climbing plant from the guttering at the rear side of the house.

We got into the Jeep, Joy muttering something about earthquakes.

'Earthquakes,' I said in alarm, quickly strapping myself in.

'There's been a warning.' She turned to me. 'Jane, don't you know this is one of the most seismically active countries. I was in the big one of ninety-nine.'

'What happened? What did you do?'

'Just carried on planting. House shook a bit, but no damage. Other rumblings have had the lights out, though. Can be a bit of a bugger; that's why I bought a few potholers' headlamps.'

She released the handbrake with a quick jerk then fiddled with the radio for the English news station—a sign that she didn't want to talk any more.

While we waited on the ground floor of the airport, Joy spoke to a couple of policemen lounging against the British Airways desk. I thought of my airport leaflet stuffed in the back of a cupboard and automatically reached for a fresh pamphlet, only to have it snatched from my grasp.

'Jane! What are you doing?' Joy stood there in reproof. 'You're not going anywhere.' To my dismay she put the leaflet back in its slot. 'Do you know why?'

'No.' For a brief terrifying moment I had the vision of Joy imprisoning me in Alcatraz forever. I would finish under a headstone in the pet cemetery, a shard of marble with a rough cross etched with: 'Jane. She died alone.'

Joy took a deep breath and raised a finger. 'Because today is the day you've passed your probationary period. Don't tell me you'd forgotten?'

'Oh, thank God,' I gasped. 'Yes. Sorry. I had. I'd forgotten.' She was correct on this one. I was thinking hard for something else to say when she rushed me to the arrivals hall.

Joy turned her attention towards the passengers off the BA flight from Heathrow. The first arrivals were coming through the wide doors and onto the concourse, wheeling their assorted luggage.

'What does Sian look like, Joy?'

'She said she'd be wearing an orange top. Hah, she's here already.'

I followed Joy to the corner edge of the metal barrier. There was the orange top emblazoned with a psychedelic print of James Joyce. Its wearer, a chubby young woman, looked around anxiously. As she went round the barrier, Joy stopped her. A quick question and answer was followed by Joy ignoring Sian's proffered hand. Instead she planted firm kisses on both her cheeks, followed by a hug.

Joy turned to me. 'Sian, this is Jane. She's been dying to meet you. I've got some Guinness waiting for you.'

Sian giggled a little. 'Well, that's lovely, I do like a tipple,' she said in a soft Irish lilt, and stretched out a hand. 'Hi, Jane.'

'Hello, Sian. It's great to see you.'

Joy looked at her watch. 'Bugger. I've not fed Wizard. No dawdling, come on.'

*       *       *

Joy talked for most of the return journey in response to Sian's questions, all of them pertinent to the garden, dealing with water conservation and drought-afflicted plants. Her knowledge and interest had Joy raising her voice in agreement.

In the face of such mutual concord and enthusiasm, I literally took a back seat. It did nothing for my self-esteem to learn of Sian's top qualification from the RHS—Master of Horticulture. I had the lowest. She'd also studied for a while at Wolverhampton University and had all the impressive terms used in biotechnology: 'microclimate sensing and datalogging systems', 'portable photosynthesis analysers' and 'basic nutrient analysis'. This, combined with the fact that she'd worked for a charity, the funds from which went into conservation projects abroad, had me ring-fenced into a pitiful silence.

Soon it was Sian who did most of the talking, during which I caught Joy glancing at me from time to time in the mirror.

At one point Joy tested her by asking if she'd heard of the Resurrection Plant.

Naturally she had, and Joy took both hands briefly off the wheel to clap her hands. 'You see, Jane! Some do know.'

Then Joy briefed her on the Neanderthal, citing his 'heinous sprinklers' and borehole as the first step to a biological *Götterdämmerung*.

'Sounds like he needs sticking up against a wall,' Sian said, her hands now clutched tightly on the hanging door strap.

'You and I will get on, Sian, I can see that.' Joy gave a big smile as she hurled the Jeep across the road to climb the hill into the garden.

As we arrived at the house, the dousing of headlamps left us in inky blackness. There was an ominous rattling of chains.

'What's that?' said Sian nervously.

'It's only Titan.'

'Who's—aagh!' Sian screamed as, out of the dark, leapt Titan. The canine burglar deterrent jumped at Joy in greeting, striking Sian's arm as it did so.

'Titan! Bad boy! Get off her!' Joy grabbed Titan's collar. 'Sorry, Sian. Titan, sit down and wait for me to fetch you in.'

It was a flustered Sian who wheeled her luggage through the alcove. But no sooner had she stepped into the house than Wizard, with a screech, flew from his open cage. 'Aagh!' Sian stepped back as the macaw flew across her to perch on a Minoan statue.

'Bad, horrible bird!' Joy hollered. 'Sorry, Sian. Forgot to close the cage. He's very sensitive. Some people aren't in tune. It's either the smell or the vibes with him. Do you smoke?' Joy offered her a cigarette.

'No, I don't.'

'I hope you don't mind me. Addicted, I'm afraid. Oh, and this creature here is Winston. He's not got the best of hearts nowadays. Have you, old boy?'

Winston eyed Sian with his rheumy eye and then lowered it to stare at her shoes.

I found it amusing and it helped offset some of the irritation I felt at Joy for never having asked my permission to smoke.

Joy went out to collect Titan. As she disappeared Winston began to lick Sian's shoes.

'No. Don't do that.' Sian bent down but didn't dare touch him. She appealed to me, her eyebrows ruffled. 'Can you stop him? Oh no, what's he doing now?'

Winston was now rutting furiously.

'Oh my God!'

I chuckled as I grabbed Winston's collar. 'You must have said that you liked animals to come here. It's a condition of contract.'

'Yes, but not weirdos. Get him off!'

As soon as she detached herself from Winston, she cried out again as Wizard flapped onto her shoulder. 'What's going on?'

'Don't move, Sian.' I slowly put out the back of my hand towards her shoulder.

Obediently, Wizard stepped onto it and was soon returned to his cage.

'Oh my God,' breathed Sian, dusting her

shoulder with a hand and looking at her shoes. 'There's a Hound of the Baskervilles outside, and inside a sex pervert of a dog and a mad parrot.'

I began to laugh. Sian began to see the funny side of it. 'Well, there's reception committees and reception committees, I suppose. I think I need that Guinness.'

Joy brought in Titan, who went straight to his sofa, lay down and rolled onto his back.

'He wants you to fuss him, Sian. Best to do it.'

'Really? Do I have to?'

'Yes, if you want to keep in his good books.'

Sian tentatively approached Titan to stroke his silky chest. 'What you do for love.'

I looked at my watch. 'I'd better go, Joy. Got a meal to get.'

'What do you mean?' She glowered at me. 'You're staying here for the meal. I told you.'

'Oh, sorry.'

'I told you we were celebrating the end of your probationary period, didn't I?'

'Yes. I'm sorry, Joy. I'm a bit forgetful.'

\*  \*  \*

While Joy settled Sian in the 'ghost room', I laid the table, prepared a log fire, then checked on the simmering saucepans in the kitchen. A few minutes later, Joy appeared, cigarette in hand.

'Sian's just been telling me about her latest correspondence course. Hydroponics, Jane. Soil-less gardening. Eighty litres of water are used to grow one kilo of cabbage grown in soil. With hydroponics it's only three litres.'

'Great for a trip to Mars.' It was Sian's voice.

210

She came in and sat at the table with an aplomb that gave me pause. She immediately began to deliver a mini lecture on hydroponics, ending with, 'So, what could be simpler? Urine is processed back into plain water. That grows the veggie. That gets eaten and some of that turns back to urine. Simple. Puts your work in the shade, Joy.'

I froze for a moment. If I'd said that Joy would most likely have thrown a village shoe at me.

But Joy seemed unfazed. 'Ah, but it's not for me because I live with the elements. And it's certainly not for Jane. Is it, Jane?'

'Why's that?' said Sian. 'Oh yes, Joy said you were a bit of a mud baby—like to eat soil. Yuck.' She grinned at me.

Why had Joy told Sian that? It was as if she was belittling me.

Joy suddenly slapped a palm to her forehead.

'Ah! Hydroponics. I remember now. Criminals use it to grow cannabis plants. They take over big houses and fill every room with them.' She sat back in her seat. 'Grass, we used to call it. Or weed. I smoked it regularly—we all did. Had me once staring at a goldfish in a bowl swimming round. I watched it, fascinated, for hours. I can't remember its name, though.'

Joy puffed on her cigarette, brought out an old ouzo bottle cap from her pocket and thoughtfully tapped a long line of hanging ash into it.

'Now what was it? Stalin. Or was it Lenin?'

I exchanged a quick smile with Sian and went back to the kitchen to collect the bowls of steaming food. Then I struggled to uncork the wine bottle. I could never work out how to use Joy's large and unwieldy corkscrew. Sian saw me

211

straining and took the bottle off me, pulling the cork out with a satisfied grunt.

'Easy. All that mud's made you soft, Jane.' She poured out the drinks.

Joy raised her glass. 'Welcome, Sian. Hope you enjoy your stay here.'

'Thanks, Joy.' Sian nodded, sipping her drink.

'And to Jane,' Joy said, stubbing her cigarette out and clinking her glass against mine. 'She's passed her probationary period. Well done.'

'Yes, good on you,' Sian agreed. She reached up to touch glasses with me, the chipped crystal glinting.

I was filled with conflicting emotions. I was glad to have passed my probationary period, but annoyed at being made to feel as if I was a schoolkid. After days and days of aching for company a part of me now wanted Sian to leave.

'And this is our very own home-grown pressing.' Joy leaned across to a small side table and picked up an ouzo bottle full of olive oil. 'The fruits of our labour. Jane bottled it.'

'Eh, that's great, Jane.' Sian was first to help herself to a wedge of bread and a spoonful of glazed vegetables. 'But in ouzo bottles? Isn't that a bit like decanting wine into vinegar bottles?'

'I wouldn't know if the taste was spoiled anyway,' I said, perhaps a little tetchily. 'All that mud's ruined my taste buds.'

Sian didn't respond. Instead she looked at Joy, changing the subject. 'Oh, I've got to provide a case study. Did I tell you? I'm hoping you can help me.' We listened to her list of requirements: photographs, plant lists, water data, flower-pressing samples and seeds.

212

'Of course,' Joy said. 'Take notes, photographs, copy records. We like people to take scientific data, but there's also something else we'd like you to take with you.'

'Oh. What's that?' Sian looked eagerly at Joy.

'The spirit of the garden, also known as the *genius loci.*'

'Huh?' Sian gave Joy a quizzical look and then suddenly said in alarm, 'Oh my God. Jesus.' She ducked her head under the table to see Winston licking her ankles.

Joy bent down. 'Stop that! Winston! Stop it!'

Sian grimaced at Winston looking up at her, a yellow-stained tooth poking out of his gums.

'Joy?' Sian hesitated. 'To be honest I'm not really hungry or a big meat eater.' She noticed Joy pause in her eating and added quickly, 'Unless you've got fish fingers? I'll grill them myself?'

Joy sat back in her seat and let loose a beaming smile, eyes opened wide in revelation. 'Trotsky. The goldfish. It was called Trotsky!'

*       *       *

The next morning, I woke early and grabbed the opportunity to see my second volcano sunrise. While inhaling a sprig of rosemary, I watched the glorious initial explosion, followed by the sun's rays spitting and striking off the mountain's ridges, shooting out long fingers of red light across the plain. As the light slowly flooded towards me I stood up and went to explore, wandering without purpose or thought.

Swirls of anemones carpeted the hillside, their delicate petals rippling in shades of red, white and pink. I lay on the ground, entranced by a swathe of paper-white narcissus swaying gently in the breeze. Luxuriating in the sweet scent of their blooms, I turned on my back to stare at a lone fluffy cloud turning orange with the rising sun. Then I climbed my favourite olive tree and, safe in its cradle, closed my eyes.

*      *      *

After lunch, as arranged, I met Joy and Sian by a prickly pear on the lower terrace. I'd brought pitchforks, axes and sacks from the tool shed as Joy had requested.

'Right, ladies,' Joy said, rubbing her hands, 'can one of you tell me something interesting about *Opuntia ficus-indica*?'

While I was floundering to come up with an answer, Sian responded immediately. 'The flat stems are called nopalitos, grown as a host plant for cochineal insects. They feed on the cactus and produce an acid used as red dye . . .'

On and on she went, until finally Joy put a hand up to stop her.

'Anything to add?' Joy looked pertinently at me.

'Isn't it used as a hangover cure?'

Sian laughed. 'They've found mescaline in it as well. You should try it, Jane. Better than mud.'

'I might.' The girl was just too knowledgeable.

Joy pointed at the cactus. 'I want you both to cut this fellow down. It's too near the compost beds. Cut off all the wet succulent pads and any wet part of the trunk. Take them to the tool shed and hack them up. Tomorrow, shred them. I'm off to the village for the afternoon.'

214

Joy waved her hand in the air and scuttled away up the terrace steps.

Sian let out a sigh and scowled at the prickly pear. 'This is going to be messy. I haven't brought any gloves. Be back in a mo, Jane.'

I worked for an hour without Sian. By then I was covered in goo and dripping with sweat. The plant's viscous solution had oozed everywhere. I'd chopped up all the succulent paddles and parts of trunk and carted them up to the tool shed to pile them on a dust sheet, ready for shredding. Then I began to worry about Sian and went to the house to search for her. She was not in her room. I stood outside and called out her name. I was turning away when I caught a flash of movement at an open window.

'Sian?' I called.

I was thinking of phoning the village shop where Joy was most likely to be, when I heard a weak voice. 'Jane?'

Sian was leaning out of the window, her hair bedraggled. 'Just got out the loo; got a tummy upset, sorry.'

'Go to bed,' I said. 'There's Imodium in the bathroom if you need it.'

She nodded and withdrew. 'Thanks.'

An hour later, she came out to find me.

'That Imodium's really good,' she said. 'I'm fine now. What do you want me to do?

I handed her the diver's mask that Joy insisted I wear when using the shredder.

Sian raised her eyes in surprise. 'Oh my Lord. Have you not got any safety goggles?'

'Do the same job, don't they?' I said, remembering that had been my initial thought

215

when Joy had first given them to me. I handed Sian pieces to stuff through the shredder, a messy job that meant we had to stop every so often to clean out the machine. After an hour I started to warm to her.

Without Joy around, it was easier to get a word in edgeways and she seemed a much more amenable character. She told me funny stories about her family in Ireland and time passed quickly. We finished the work and, using wheelbarrows, transferred the resultant gooey mess to beneath my favourite olive. This was a temporary spot. Once dried out it would be put through the shredder again and used as mulch, a process taking around three to four months, depending on the weather.

Joy came out at 4 p.m. bearing a tray with three mugs of coffee. 'You two did a great job. Not an easy thing to chop up.'

Sian sipped her coffee and rubbed her face where the mask had dug in to her skin. 'No. In actual fact, Jane did most of the work. I felt a bit sick at one point.'

*       *       *

Joy had invited Charles and Rachel over for tea and, since she and I were now on reasonably good terms, I asked if it was all right if Sian joined me for an evening meal in Alcatraz. Joy said it was fine and Sian enthusiastically accepted my offer. 'Great, I'll bring fish fingers and Guinness.'

As we approached Alcatraz, Sian jumped back in shock as Orwell charged out of a shrub and dashed under my washing line, bed sheets and shirts

216

billowing like sails.

'It's only Joy's cat. Come in, I've got another one waiting.'

I shoved open the door and gestured for her to enter before me. Zeus could make his own introductions.

'Oh my God!' Sian stared in disbelief. 'What's a stuffed lion doing here?'

'Say hello to Sian, Zeus,' I said, telling her about Joy's zoo, but not revealing the part about him injuring Christos. I felt that would be betraying Joy in some way. Sian was amused at first then quickly lost interest, casting her eye around my cell. 'Do you actually live in this place?' She clasped her arms around her chest. 'And it's freezing.'

'Oh, sorry.' I put the heaters on and lit a few tea lights.

Sian pushed apart the bead curtain across the cubicle and withdrew her head, nose wrinkled in disgust. 'That mould's jumping off the walls. How you can sleep here, I don't know, Jane. I couldn't do it.' She pointed to my laptop. 'But you have the internet. That's something.'

I told her there wasn't a connection and never would be if Joy had anything to do with it—it was Satan's work according to her—then set to frying the fish fingers on the camping stove.

Sian blew her cheeks out, ripped the ring pull off her Guinness can and took a quick sip. 'I could never do it. And Joy! God bless her, but how you can live with her, I don't know.'

While attending to the fish fingers I listened to Sian's criticisms, torn between agreeing with her and wanting to shout her down. Instead, I was caught in a no-man's land of traitorous nods and

217

half grins, as I had no wish to cause friction. Sian was only here for a short time and I would probably never see her again.

'And there's something strange about that room.'

'Sorry?' I paid attention.

'I don't know; it's just a feeling.'

I hesitated, almost tempted to tell her about Joy and her ghost story, then my conscience overcame me. If she was alarmed by Orwell jumping out of a shrub, she'd be troubled by tales of phantoms.

'It's the wind. Can sound like a tidal wave's coming in sometimes.'

We ate in a companionable silence. Sian chomped on her fish finger sandwich, while I enjoyed lentil soup, with a side serving of chunky bread dunked in Helikion olive oil.

For the rest of the evening she talked about the outside world, pubs, parties, friends, scandalous news, holidays and her Christmas plans. To all these I made comments, but offered little of my world before Alcatraz. I couldn't. It would have been too painful.

At midnight I escorted Sian back to the house, Joy's potholer's lamp on my head. I returned to Alcatraz, homesick.

*　　　*　　　*

During the next few days I saw less of Sian during the day, as she was always in Joy's company, either huddled over her desk and looking through the microscope, or taking a walk around the garden while earnestly discussing scientific topics. Joy would wave a hand at me and say hello, but that was all, our 'walkabouts' set aside in favour of Sian and her college project.

On the Friday evening, Sian, as usual, joined me in Alcatraz. She admitted having benefited from Joy's knowledge during the day, but at night said she couldn't wait to be free of her.

'Joy's a mad bat, God bless her,' she said, watching me fry another batch of fish fingers. 'Oh, and we're going to Athens, Jane. She told me to tell you.' She flopped onto my bed and opened a can of Guinness. 'We're going by bus. Your guy Pavlos is coming along as well. A tour of the National Gardens is organized.' She looked around Alcatraz. 'Bet you're glad to get away for a bit.'

'Yes, I'm glad. We'll enjoy it. Was it her suggestion?'

'Yes, it was.'

I poured myself an ouzo, hurt and resentful. I'd told Joy more than once that I'd like to visit the National Gardens, but she'd always found the demands of work an excuse not to take me.

The next morning, as Joy drove us to the bus stop, dark clouds bustled over Mount Hymettos and the hidden city of Athens. Pavlos sat in the front passenger seat, while Sian and I were belted into the back seat. Encouraged by Joy, Sian was telling Pavlos about her endless qualifications, tossing in something highly technical from time to time.

'There's your stop,' Joy said, bringing the Jeep to a halt and pointing to a bent metal sign. It poked above a wire fence straddling the busy highway.

She delved into her purse and brought out thirty euros, holding it out to me. 'Go on, take it. For drinks and snacks.'

I politely refused. I knew that Joy had little money.

'I insist.' This time Joy shifted in her seat and looked at me with a steady gaze, eyes unblinking.

I took the money and joined Pavlos and Sian, turning around to wave, but the Jeep was already on its way, a puff of cigarette smoke flying from the driver's window.

\*       \*       \*

It took an hour to get into Athens, traffic snarled on the outskirts. Reaching the city centre, we passed down Leof Vas Sofias, the road leading to Syntagma Square and our last stop. White mulberry trees, their tops savagely pollarded, lined the street as we approached.

Sian had nodded off, her head resting on Pavlos's shoulder.

'Joy got her workings too hard?' Pavlos grinned at me.

I smiled and looked out of the window at an increasingly darkening sky. Shortly after stepping off the bus, a piercing crack of thunder and flashes of lightning had us running for cover. A smattering of fat droplets suddenly turned into a torrential downpour.

We dived under the awning of McDonald's to brush ourselves down amid a sheltering crowd. African immigrants appeared, weaving their way through the mass of bodies, holding up cheap umbrellas in polystyrene sleeves, shouting out prices in Greek and English.

Then, just as quickly as it started, the rain stopped, thunder rumbling in the distance.

220

'Rights. National Gardens. This way.' Pavlos headed for the peach-coloured Parliament Building, a long neo-classical building that loomed over the square. Already the café tables were filling on Syntagma's marble plaza. I gazed enviously at people drinking coffee, talking over each other, arms flapping. Old men with bent legs wound their way around the metal tables carrying lottery tickets pinned to boards on tall poles, trying to sell the odds. A couple of stray dogs milled around the entrance to the underground, scattering pigeons. I felt like an alien.

After crossing the road, we followed Pavlos past a small crowd gathered in front of Parliament and the Tomb of the Unknown Soldier.

'They are changing of guards,' said Pavlos proudly, leading us down Amalias Avenue. 'You have same in England. We call ours Evzones. Means well-belted.'

Beneath a grand row of soaring desert fan palms we met a short stocky man with beetle brows and a wide smile. He had a few tourists waiting for the tour, standing nearby. One I recognized as a volunteer at Helikion. We acknowledged each other, smiling, raising our hands at each other.

'This is my friend, Loska,' said Pavlos, handing us over.

'Ladies and gentlemen,' said Loska. 'You are standing in the heart of Athens. The gardens are its lifeblood, its oxygen. Fifteen and a half hectares, envisioned by Queen Amalia, now owned by our great City of Athens. The first planting began in eighteen thirty-nine. Many of the plants were imported.'

Sian raised a hand to intervene. 'So they didn't

use indigenous plants?'

'Good observation! Many of those imported could not cope with our harsh climate. So species were collected from Sounion and the island of Euboea. Some plants may not have survived but the animals they brought in did. We have peacocks, turtles, ostriches ...' He carried on talking, gesturing for us to follow him.

We followed his bounding stride along paths that wound through a shady, evergreen oasis.

In the garden's heart Loska stopped with a dramatic gesture. 'Let the air from the plantings flow into your body. It clears the vision and removes thick humour from the eyes.'

He breathed in, swept his arms upwards and then slowly exhaled, letting his arms drop. 'Words from the great Roman architect, Vitruvius.'

'Yeah,' said Sian in an aside to me, 'who's he kidding?'

Through Loska, aided by Sian, we learned that the gardens had access to water by virtue of two underground aqueducts, the earliest Roman built, dating from the sixth century BC.

At the end of the tour I was surprised when Loska took me aside to hand me his card, saying that if ever I needed a job he would provide me with one. But how did he know who I was? I hadn't even been introduced to him.

His eyes twinkled. 'Oh yes. You have.' He refused to elucidate further. 'But not your friend.' He was pointing at Sian.

Pavlos decided we had time to climb Mount Lycabettus, an easy journey, he said, not requiring special clothing or equipment. On the way up I engineered it so that Pavlos and I were behind

Sian and out of her earshot. I spoke quickly and in a low tone. 'Why did you tell Loska I might need a job?'

Pavlos was silent for a moment, getting his breath. 'Jane,' he said, 'Joy worries the garden may finish. If Tom sells the garden and you stay with Loska to finish your year she will gives you testimonials as if you'd stayed all time at Helikion.'

'So it was you who told him what a hard worker I am?'

'Of course. You are.' He looked at Sian, who had stopped to rest. 'Some hard workers in other ways.'

After twenty-five minutes of climbing we finally reached the peak and headed for the restaurant that nestled below the tiny chapel.

'I'm gasping,' Sian puffed, and sat at one of the outdoor tables to rub her feet.

I took my drink to the parapet and stared at the mighty sprawl of Athens. I was not marvelling at the view, but thinking about Joy. She hadn't sent us to the National Gardens for Sian's pleasure, as I'd suspected. She'd done it for me. She must have briefed Pavlos beforehand.

Pavlos joined me. 'Now, if Joys was here she'd be telling you that it was the Roman Emperor Hadrian who solved the problems of water supply for whole of Athens. He builds great reservoir on slopes of Lycabettus.'

We stood in a comfortable silence, shoulders touching, the light fading. Pavlos pointed to the flank of Mount Hymettos and spoke quietly in his deep bass voice.

'Oh, glorious Athens, shining violet-crowned, worthy of song, stronghold of Greece, city of the gods.' He smiled at me. 'Fifth century BC. Poet

223

Pindar.'

As the sun set, Mount Hymettos slowly transformed from bluish-grey to violet-rose, the colour seeming to flood the atmosphere. Sian sidled alongside me and sniffed. 'That's the pollution gives that effect.'

On the journey home I glanced at Pavlos as the bus took us away from the city. For all his warmth and sense of fun I detected an inner sadness. It wasn't the first time I'd thought this. I had seen him more than once, lost in reflection. His eyes would be fixed upon something, but not looking. Like Joy, he never revealed much about himself, his past life or his family—if he had one. I'd raised it with Joy more than once and she would conveniently find some excuse not to answer or pretend to be too busy. Nevertheless, I made a mental note to raise it at a moment when she would have to give some sort of answer.

Sian, who was sitting across the aisle, caught my glance and smiled. 'Give me Dublin any time. All that stuff about breathing in the air. The pollution, more like. I know. I can give you the exact volume per cubic metre.'

Joy was in bed by the time we returned to Helikion, but there was a note pinned to my door. It was scrawled in red crayon: '8 a.m. Meet me by the pine that Tom's window men decimated. We have pests to destroy.'

*       *       *

After breakfast the next day I walked to the house and looked down the track to find Joy standing beneath the damaged pine, a pair of telescopic

224

loppers gripped in her hand.

'Hello, Joy.'

'Morning, Jane.'

'I enjoyed the National Gardens. Thanks.'

She ignored the comment, too busy staring upwards. 'You see that thing that looks like a hunk of sheep's wool?'

I peered upwards. 'Yes, I can.'

'It's a processional caterpillar nest. Full of furry toxic caterpillars. Soon as they're out they'll eat all the pine needles. They need removing and burning. I don't like doing it, but it has to be done. Their predators have disappeared—climate change, people, for whatever reason.' She coughed, then lit a cigarette and looked to the house. 'Sian said she was sick this morning, so she's staying indoors. Any idea what's wrong with her?'

'I don't know. Haven't seen her since last night.'

For the rest of the day Joy and I patiently removed the caterpillar nests, many hanging high in the pine branches, taking turns to use the telescopic loppers. By early afternoon we had a pile of them stuffed in a large metal bucket. Joy left me to light the funeral pyre, while she walked the dogs.

As soon as she disappeared behind the house I heard Sian calling me from the driveway.

'Jane? Has Joy gone with the dogs?'

'Yes, just. Where are you?' I walked down the hillside path to find her standing on the driveway by the side of a bright yellow taxi. The driver was loading her luggage into the boot.

I walked down to her. 'I thought you were ill. Are you OK?'

225

'No. This isn't what I expected at all. I booked a flight back late last night. Sorry I didn't tell you. I told Joy I was sick this morning so I could phone for a taxi. Feel awful, but I can't bring myself to tell her. Can you do it for me? I'll write to her, of course.'

'Yes. Yes, of course I will.' I stood at a complete loss.

'Anyway, thanks for the fun evenings. I'll send you a postcard.' She made to get into the taxi, hesitated and trotted over to give me a kiss.

'Bye, Jane. Thanks for everything.' She waved, getting into the taxi. 'Keep eating the mud and good luck.'

The taxi drew away. I watched it disappear then walked back up the driveway, my head bowed in deep thought.

'Jane!'

I looked up to see Joy being pulled down the hillside path by Winston and Titan, straining on their leads to greet me. I bent down to make a fuss of them, then stood upright.

'Sian's gone, Joy. She's booked a flight home. The taxi just picked her up a minute ago.'

'Oh.' Joy pursed her lips. 'I see. Oh, well.'

'She apologized and is going to write to you.'

'Oh, that's good of her. I may be nearing the knacker's yard, Jane, but I still have half a brain intact. I knew she wasn't ill. I see more of what's going on around here than you might think.'

She gently pulled the dogs away, then stopped. 'I saw you out early the other morning, wandering about, sitting in the olive tree. Did you get it?'

'Get what, Joy?'

She slowly turned her head and looked around

226

the garden, then to the sky, and I instantly knew what she meant.

'*Genius loci*?'

'Yes. Describe it?'

'Just the feeling. The volcano sunrise, the light, flowers, everything really. The past, the future, nothing mattered but then.'

I thought of Sian making her way to the airport, but rather than feeling envious I was surprised to feel relief. I was staying and would have 'mad bat' Joy back to myself. Sian may have known all the right scientific terms and have a ream of qualifications, but I had tapped into something that she was not yet aware of—a sense of place. And Joy had shown me how to appreciate it. It was then I made a decision. I would stay at Helikion for Christmas.

I watched her walk away, a hand of acknowledgement briefly raised in the air then brushed caressingly through the dark green leaves of a spurge olive.

# 11
# The Wrong Tree

Narcissus
papyraceus
'PAPER-WHITE NARCISSUS'

Two weeks had passed since Sian's visit, and the smell of burned fish fingers still lingered in Alcatraz. I didn't mind so much. It reminded me to stick to my new-found resolution, which I'd written in my diary after she'd left:

*I will NEVER moan about being alone here again. Sian made me think about home far too much. Solitude strengthens the mind— think that's another of Joy's Churchillian quotes. I keep repeating it to myself. Helps me to keep on track. Can't say Joy is. She's off her trolley, drifting around the garden in hippie dresses and pink wellies, muttering to herself. Maybe talking about her 'grass'-smoking days caused it? I can imagine her, the beautiful model with all her Carnaby Street friends, puffing on pot.*

It was late morning and I was weeding on the lower terrace when I became aware of Joy's presence and that she was watching me. I was used to this and pretended I hadn't seen her.

'Can you tell me why it's such a beautiful colour?'

I looked round enquiringly, but her gaze was now fixed on a blowsy *Iris germanica* bloom, the sole flower amid a sea of bright green leaf blades.

'Just look at that purple,' Joy breathed, looking up at me and smiling. 'It's easy to stop looking, isn't it? Let's gaze a bit more. We don't do it enough. Come on.'

I followed her, soon stopping as she pointed out

231

the blue-veined flowers poking out of a mandrake's large crinkled leaves.

'Like baby birds, aren't they? Squashed in a nest, eager for food, beaks wide open. Can you see that, Jane?'

'Yes, I can,' I said.

Orwell brushed past me and nestled against Joy's legs, then plodded after her as the tour continued.

She stopped to marvel at the daisies on a blue marguerite. 'Look at them. I need sunglasses they are such a piercing colour. Now, Jane, what's the Latin?'

'*Felicia amelloides.* From South Africa.'

'You're coming on. I'm presuming you didn't take a peep at its marble sign,' she said with a wry smile, then suddenly a frown crossed her face. 'Marilyn never kept a plan, you know. No plan or sketch of the garden layout. She must have thought she'd be here forever.'

She sat down on a terraced wall, stroking Orwell, and composed herself.

'I was in England for a month—my sister's funeral. And I missed the garden. How I missed it. I found a poetry book in her bedroom. Wordsworth. It brought the garden back to me and made the whole affair more bearable.' She paused and then began to recite from 'Lines Composed a Few Miles Above Tintern Abbey':

'These beauteous forms,
Through a long absence, have not been to me
As is a landscape to a blind man's eye:
But oft, in lonely rooms, and 'mid the din
Of towns and cities, I have owed to them
In hours of weariness, sensations sweet,

232

Felt in the blood, and felt along the heart;
And passing even into my purer mind,
With tranquil restoration.'

She bit her lower lip. 'I sometimes forget when I'm
spouting off about water and illegal boreholes. I
do forget how *spiritual* it all is.' She patted my
hand then lifted Orwell off her lap, gently placing
him on the gravel path.

*     *     *

The next day, Joy joined me in planting out on the
terraces. We said little and after a few hours she
went into the house to bring out home-made cakes
and a flask of coffee. We sat underneath a sumach
tree and listened to the drone of bees collecting
nectar from its flowers. A robin sat on the handle
of my garden fork while chaffinches gathered in
fluttering circles.

'Have I ever told you about Wordsworth's poem
"Lines Composed a Few Miles Above Tintern
Abbey"?'

I glanced at her. 'Yes, you did—yesterday.'

'Did I? Oh yes. I remember.' She finished her
coffee. 'Everybody knows the daffodil poem, don't
they—"I Wandered Lonely as a Cloud"? But do
they know the last verse?

"For oft, when on my couch I lie
In vacant or in pensive mood,
They flash upon that inward eye
Which is the bliss of solitude;
And then my heart with pleasure fills,
And dances with the daffodils".'

In a gust of wind, a spray of petals and pollen fell from the sumach tree to land on our heads and the gravel path. Joy gave a little sigh and stood up.

'Right, I'll leave you to it.' It was as though someone had pressed a button, switching her on to busy mode. After a few steps she turned round.

'Oh, I know what I wanted to tell you.' She pointed towards a couple of trees. 'I want you to chop down that dead tree over there. You remember, I showed it to you yesterday?'

I followed her pointed finger. It was about twenty yards away beyond a rosemary shrub.

'Do it now, before you forget.' Joy turned away and went back towards the house.

I went to the tool shed to bring out a strong handsaw. Joy loathed chain saws, seeing them as instruments of the devil, for the noise they made and the danger to life and limb they posed.

I approached the tree, deep in thought. Joy's choice of Wordsworthian poetry was intriguing. I wondered if it had anything to do with the possibility of her losing her beloved garden. She'd be as empty as the poet in a big city. It all fitted—the awfulness of being ' 'mid the din of towns' and finding solace in the memories of the plants and landscapes he'd once roamed.

It gave me an uneasy feeling. As I made the first cut in the base of the tree I thought of Pavlos, the gentle giant who radiated warmth and always made me smile. He would know what was going on in Joy's life. I would ask him about her. As I continued to saw into the tree trunk it occurred to me that I knew more about Joy than I did about Pavlos. He reminded me of Pavarotti or of a grand

234

restaurateur. His charisma allied to his deep resonant voice always lit up any room of people.

Horror!

I stared at the deep cut I'd made in the tree trunk. It was moist and there was a green tinge to it. Blood rushed to my head. My hands prickled. I started to sweat and stepped backwards to stare at the tree. It was its absence of leaves that had given the impression it was dead. In my daydream I'd dismissed the fact that it might be deciduous. It was a Chinese elm, the only one of its type that tolerated these conditions. What excuse could I muster? None. Squatting down, staring hard at the ground, I tried to remember Joy's instruction. 'That dead tree over there,' she had said. Was it possible that Joy had thought it was an evergreen Chinese elm, showing its death in the absence of leaves? Never. Joy may have been forgetful sometimes but she knew her plants.

I stood up and found myself staring at an Italian buckthorn tree, ten metres or so away. Oh God. I remembered what she'd said yesterday. 'I want you to remove this buckthorn. Poor thing's given up the ghost.'

The buckthorn was an evergreen tree but the dark green leaves that would normally adorn it were stained yellow and brown. It had given up the ghost, all right. I'd killed the elm without thinking; I'd not even carried out the standard procedure of nicking the bark to see if it was dead or not.

I examined the cut. It was far too deep, way beyond a remedial patch or any kind of bandage that could cover up what I'd done. The tree would die. And Joy would know the reason. Then, salvation! The Neanderthal. He'd already committed acts of vandalism in the garden, or at least been accused of them. This would be another of his crimes. It was a godsend. My story would be that, after cutting down the buckthorn, I'd walked in the direction of the elm on my way back to the house. I'd spotted the damage and rushed to tell Joy that the Neanderthal had struck again. I picked up the saw and was about to move towards the buckthorn when I stopped dead. There was Joy striding towards me in a purposeful manner, her face set and hard as a brick.

I stood still and awaited my fate.

'What have you done? I saw you from the top terrace,' she croaked, rushing past me to stare down at the damage I'd done, letting out a cry of anguish. She clasped a hand to her mouth and, in a coughing fit, put her hands on her knees, waiting for it to subside.

'I'm terribly sorry, Joy. I wasn't thinking.'

'No, Jane!' Joy was on her feet. 'You were obviously away with the fairies. If you can't tell the difference between—'

She broke off and in a thin, taut voice spoke quietly and deliberately.

'I suggest you go and study your books. I did point out the buckthorn yesterday.'

'I know. I'm so sorry. I really am.'

I was mortified to see Joy's eyes fill with tears as she crouched down at the tree's base and embraced its trunk.

'You don't realize . . . just go, please.' She waved her arm for me to leave.

I stumbled away. On reaching Alcatraz I threw myself on the bed and crushed my head into the pillow, sobbing uncontrollably. So much for passing my probationary period. How could I have been so stupid? That was it. I was finished at Helikion. Joy certainly wouldn't want me around any more.

I struggled to sit upright—and to think. I didn't need an airline leaflet. I would just go to the airport and catch the next available flight, no matter whether it was day or night. Sleeping on an airport bench would hardly be less comfortable than Alcatraz, probably warmer. But wait—the National Gardens. Loska had said he would hire me. I thought about where I might stay and the cost of living in the city. I decided to contact him and see what my prospects were before making any decision.

I seized a pad of notepaper and did something my dad had taught me to do when faced with a big problem. Write down all the pros and cons, and in the end add them up in points scored. I scribbled down that life in the city would be what I made it. There were young people there and cafés and clubs. There was an English website acting as a meeting place for ex-pats. I felt a surge of excitement. I moved to go to the cubicle—and stopped.

Joy was outside again, sitting on the wooden chair. I crept closer to peer through the small paned window. She was holding a large jug full of twigs. As I watched she stood up and walked round to the door. I flattened myself against the wall to avoid being seen.

There was a knock. 'Jane?'

I hesitated and then slowly went to open the door.

Joy stood in the entrance, expressionless. 'I

237

thought you might like these.' She held out the jug. They held elm twigs from the wounded tree. 'We might as well use its benefits.'

I gave a gasp of relief. 'Oh, Joy. I'm really, really so sorry, I—'

I broke off as Joy stepped forward, put both arms at my sides and gave me a brief hug. 'I thought you might like to wind some Christmas lights around them. I've got some in the house.'

'Thank you,' I said, tremulously. 'Thank you so much.'

Joy seemed to be having difficulty finding what to say next. 'I didn't tell you, but I only found out a week ago,' she said awkwardly. 'I knew that Tom's mother, Marilyn, had ordered him to look after the garden in his lifetime. That's why I found it strange that he even talked about selling.' Joy paused as if it caused her pain to say it. 'But Charles brought me another email from him—you know he's coming over soon—and he mentioned that she hadn't specified it in her will. He can do what he likes with it. The garden could return to just scrub.' There was another pause. 'You do understand.'

'Of course I do. I'm so sorry. I didn't realize—'

I broke off as she suddenly strode past me and grabbed hold of Zeus.

To my astonishment, she dragged him backwards towards the door.

'Give me a hand. Just this once we'll have Christmas early. Get the wheelbarrow.'

Confused, but elated, I dashed outside.

A few minutes later, Zeus sat in the wheelbarrow being wheeled to the house. It had me giggling with the kind of nervous hysteria that comes with a sudden release of tension. But it was indeed funny and Joy was chuckling as we went. At the house Joy asked me to collect some laurel leaves while she went into the ghost room to fetch out the Christmas decorations box. Soon Zeus sat in the alcove, ready to welcome visitors. On his mane he wore a crown of laurel leaves and he had a string of fairy lights around his body.

Joy stood back to admire our handiwork then went inside the house. She came out with two tall glasses of cloudy ouzo. 'To Zeus,' she said, raising her glass.

'To Zeus,' I said.

We touched glasses.

'You know,' said Joy, sipping ouzo, 'it's not outside the realms of possibility that the elm might re-sprout.'

'Wouldn't you rather plant a new one?' I asked innocently.

'No.' She tightened her shoulders. 'No, I wouldn't.' She turned away and went quickly into the house, closing the door behind her.

I looked at Zeus sitting proudly inside the alcove and patted his head.

'Happy Christmas. Behave yourself here. It's a proper house.'

After lunch, I cut down the buckthorn and then went to remove the Chinese elm. With quick sawing actions I was able to push the tree over. I blew sawdust away from the top of the stump and prayed that it would re-sprout.

When I opened my eyes I noticed a metal tag partially embedded in the earth. I pulled it out and removed the green wire that attached it to the base of the stump. It was dirty and difficult to read so I cleaned it with a tissue taken from my pocket. There were two words and a date underneath. The first letter stamped into it was 'F'. I had to give it a spit and a polish to reveal the next two letters.

'For.'

The next letter was 'C'. Another spit and a wipe and it revealed the name: 'Christos'.

'For Christos'.

The date underneath was '21.3.91'.

'I see you've found it.'

I turned round.

Joy held out her hand. 'I'll fix it to the next tree we plant,' she said.

# 12

# Merry Mezethes

A foul smell arose inside Alcatraz. I first noticed it after taking one of my quick showers, spending no longer in the mouldy cubicle than was necessary. I went early to the house to inform Joy of the unpleasant odour. She came back with me to 'sniff for herself', not that she doubted me, but a previous intern had left a small waste bin under the bed, the resulting stink being the product of a pack of writhing maggots amid rotting bread, meat and bits of fish.

Having confirmed that I had not been so 'bloody stupid', as she put it, Joy called Spiros. A recorded message informed her that he was recovering from a hernia operation and would not be available for some days.

'There's no other plumber available,' Joy said, then added darkly, 'nobody we can trust, anyway. They come from miles away and charge the earth, so we'll do it ourselves. In the meantime you'll have to stay in the ghost room.'

I made no reply but hesitated. Joy looked at me with a teasing smile. 'Scared of the ghost room, are we?'

I should have replied, 'No, Joy. Scared more of you, actually.' But I merely gave a silly grin in return. 'Not really.'

My future at Helikion was now die cast. I would last out the year. But if I lived in close proximity to Joy by night as well as by day, it might cause more friction. On the other hand, I was eager to know more about her time with Christos in the hope that it might shed some light on her strange behaviour—living in the house might provide me with a chance, in a relaxed moment with her, to ask about those days.

However, on balance I settled for staying in Alcatraz if the stink could be removed. In a perverse sort of way I'd rather taken to my cell, for all its poverty. The red shag-pile rug and the orange lampshade, which Joy had bestowed upon me, had made it look a wee bit cosier and in the evenings I would set tea lights aflame and enjoy relaxing in their soft glow. I'd also bought some multicoloured muslin cloth from the market and draped it over the window—something my Moroccan boyfriend had done in his gloomy flat in London.

Joy had had the foresight to cater for plumbing problems when she'd made Spiros write out simple 'plumbing notes' for when he was unavailable. To my surprise, instead of going to her desk to collect them, she went outside to the garage to search her 'archives'. Apparently, all the important documents relating to the property had been transferred there after Winston, in a vigorous sexual affair with a pair of sandals, had knocked over a candle during a power cut. The fire had been short-lived, but the next day Joy had dumped the archives inside a filing cabinet and garaged them between the olives' storage space and two old bicycle frames.

After stuck drains, stuck filing cabinets. Try as she might, not one drawer would open. After much tugging and swearing, plus a broken fingernail, Joy called for my input. In an inspired moment I suggested brute force. Joy agreed and so I went to the tool shed to return with a crowbar. After insertion between drawer front and cabinet top and followed by violent levering, the drawer was eventually released. It was after withdrawing its contents that I noticed a key on a hook adjacent to the cabinet. It fitted the lock exactly.

I put it to Joy that perhaps the drawer wasn't stuck but locked.

'Bugger,' said Joy. 'I now remember putting the key there. But why didn't I remember before?'

'Perhaps there's a key for a lock to open the drains,' I said, hoping to make her smile.

But she was too busy scanning the notes. 'Now then. Here we are. "Drains and pipes".' After a quick read-through it became clear that, according to Spiros, it was all a question of the U-bend.

We stood in Alcatraz, Joy in the cubicle reading the notes. 'The blockage would be in the bottom of the trap,' she announced, translating as she read. 'Step one. Place a bucket under the U-bend. Two. Unscrew the retaining caps using a pipe wrench. Three. Let the trap fall into the bucket. Four. Empty the water. Five. Fish inside the pipe using a length of wire.'

'What about step six?' I said. 'Find a pipe wrench. Have we got one?'

'No. He keeps his tools at home.' She phoned Spiros again, this time making contact. '*Andio*,' she said at the close and put down the phone. 'I've got to go and fetch a pipe wrench.'

Half an hour later she returned waving the wrench and marched me back into Alcatraz. She stepped inside the cubicle, picked up the plastic shower bowl and gazed sombrely at the metal drain stuck in the stone floor. 'You can't get a flea, never mind a bucket, under that,' she said, and so we went outside. A few bricks, stacked together against the bottom wall of the outhouse, protected the drainage pipe that led from the cubicle. I removed them to unveil a junction with another pipe that ran at a downward angle towards a manhole three metres away.

'No U-bend under that,' I said. 'It's a simple pipe draining into that manhole.'

'Not a job for a bucket,' said Joy. 'And we've no rods either.'

And so I came to be domiciled in the ghost room, pending the recovery of plumber Spiros.

My diary entry for my first night in the ghost room read:

*1 a.m.: Determined not to let the thought of a 'ghost' affect me. 2 a.m.: Can't help but think something's going to leap out at me. 3.20 a.m.: Angry now. Why did Joy have to tell me about a bloody ghost, real or not? 4 a.m.: Cracked open one of the plastic mini bottles of whisky that I've saved from my air flight. Watching episode six of* The Sopranos, *series three.*

In the light of the morning I found the ghost room not so alien a place now that Sian had stayed there. The mothball smell had gone and the double bed, which I had tossed and turned in for the majority of the night, was far more comfortable than the narrow mattress in Alcatraz.

I was correct in my reservations about living with Joy. On one occasion I went to the toilet and found her, in a long silk nightdress, slathering Vaseline all over her lips. She remained at the washbasin to brush her hair and said, 'Don't be shy. I won't look.'

*     *     *

Tom's impending arrival kept Joy on the ragged edge of irritability. Her nervousness soon showed by her diverting me from whatever job I was doing to some new task, and then either back again to the original work or to something entirely new. Thus, no sooner had I mixed the cement for the building of the path through the herb garden than I was called upon to weed the terraces, except that I was no more than a few hours into that project when Joy would ask me to help collect the bitter oranges for making marmalade. When I returned to building the path, the cement had set and was useless.

Still, I reasoned, there were pleasures to be had in between the frenetic activity; in particular I enjoyed the pungent sweet smell of boiling fruit drifting out of the house and across the garden. It had me lifting my nose in the air, sniffing dreamily like one of the Bisto kids in the old gravy advert.

I was on my third attempt to start work on the herb garden path when Joy hailed me from Alcatraz to join her. With a patient sigh I put down my mortar trowel, poured a little water on the pile of mixed cement to keep it from drying, and went to join her.

At long last Spiros had arrived, his hernia operation no longer a hindrance to work. Dressed in working jeans and a droopy brown sweater, he raised his hand as I approached, while keeping a fixed eye on the open pipework, now minus its brick covering. With a chuckle, he pushed up his grey cloth cap.

'Joy?' I wondered what Spiros found amusing.

'He thinks it's funny, him telling us to put a bucket under it.'

'Isn't the blockage caused by the pipe running down too shallow,' I said. 'Isn't the simplest thing just to make it steeper? After he's cleared it out,' I hastily added.

'Spiros?' Joy put my question to him.

'Hah!' Spiros put up both hands sharply and began lecturing Joy in rapid dramatic Greek, his expansive gestures embracing, it seemed, a whole universe of common knowledge. The translation, when I heard it, would have pleased Aristotle. It was not true, according to Spiros, that the simplest way was always the best. 'No man should claim to have an answer by taking the obvious and easiest of cures' is the gist of what he said.

I asked Joy what all that had to do with a blocked drain. 'He's saying that a steep pipe drop, though it seems the obvious thing to have, is actually the wrong thing to have. But nobody learns, the whole world over.'

Joy broke off as Spiros added something. 'He says that the fall has to be no more than one centimetre in forty. The reason is that if it's a steeper drop the water will fall away quickly but it will leave solids behind.'

'But it's not a foul drain. It's only taking away water from the shower and sink.'

Joy spoke again to Spiros. He pointed towards the cubicle, then down at the pipe run.

Joy translated. 'He says there's always solids after washing. You get hair, dirt and bits of towel building up over time. And then you've got a

248

blockage.'

'So when's he going to clear it?' I asked, perhaps too urgently.

Joy grunted. 'After he's picked up his grandchildren, Jane. No earlier.'

'*Dodeka*,' Spiros said, lighting a thick cigar.

'Twelve children. And still counting,' Joy said. 'Each Christmas he takes them to Athens Zoo.'

\*　　　\*　　　\*

It was early on Christmas Eve morning. Joy had insisted she make me breakfast after I'd drearily confessed to another sleepless night. It had nothing to do with ghosts, I insisted. It was a phase. It would pass. And it didn't matter a jot because I was free from work for three whole days. Joy, who had already walked the dogs, peered at me. 'Jane, you look awful. Go outside for some fresh air. Go on.'

As I stepped outside, blinking in the daylight, I performed my usual habit of peering up at Mount Hymettos. Standing at 1,026 metres, it sometimes played the role of a weather barometer, giving a rough height for any cloud base that ringed it.

Today it was crowned by a sunlit covering of snow and plainly defined against a clear blue sky. Recently I'd been reading a history of the mountain, interested to learn that it was famous for its thyme honey and that many English fireplaces were made from the marble cut from its slopes. Since 1995, however, the industry had been banned.

I was not out of the house more than a few minutes when I heard a vehicle mounting the driveway, coming to a stop outside the Neanderthal's gates. It was a large blue Mercedes estate car. The driver, a young man with dark hair and wearing designer jeans and sunglasses, got out to press the gate speaker button.

As he turned to get back into his car I nipped behind an olive tree to watch him slowly drive through the opening gates. Through the car's rear window I could see two identical wooden cabinets. They were made of a dark polished wood, but much of their facing was comprised of some kind of tight mesh, something like fishing net material, or something like two speakers ... like part of a sound system.

After breakfast Pavlos and Vassili arrived with a tall Christmas tree, bought from the village market. While I brought the decorations from the ghost room and helped them dress the tree, Joy got down to the business of making almond cookies—called kourabiedes. Pavlos, I noticed, kept glancing towards the kitchen with a frown on his face while letting out little rumbles of discontent from time to time. I couldn't decide whether he found the smell unpleasant or if it meant he was starving. When Joy moved on to cooking honey cakes—melomakarona—his torment drove him to slap his forehead with the palm of his hand.

'*Blasfimia!*'

'What did you say, Pavlos?' I giggled, looking down at him from the top of the ladder.

'Hah, Jane,' he sighed, spreading his arms in misery. 'I said damnation. Before Christmas I fast for two weeks. Used to be four weeks. For religion ...' he paused to pat his girth, 'and to remove fats.'

'Darling Pavlos, be glad you don't have my metabolism,' said Vassili, who more and more reminded me of Toad of Toad Hall. He reached inside the decorations box to bring out a dusty Christmas tree fairy. He tried to straighten its crooked wand, but to no avail.

'Here, Jane, put this on top. Like Joy, she's as old as this hill.'

'I heard that, Vassili,' shouted Joy, walking out of the kitchen with a plate of small sausages. 'I'm not that ancient. Now Pavlos, if you're hungry I'll let you have a tiny present. Your fasting ends tonight, so why worry? All my own work. Better than from any supermarket.'

Titan and Winston trotted alongside her, noses twitching, tails alert.

'Well, a few hours won't matters.' Pavlos made yum-yum noises as he ate first one sausage then another. 'But this is sad day for my bellys.'

'They're made of pork, Jane,' said Joy, offering me the plate. 'I add herbs, a dash of Tabasco and a secret ingredient only known to myself and my dear Christos. My own recipe. In the old days every family had a pig and slaughtered it on Christmas Eve. Out of fashion now, of course. But we believe in keeping traditions, don't we, Vassili?'

'My darling, one hundred per cent.' Vassili held his hand out for a sausage then let out a yelp as the fairy clattered to the floor. 'Well, *that* hasn't gone out of fashion, has it? Every year she falls, Jane. It's time for a new one.'

Joy went to pick up the fairy and stood quietly, looking out to the garden.

On Christmas Eve night, Joy and I were left alone in the house. We played Scrabble, the Bing Crosby record of 'White Christmas'—a must for Joy on this special day—softly playing in the background. Flickering candlelight danced around the room and the tree's lights twinkled, the fairy now Sellotaped to its top. Wizard was perched on his swing, while Winston lay curled against Titan's belly on the sofa. Joy was quiet and, unlike the previous games we'd played, quick to make her words. She was delving into the bag of tiles when suddenly there came the thunderous 'boom-boom' of disco music accompanied by the screaming voice of a disc jockey through a PA system, undoubtedly part of which I'd spotted inside the Mercedes estate car.

'What the blazes!' Joy mouthed, looking at me.

I told her of what I had seen earlier in the day. Incensed, she scraped back her chair and scurried towards the alcove. She was out of the house in a flash and I chased after her down the driveway and onto the track. The entire area around the Neanderthal's house was illuminated by floodlighting. We peered through the bars of the fencing. Party-goers could be glimpsed, shouting at each other, laughing as well as jigging to the bass rhythm. As the PA faded, I could hear the splashing of water amid shrieks of laughter.

'The brute. Jane, did you hear that? It's a swimming pool.'

Joy went to stand outside the gate, shaking her fist at the CCTV camera. As she did so a couple of chained guard dogs appeared, leaping at the bars, snarling and barking.

The PA resumed its bombardment. Joy stomped back furiously to the house. 'It's the season of goodwill and that bloody man's declared war!'

We put cotton wool in our ears to finish playing Scrabble. While picking out tiles from the bag, she suddenly said something urgent. I stuck my head forward and to one side to hear her repeat her statement.

'I said Charles had an email this morning,' Joy shouted. 'Tom will be here on January the seventh.' She paused and then resumed her shouting, stuffing her fingers into her ears. 'There was a study done. They found that sixty per cent of people living in Athens suffered from noise pollution! They never do anything about it if you complain. I think you have to kill the noise-mongers. Shall we go back down and throttle him?'

I went to bed envious of the young people at the disco, still thumping away. In between thinking of friends back home, parties I couldn't attend and imaginary ghosts, I shed a little tear.

\*       \*       \*

I awoke early on Christmas Day morning. The noise had lasted until 1 a.m. I found Joy still in bed, so I slipped out into the garden, which lay still and quiet. The Neanderthal's house was also mercifully silent, no sound or sight of dogs or people.

I held my nose, the smell from the shower drain even more pungent, and went into Alcatraz to bring out a gift-wrapped package I'd kept hidden

253

in the back of a cupboard. I brought it back to the house and found Joy, in a bright red kimono, making breakfast. I was momentarily halted in my tracks when she turned around to face me. She had applied a mud pack to her face, which had nearly dried out and was cracking in places.

'Er, Happy Christmas, Joy,' I said, holding out the present, staring at her.

Joy held up her hand to ward me off and spoke, her lips barely moving. 'Happy Christmas, Jane. No presents until after breakfast. Another custom.' She tried to smile but quickly stopped herself.

'Oh . . . is it a Greek custom?'

'No. Mine. I want to concentrate on what I've been given. Can't do that if I'm hungry.'

I ate feta cheese and bread dipped in olive oil, while Joy carefully nibbled toast with honey from one of Nikiforo's beehives. After she had finished she bustled off to change and returned rosy-faced, blueberry lipstick applied.

'Now, Jane. I insist that you try one of my *melomakarna* cookies.'

Were they too sweet, she wanted to know? I shook my head. 'Pavlos will go bananas with these.' It was at that moment that the question I'd wanted to ask for weeks suddenly rushed out. 'What does Pavlos do, Joy? Has he a job or what?'

Joy was silent for a while as she put the breakfast dishes in the sink.

'If I tell you, you must promise not to tell anybody—promise now and I'll tell you why.'

'Of course, Joy.' I was enthralled. 'I promise. Go on.'

'His father owned a ferry company in Piraeus.

254

He sent Pavlos to school in France because he was frightened he might be kidnapped—the Greek mafia have been doing it for hundreds of years. There've been twenty-five kidnappings this year—mostly in the Athens area, all rich people. Huge ransoms have been paid; in one case forty million dollars. Often the police aren't told and the money's paid. So it encourages more kidnappings. It's been going on for centuries—a custom if you like. A cousin of Queen Victoria was taken and murdered because the ransom wasn't paid. There was a bestselling book about it called *The Dilessi Murders*.'

'That's amazing. I'd no idea,' I said, shaking my head.

'Anyway, Pavlos got a degree in music. Then he married a French girl. She died in an accident. They had no children. He was heartbroken and came back here to live when his father died. Inherited a fortune but keeps it all low key, for obvious reasons. But he does stand out in a crowd, doesn't he? Easily recognizable. So he doesn't go out a lot. He's taking no risks and I don't blame him.'

My mouth remained open. 'Good grief,' I said slowly. 'Incredible.'

'By the way, it isn't Pavlos's real name. He changed it as soon as he came back.'

'So how does he live, Joy? I mean, what kind of house?'

'He lives modestly in an ordinary house. He supports charities through an English contact, writes music and does some private teaching.'

Joy began washing up the breakfast things. 'He does put some money into Helikion to help keep the garden running. But it has to be small, in keeping with his lifestyle.'

'The accordion,' I said, helping her to wash up. 'He plays it beautifully.'

'You ought to hear him play the cello.'

On impulse she went to pick up the phone. 'Jane, I'll ask him to bring it.' She hesitated. 'But you mustn't talk about his father, or his past. He's very nervous about it.'

'I promise, of course. Where does he live?'

'About a kilometre away. Nothing fancy. Small house and garden. His views outside are the same as ours.'

While Joy made her phone call I went to stand at the veranda doors, looking out over the garden, reflecting on what Joy had told me. It was the stuff of fiction. And to think that, in Alcatraz, I'd been pining for the outer, better-off world, whereas Pavlos had left it to—well, join me in mine. I remained there lost for several minutes in a daydream.

'Oh, how marvellous! Thank you, Jane.' Joy's excited voice brought me back. I turned round to find that she had unwrapped her present.

'*Birthday Letters* by Ted Hughes. It's exactly what I wanted. How on earth did you know that?'

'I know you love poetry. And you told me—a month ago.'

'Did I?' Joy stared at me, then dismissed her forgetfulness and grabbed me by the shoulders to plant a big kiss on my cheek. 'Thank you so much! But how did you get it?'

'I got my parents to send it over.'

Joy promptly went to her desk, opened a drawer and brought out a medium-sized parcel wrapped

256

with newspaper covered in glued-on stars and sparkles. 'That's one pressie.' She brought a second package. 'And there's the other.' I was touched and surprised. I hadn't expected anything from Joy, given her worries.

'Joy, they're great! Thank you so much!' I gave her a quick kiss on the cheek.

I now had a pair of tough gardening gloves and a large sketch pad with a packet of drawing pencils. There was a caveat. In return she wanted permission to look at my sketchbook, not just of the plants but also her pets. I promised to bring it over.

'And could I read your gardening diary?' she asked.

'Course you can.' I didn't tell her that I had another, a more personal diary.

'Now you must light the fire, Jane. I've laid it. Pavlos loves his log fire.'

'So do I,' I said, going to the fireplace. When I struck a match, Wizard made a fuss in his cage.

'I forgot,' said Joy. 'Wizard loves it too.' She opened the cage door. Wizard took a speculative step forward to perch in the open doorway and then flew to land on the brass fender where he sat ruminating at the rising flames.

'It's a pity he doesn't talk. Mind you, with my swearing, perhaps not.' Joy chuckled then let out a small sigh. 'Christos rescued him. Poor thing was mistreated when he was young. That's why he's a little devil now. It's a lesson, isn't it?' She looked kindly at the macaw and made a soft cooing noise, which Wizard reciprocated.

At midday the clanking cowbell proclaimed the arrival of Pavlos, Demetri and Vassili, the trio

257

entering to an exchange of seasonal greetings. While Pavlos and Demetri lugged in a crate of champagne, Vassili, holding a lightweight cardboard box to his chest, strode in majestically, placing it reverently on the table as if it were the Crown Jewels.

'Darlings. The *pièce de résistance. Voilà!*' Reaching inside the box, he pulled back a layer of tissue paper protecting its contents. 'A tree fairy made by the finest hands.' He looked at Demetri, who grinned sheepishly.

The rest of us gathered round to look. Nestled inside a bed of newspaper there lay a small figurine carved out of balsa wood. A small spade, its shaft made out of a pencil, its blade a square of thick tinfoil, was attached to its tiny hand and held aloft.

'A gardening fairy for your every wish,' Vassili said quietly, his eyes milky.

'Oh, how lovely!' Joy hugged first Vassili then Demetri. Pavlos picked the fairy out of the box and went to place it on the tree. He then went out to fetch his cello, but on his return turned down my earnest supplication that he play it immediately. 'Janes. My heart responds to sparkles.' He laughed heartily. 'I only play well drunk.'

'You shall have *your* wish, Pavlos.' Joy went to the crate on the table, took out four bottles of champagne to cool in the fridge then opened a drawer to bring out a huge corkscrew. A large platter of tiny rounds of goats' cheese marinated in herbs and olive oil was placed on the table. 'Mezethes from Nikiforo's goats,' Joy said. 'Makes the cheese himself. Perfect with champagne.'

In the space of twenty minutes three corks were

popped with the fourth bottle on standby in readiness. As we gravitated around the log fire, I prompted Joy to relate the dreadful tale of the neighbour's Christmas Eve party.

'It went on until one o'clock this morning. And that swimming pool. You heard it, Jane, didn't you? If I could have got over that fence I'd have drowned him in it.'

The dark business was listened to in a deep and respectful concern, despite Vassili being squashed into the side of his armchair by a recumbent Titan and Demetri having trouble sharing his new Italian shoes with Winston. Wizard remained aloof, perched on the rafters, uttering low chortling squawks from time to time.

As minds became liberated by champagne and the senses stimulated by the scent of burning pine and the taste of Nikiforo's mezethes, the conversation became louder, more excitable and light-hearted.

By the time the fourth bottle of champagne had been consumed anybody who had anything to say either forgot it, or couldn't be bothered, pleased as they were in a general haze of self-satisfaction. And the bodies, once upright, had now sunk perceptibly into the depths of the cracked leather armchairs and belching sofa. It was Demetri who was first lulled into sleep, his 'daddy long legs' stretched out, his head lowered and arms drooping over the sides of his armchair. Then it was Pavlos's turn, his head falling to his chest, letting out little rumbles and wheezes, gradually transmuting them into a stentorian snore.

I stared into the flames, making pictures as I did as a child in the heart of a coal fire but finding it

259

difficult, my eyelids dropping, having to blink hard to stay awake, determined to enjoy every minute of the day. But then I too finally succumbed. The last thing I remembered was the silence broken by Wizard's soft mutterings and the crackling of burning logs.

'Bugger!'

Joy's shout jolted us all upright in a bewildered state of a pulse-racing dizziness. Vassili, thinking he'd had a heart attack, clutched his chest and flopped back onto Titan's shoulders. Joy, meanwhile, had rushed into the kitchen from where there came a despairing wail. In alarm we stumbled to her aid and stopped dead at the sight which greeted us: Joy staring into the open freezer cabinet in which sat a very cold, greasy-looking— and definitely uncooked and raw—turkey.

'How did that—Jane—I cooked it!' she stuttered in appeal. 'You saw me start it, didn't you?'

Squirming in discomfort, I was forced to say, 'I didn't actually, Joy, no.'

'What? It's ridiculous.' Joy's distress had Pavlos putting his arm around her.

'Joy-bells, no problems. We cut bits of it off and cook with blowtorch.'

'No, no, no, Pavlos. I can't believe this.' Joy broke free, grabbed her champagne glass and tossed what remained down her throat. Then she drew herself upright. 'Right,' she said toughly. 'What's done is done. We'll have to have the lamb. I saved it for tomorrow. But it's Christmas Day and I'm an idiot. Now everyone shoo!'

She harried us out of the kitchen, clapping her hands. 'Pavlos, get my gramophone and put on Louis Armstrong. He's always good for cooking in

260

a crisis.'

Joy set about preparing lunch with a brisk efficiency, refusing any help. It was her penance, she said, popping her head out of the kitchen entrance. On her head, courtesy of Pavlos, was a chef's white top hat.

Half an hour later an ad hoc spread covered the table, comprised of fragrantly spiced lamb with vegetables, side plates of olives, walnut bread, cheese and biscuits. More champagne bottles were popped and, apart from Joy, who kept on her chef's hat, we all wore paper hats and wished each other a Happy Christmas—and then dug in.

'It's wonderful, Joy!' squeaked Vassili. 'Delicious, darlings. So good of you to wake us all up.'

Joy smiled, screwed up her napkin and threw it at him. Vassili ducked and tossed it back with a mischievous yelp.

'Best thing to happens,' pronounced Pavlos. 'Who wants turkeys when we haves all this?'

We toasted Joy fulsomely. As if not to be left out, Titan wandered over to nuzzle against Joy's legs. The sole occupant of the sofa, Winston, cast a soulful eye on the proceedings, a red paper hat scrunched up around his neck.

\*       \*       \*

After lunch, my pleas for Pavlos to play his cello were, at last, rewarded. He sat some distance from the fire, the instrument resting against his thighs. Composing himself, the big man held his bow with a relaxed yet firm grip. Looking up to see that we were ready, he said, 'I make mistakes. I don't know

261

it all. But I will try.'

He placed the bow hairs across the cello strings. I took a sharp intake of breath at the dramatic, yet melancholic, first drawn-out note of Elgar's *Cello Concerto*.

As the romantic piece developed in all its light, shade and feeling, the picture in my mind was, as always when I heard it, the English countryside in all its autumnal colours and glory. I brushed away a prickle of tears. When the final note ceased we sat in silence. Joy then led the clapping. Moved and swept up in a moment of homesickness, I clapped the loudest.

Late at night, after a slow and unsteady walk back into the ghost room, I found one more present lying on the bed. It was a tub of mould-killing paint and a brush, to which was attached a note: 'Spiros will paint your cubicle once the drain is fixed after Boxing Day. Happy Christmas, Joy.'

\*     \*     \*

On Sunday, 6 January at 7.15 a.m., I was woken by Orwell scratching and hissing at Alcatraz's door. I blinked hard and looked at him.

'What's wrong?'

He flattened his ears and arched his back, hackles raised.

Then the bed shook violently. Shocked, I rolled out and placed both hands flat on the floor, but that too was moving from side to side. I quickly joined Orwell at the door, scrambling outside to look back at Alcatraz, stupidly hoping that it was the only thing moving. But the ground continued to tremble beneath my feet.

Scared, I was forced to adopt the pose of a surfer, arms stretched out, legs bent, one in front of the other. For a fleeting moment I thought how silly I must have looked, but that quickly transmuted into a desperate prayer. 'Please, God, don't let the ground open up and swallow me whole.' I didn't want to die in my pyjamas.

Then all was still.

'An earthquake off the Peloponnese coast,' Joy said breathlessly as I met her outside the house, having hurriedly changed. 'I've just heard it on the news. I did warn you we might have one. Quite a biggy. Six-point-five on the Richter scale.' Anxiously, she surveyed the roof of the house, looking for signs of damage. 'Jane, I'm going round the house. Can you go round the garden? See if there's any damage?'

'Yes, I was going anyway.'

I was on my way up the hill when Joy called out to me. 'Oh, and Jane?'

'Yes?' What now. Wasn't Sunday supposed to be a day of rest?

'Your jumper's on inside out and back to front.'

*     *     *

I made my way to the hilltop, walking in diagonals to cover as much of the garden as I could in one ascent and descent. But the only damage I could see had been caused by a dislodged boulder forming part of a decorative feature at the bottom of the phrygana. It had run a few metres downhill, crushing a few plants en route before it stopped perilously close to the edge of the wall overlooking the steep driveway. If it fell from there it could run

263

out onto the road. When I told Joy, she tutted and hastened down the driveway to look for herself.

'Of course, this would happen when we've got Tom coming tomorrow.' She stood looking up at the boulder, shaking her head. 'It's one thing after another. It could fall off if we have an aftershock.'

As a temporary measure we rammed some small stones under the front edge of the boulder, using a piece of wood as a battering ram.

'I'll ring Spiros. He'll know what to do.' Joy stepped back, shaking her head once more.

The following morning Tom telephoned Joy.

'He's landing at one o'clock,' she said, joining me in the garden. 'He'll be here round about two.' She drew the palm of her hand across her mouth, something she often did when feeling disturbed.

Winston, having spotted a few green toads bouncing in the vicinity of some damp rocks, vied for her attention, his tail wagging furiously. Joy took a look. It was one of those special moments in the garden that she would normally enthuse over, but on this occasion she stared blankly and ignored it, her mind elsewhere. She came round to make a cynical remark.

'Toads have to mate in water. Let's hope they do it in the Neanderthal's swimming pool.'

When Spiros arrived he was taken to see the errant boulder. He scratched his moustache and automatically took out his worry beads to click them as he meditated on the situation. Did it pose a risk to life and limb? asked Joy.

Yes, there was the matter of public liability insurance, Spiros told her. The rock could fall with any aftershock. Millions of euros could be involved. Lawyers specializing in everything,

264

including fallen boulders, would demand the earth. The garden would fail. Joy would be put in prison.

All that Spiros's doom-laden warning did was to make Joy force him to promise on his mother's grave that he would turn up the next morning and make the boulder secure. He promised.

'Spiros. Promise once more. Promise.'

Spiros promised. He'd taken his twelve grandchildren to the Athens Zoo and in the early morning their parents would arrive to take them back to their homes. It was all very simple and straightforward.

That evening Joy and I were invited for a 'calming down' meal with Charles and Rachel, both privy to the stress that Joy was under and eager to help.

It was bitterly cold, as well as pitch black with a moonless night, so Joy decided she would drive the short distance to their house. On arrival I paid a visit to the toilet and was washing my hands when the white sink appeared to move left and then back again.

For a moment I thought my eyesight was faulty but Charles, Rachel and Joy had felt the actual tremor of the aftershock. The net result was that, for the rest of the evening, Joy worried about the boulder. No sooner had we sat down at the dining table than I could see she wanted to get away, turning the 'calming down' meal into a stressful affair. No matter how much Charles and Rachel reassured her, Joy would not be satisfied until she had paid the boulder a visit.

Arriving back at the house, Joy's anxiety was compounded by frustration as, in her rush, she had difficulty steering the Jeep into the garage. After much manoeuvring, it was impossible for her to drive forwards or backwards without causing damage to the Jeep's front wing. Since this was the least of her worries, she abandoned the task, got out and hurried me downhill.

The boulder now lay in the middle of the driveway, bits from it scattered all around from its impact. At least it hadn't run into the road.

'Bugger,' I said, shaking my head and tutting, an affectation of Joy's that I had found myself imitating more and more. Joy caught me doing it, smiled dryly and lit a cigarette.

\*        \*        \*

The following morning light snow had started to fall as I stepped out from Alcatraz. I pulled down my woollen hat, then went to check the plants that we had covered with horticultural fleece for protection. As a consequence I arrived at the house slightly later than usual.

Joy was sitting at her desk, drinking strong coffee and smoking, wrapped up in her matrix of problems. Dwelling on them had added another two problems to her sorry list. She had forgotten to go shopping.

This, in turn, had given her even more anxiety, in that she'd been determined to provide Tom with a good meal when he arrived on the basis that the way to a young, healthy and baseball-playing American jock's heart was by way of his stomach. That thought led to her worrying about Spiros. Grandchildren in Greece were doted on, in much the same way as in other Mediterranean countries. But it didn't mean that their parents, four pairs of

266

them, would all be on time.

If they were not, the boulder, a priority for Joy, would become of secondary importance to the fulfilment of his grandparental duty and he would fail to arrive. And the boulder would remain, blocking the driveway. She was also concerned that the Neanderthal might make an issue of it and she didn't want to award him that privilege.

'Perhaps you should ring Spiros?' I suggested, taking her cup away. She had a look in her eye that suggested that if she drank any more Greek coffee she'd end up perching on Bosch's triptych.

At 10.30 a.m. she rang him. There was no answer there, nor from his mobile phone. By midday she'd given him up. Tom was due within two hours and drastic action had to be taken. She rang Charles and Pavlos, as well as Nikiforo, asking for their help, a desperate plea. The three men said they would drop what they were doing and be there post haste.

On their arrival Charles and Joy set to the task of releasing the jammed Jeep, while Pavlos and Nikiforo tackled the boulder. On first seeing it, the small man with the low-fitting cap under which sprouted newly grown sideburns walked around its girth, assessing its weight and muttering to himself.

'Epikindynos!' he declared with a gesture. It was too dangerous to be moved. But he had the solution. There was only one course of action available, he told Pavlos, and strode off to his van, returning with a sledgehammer. He heaved it over his head, about to take a great swipe at the rock, when Pavlos stopped him, remembering there was an iron spike in the garage. It was equally fortuitous that the boulder's fall from the wall had caused it to split a little, creating a slot into which the spike fitted and held firm.

Pavlos, the much bigger man, insisted that he limber up with the sledgehammer to deal the first bash. Taking a deep breath, he placed the sledgehammer on the flattened top of the spike, drew it back over his head and, in the manner of an executioner, delivered the decisive blow. But the boulder remained a boulder. It took several hits before it began to split.

While the boulder was under attack Joy was sitting in her car observing the fractional sideways movements of Charles' rigid upright hand. It was a matter of judging how far Joy had to turn the front wheels and then how far to reverse the car and then go forward. It was all about centimetres. Gradually a small gap was created in which, by one careful manoeuvre, Joy managed to free the Jeep. She leapt out to kiss Charles, thanked him profusely, then set off down the driveway, bound for the village.

Her mission was suddenly halted as, cresting the rise in the drive, she was confronted by the roadblock created by Nikiforo and Pavlos. The boulder now lay in many pieces, scattered all around them. As Joy leaned out of the window to enquire how long it would be before the drive was cleared, another vehicle, a taxi, pulled off the road and into the drive, also stopping abruptly at the sight of the roadblock.

The taxi driver, a man with a saturnine-looking face, spread out his arms and shook his head at the two labourers. Nikiforo went to explain to him what had happened. It looked like one of his charades as he first pointed to the house, then to the taxi's driving wheel, back to the house and then at the remains of the boulder.

Joy got out of her car, but she was no longer concerned with the log jam. As she picked her way through the debris she made for the passenger side of the taxi. Sitting inside was a young man with a mop of scruffy brown hair, wearing a denim jacket and an open-necked shirt. He was laughing at the efforts of Pavlos and Nikiforo to clear the driveway. As he saw Joy approaching he pressed a button and his window descended. He beamed at her.

'Hi, Joy.' He stuck out his hand.

'*Ya su*, Tom,' said Joy, taking it. 'I'm awfully sorry about all this.'

## 13

# When the Saints Go Marching In

snow &
branch skeletons

The first feeling I had when I awoke was that of a solid, utter deadness in the world around me, such as I'd never experienced before in Alcatraz. Wonderingly, I poked my head above the blanket to see my breath steam in the freezing air. Then I stretched up to peer out of the window—except the window had been replaced by two iced panels of exquisitely etched pictures and patterns of white frosted trees, ferns, leaves and whorls.

I looked at Zeus, safely back from his festive sojourn in the alcove. 'Typical of January at home, but I didn't expect it here. If it's like that inside, what must it be like outside, eh?'

I dressed quickly. It had been a freezing night and in addition to my pyjamas I wore thermals and a woollen hat, plus a pair of socks as gloves. I whipped them off to put on a long-sleeved top, jeans and waterproof over-trousers then my puffa jacket and the wellington boots that Joy had given me.

I found that the tap, which spluttered and coughed, issued forth no water. The toilet was similarly frozen. Grabbing a cloth I rubbed away a patch of ice from one of the windowpanes and peered outside. Thick snowflakes drifted and swirled in the air. The garden was no more, replaced by a magical land of moulded sculptures and white humps, out of which protruded the skeletons of bent, snow-laden trees, their black branches exposed like bones through skin.

I opened the door to be faced by a wall of snow. I punched and kicked into it, but it refused to give way. There was a gap between the top of the snowdrift and the doorframe. I put my face to the opening and shouted for help—and kept shouting

273

until, minutes later, I heard a strong male voice call out in an American accent, 'OK, Jane. Joy sent me to come and get you!'

I caught a glimpse of Tom ploughing slowly towards me, carrying a spade. I relaxed and waited. Soon I heard the crunch of his boots compressing virgin snow and getting louder. Then came his heavy breathing as he reached the snowdrift and began to clear it away from the door.

'I thought I'd come to Greece, not Alaska,' he panted cheerily.

While Tom huffed and puffed outside, I put on a bit of make-up and smiled to myself as I imagined that, after the rescue, he'd whisk me away to the south of France and a life of bliss. After a few minutes Tom called out that I was 'free to leave'.

I checked my appearance in the mirror one last time, stepped through the beaded curtains, past Zeus and out of the door.

'At last. My escape from Alcatraz.' Tom raised his eyebrows in query.

'Did I hear you say Alcatraz?'

'It's a joke.' I suddenly flushed with embarrassment. Had I offended him? I prayed that he wouldn't tell Joy. She might not be amused, either, calling 'her' outhouse after the infamous island prison.

Tom's face broke into a wide grin. 'Oh, you're Mrs Capone? Can I see?' He stepped inside and looked round then came outside to join me. 'Dead right. No room to swing a cat. Mum said it needed an overhaul.'

'Please don't say anything to Joy. I've never told her.'

'Don't worry. Your secret's safe with me, prisoner Jane.' He laughed at my embarrassment. 'I've come to escort you to the Governor. Handcuffs aren't necessary. You look friendly enough.' I laughed in relief, and we set off, slowly making our way to the house.

Tom pointed to the overhead telephone line leading to Charles and Rachel's house, except that it was no longer overhead but trailing to the ground, having fallen under the weight of snow.

'Electricity's off and the water. It could be the main outside that's frozen but if it's pipes in the house, expect fireworks when it thaws—I should say waterworks,' he added with a grin. 'At least Joy has the fire going. You'll get warm.'

Despite feeling the cold I had to stop when we came to the nursery and a point where we had the best view of the garden. The grandeur of the scene was breathtaking, a beautiful world seemed to have been given an extra layer of insulation. It was as if the whole area had been soundproofed. But despite the continuing snowfall, there was proof of life in the recent tracks left by a rabbit that had run a straight and purposeful line, disappearing into the white void.

'Isn't it fantastic?' I said.

'Yeah, quite something. Better than when I went skiing up in Colorado.' I looked at him and saw that he was genuinely appreciative. He caught my glance and his expression suddenly became serious.

'I'm not here to throw Joy out, honest to God,' he said sincerely. 'Do you believe me?'

'Of course I do.'

'And I don't want to ruin your year.' He drove a

275

gloved fist into a waist-high snowdrift. 'It's money. That's all it is.' There was a loud crack like gunshot close by. Tom looked about in alarm.

'It's OK,' I said. 'It's that tree over there. The snow's snapped an olive branch. Can you see it, look?'

'Yup, I can see it. Hey, I was scared there. Thought it was a bear!' He raised his arms and took a step towards me in imitation of a wild beast. I grinned and backed off to gather a snowball to lob at him. It was a perfect hit, right on the nose.

'Ouch!' He wiped the snow off his face. 'Great shot. You should play baseball.'

'I played rounders,' I said, quickening my pace, expecting him to retaliate. 'You Yanks call it baseball.'

'Oh yeah, well you insult our national game.' He quickly cupped his hand into the drift and hurled snow at me. 'Take that, you cricketer!' It was my turn to wipe snow off my face. We laughed together and resumed our plodding, bumping shoulders.

As we neared the driveway and civilization it seemed right and proper that the snow lay not as thick, allowing us to stamp our boots on hard ground all the way to the alcove, where we removed them.

Joy had a warming breakfast at the ready, porridge together with mugs of hot tea, all prepared on a two-ringed gas camping stove brought from the ghost room. 'Enjoy your tea. Did Tom tell you we've no bottled water left?' she said. 'We can't wash up. And the toilets aren't working. But we will not be defeated. We'll bring in buckets of snow and melt it. Easy.'

During breakfast Tom kept glancing at me, as if wanting to speak, but it wasn't until Joy had gone outside for a moment that he opened up.

'Quite a tough job you took on here, Jane.'

I looked into his deep brown eyes, his broad strong face set in a calm smile.

'Yes, it is, especially today. Don't think there'll be much weeding going on.' Tom laughed and gave a sideways glance as Joy re-entered, his smile fading a little.

Later, I came out of the bathroom to find Joy beckoning me into her bedroom. She closed the door. 'Sit down, Jane.' She took a deep breath and spoke in almost a whisper. 'Last night he said he plans to buy an apartment in Athens.' She paused for another intake of breath. 'It's exactly what I feared. He says he might get a job here but he hasn't enough money to keep the garden going as well as me as curator and interns like you.'

She held her hands tenderly together and caught me looking. 'It's the cold weather, Jane.' She dropped her voice again. 'He says he might have to sell it. Or turn it into something that makes money. "Could I charge visitors?" That kind of thing.' Joy shook her head. 'I said it wouldn't work. We haven't got the labour to show people round and maintain the garden as well. And it wouldn't make much money.' Joy looked irritated with herself. 'He knows how important the garden is— his mother created it, for God's sake. He says he might try and sell it to an organization or anybody in our kind of world who wants to, well, do what we're trying to do . . . hopefully keep me on.'

Joy tailed off, but perked up a little as she remembered something. 'Oh, yes. He did say if he had to sell it he'd give us at least six months' notice. You'd just about serve your year out.'

I was quiet at first. Then I said, 'Why can't he put adverts in the American and English press—better still, get a newspaper to champion it?' I became excited at the idea. 'Why not? There's bound to be somebody, or some society, who would keep it going, surely.'

Joy looked at me steadily, then put out a hand and pressed my knee. 'Thank you. Jane. That's what we need now. Moral support.' She stood up. 'Come on, let's do things, else he might think we're plotting. Oh.' She stopped suddenly and peered at me.

I squirmed a little under her close scrutiny. Joy raised her eyebrows in a coquettish tease. 'You look nice today. I think he finds you attractive. Maybe that's a way we could sort it out. You two get married and employ me. We'd be just as we were. What do you think about him?'

I quickly laughed it off as a joke and left the room to find Tom staring out of the window. It reminded me of the scene in *The Shining* when Jack Nicholson is descending into madness.

Joy soon followed me, looking as though she had no cares in the world.

'The double glazing you had put in, Tom. Was it very expensive?' She put the question casually.

Tom turned round, smiling. 'Yes, but it was a draughty old place. Don't know how you got on without it.'

Joy stretched herself upright. 'I'll have you know that we Brits are tough. Aren't we, Jane? None of your air conditioning and stuff. We live with the wind and the rain!' Joy finished with a triumphant poking out of her arm.

'And the snow,' Tom laughed.

Joy went to join him at the window. 'Yes. That's a job we've got to do—and soon—get that snow off the trees. We need to do that before we collect snow for melting. It can break branches.'

'It already has, Joy,' I said. 'I forgot to tell you. One snapped on the olive tree by the aloes on the hillside.'

Joy frowned for a moment and then outlined her plan of action. Given that we couldn't call for Spiros to fix the plumbing since the land line was out of order and mobile phones were out of signal range from the house, the only solution was to get as much bottled water as we could. But the only source reachable, Joy affirmed, was that owned by Charles and Rachel who lived at the hilltop. 'They always keep themselves well stocked up,' Joy said. 'They've got a big store of five-litre bottles. They buy them in bulk.'

Tom pointed out a problem. It entailed a hill climb which, in the prevailing conditions, would prove hazardous as well as exhausting. 'And how do we carry the water?' asked Tom. 'The amount we need is going to be really heavy.'

'Rucksacks. We take a rucksack each. I've got three.' Joy was unabashed.

'There's a lot of snowdrifts up there, Joy,' I said, cautiously.

Tom agreed with me. 'Could be impossible to get up there.'

Joy exclaimed, 'Phooey! Did that put Scott or Shackleton off? Come on; let's do it!' She went off to put on her foul-weather gear. 'Come on, Jane. Tom?'

'Yeah, OK. Let's break a leg.'

'Not mine,' called out Joy. Checking that we were properly dressed, each with a rucksack on our backs, Joy opened the front door. As if bang on cue, there stood Pavlos, about to pull on the cowbell.

Joy was amazed and delighted to see him. 'Pavlos, you hero! You've walked here in this?'

'Ploughed. I am a plough.' Pavlos grinned and with his hand wiped his black swirling beard free of snow. He wore an ex-Soviet army bearskin hat, the flaps down over his ears, a Barbour jacket and a thick yellow scarf around his neck.

'Joys. I worried because I tried to call, but line was dead,' Pavlos said. 'Worst part was roads outside here. Got here—' He looked at his watch. 'Thirty minutes. When I was young I'd come on skis. Now too heavy. I would break them.' He let out a belly laugh.

The mention of skis had Joy shaking a fist enthusiastically. 'Skis! Of course! They're in the tool shed. They belonged to Christos. Of course. That's the way to do it!'

'Oh gods, Joy. You're not going on skis—' Pavlos pointed. 'Up there?'

'Yes,' she said firmly. 'They'll stop me sinking into snowdrifts.' She said that the rest of us 'young guns' would have to take our chances. 'Pavlos. Brush that snow off your legs and get in here, now, and make yourself a hot drink before we go.'

Pavlos brushed the snow from his trousers, then let out a big sigh as he stood upright to give Joy a grave look. 'I am not lettings you go up there on skis. You kills yourself.'

'No, I won't. Jane, would you mind fetching the

280

skis?'

When I returned, Pavlos was still arguing with Joy, but she ignored him and told me to bring a bottle of olive oil with which to grease the ski runners. No matter how much Pavlos argued with her—and he was backed by Tom in his polite way—Joy remained resolute. She would make her ski journey, come hell or high water.

As I watched her adjust the bindings, aided by a defeated and muttering Pavlos, it occurred to me that whenever Christos came into her head she had to demonstrate her loyalty to him, if she could. She would say to herself that Christos would certainly have used the skis in this situation. And, therefore, so must she.

We set off up the hillside, but without any path to guide us, it was a matter of guesswork as to what lay underneath our feet. Tottering and stumbling, sometimes taking one step forward then two steps back, we broke into constant laughter, turning hysterical when Joy plonked a ski in front of Pavlos, causing him to lose his balance and fall backwards into a snowdrift. With his arms and legs spread out, and his body inclined downhill, he was unable to move. His expression reminded me of Oliver Hardy, whenever a dim-witted, tie-fiddling Stanley had dropped him in it. Pavlos gave Joy, who was laughing heartily, the same kind of wry, world-weary grimace, as if about to deliver the classic line, 'Another nice mess you've got me into.'

'You shouldn't have got in my way,' said Joy. 'Get up, you look silly down there.'

Titan, who had followed us, as though infected by the hilarity, plunged into the drift and then out again to buck his way in great, frothy leaps in a large circle, finally landing astride Pavlos's legs, his tongue hanging out and puffing, his face and body flecked with snow.

'Come on, Tom,' said Joy. 'Jane, give us a hand. Get off him, Titan! Good boy.'

Tom suggested that I pull one of Pavlos's arms above the elbow and Joy the other, while he took the greatest strain by pulling on both of Pavlos's hands. We would pull on his count of three.

'One—two—three!' If it had not been for Tom's muscle power Pavlos would have lain in his snowy pit until the thaw, but his bulk arose slowly with great effort and much panting of breath. After dusting him down we resumed our slow snakes and ladders of a journey.

Still laughing, without anyone breaking a leg, or dying of a heart attack, we managed to reach Charles and Rachel's house.

From below it looked impressive, built in a totally different style to Joy's house—more like a Swiss chalet with steep roofs and a suspended covered terrace, surrounded by railings on its three sides and standing on attractively fashioned wooden piles.

'Ahoy!' Joy cupped her hands to her mouth to bark out her alert. 'Anybody at home?'

She broke into a relieved smile when Charles appeared, dressed in a thick white sweater and black trousers. He put his hands on the railing to look down on us.

'You have reached one-ton depot, eleven miles to the South Pole. Welcome. A warming tipple, anyone?'

Drinking coffee laced with whisky, we sat around a blazing fire in the living room, their dogs and cats dotted around on the rugs and furniture. Charles and Rachel told stories about their time in India, amusing us with recollections about their encounters with the wildlife.

For some of the time, Tom stood outside with his hands on the terrace railing, deep in thought as he gazed out over the blankets of snow. We would have stayed there longer had Joy not been startled by the loud crack of a heavily loaded branch falling from a tree. 'We must get back. Our trees. I completely forgot.'

When we left, we brought away twenty litres of spa water in packs of four. Pavlos and Tom were adamant that Joy carry nothing. Not only that, they ordered her not to wear skis on the downward journey.

'Don't be loonies. It's what they're for,' said Joy, apparently cross with them. But then she mellowed and smiled. 'Pavlos, if I die you can have my job. Think how much better the garden will be without me.'

Pavlos put up his hands in despair but insisted that he and Tom held her arms on the way down. 'We stop you falling or going too fast.'

Tom put it humorously. 'I've got to stop you breaking your neck, Joy, because if you do I'll have to look after the garden to stop you haunting me.'

'Ha,' said Joy, 'that's the answer. Problem solved. Off to break my neck, then.'

Without warning Joy put a ski forward and then the other, Tom and Pavlos having to react fast by grabbing her arms.

Pavlos took a deep breath. 'Joy, you gives me heart attacks.'

A compromise was reached. By pushing out each

ski a short slide at a time, while restrained by her two helpers, Joy was allowed to descend the hillside, for the most part, safely. It was only when the trio neared the house that Joy took a tumble, the skis shooting forwards, sending her backwards. It was Pavlos who managed to catch her, but instead of pulling her upright he laid her gently on her back so he could wag his finger at her. 'Get up, Joy, you looks silly down there.' He broke out into loud laughter.

It was Joy's turn to give a wry 'OK, you've got me' look.

We arrived back at the house in good humour. I was glad we'd had our little adventure. I felt that the fun and the bonding between us, as well as Joy's bravery and never-say-die attitude, had impressed Tom. Their mutual desire to help one another on a snowy hillside might continue in negotiations over the garden. Together, they would find a way for Tom to keep ownership of Helikion. At least, that's what I hoped might happen.

'We're not having any lunch till we've got that snow off the trees,' Joy said. 'We must get cracking. We have water to drink, courtesy of Charles. Anybody?' Joy opened a bottle.

'Yes, please,' we said in unison. Labouring up and down that hillside had made us thirsty, but we rationed ourselves carefully.

Shortly afterwards, having mustered two rakes and two olive tree 'knocker' poles, we set about the job of dislodging the snow from reachable branches. Tom brought all his strength and stamina to the task. Using his rake to catch hold of a branch, he would shake it vigorously from side to side, then move quickly on to the next, frequently slipping or falling over in his enthusiasm. At one point in his excesses I saw Joy giving him an appreciative look.

The task was made more difficult by it being necessary to stand away from each branch, not underneath it. If you didn't, the snow would cascade on heads and necks, melting and trickling down backs and chests, an icy unpleasantness which meant perpetually wet underclothes, the awfulness only ameliorated as the moisture warmed against sweating skin. But it was pointless.

The snow, when dislodged, fell in clouds, drifting onto us, no matter how much we tried to keep clear. Amid much moaning and groaning we soldiered on, under Joy's command. She remained indefatigable. 'Don't worry. I've got a nice treat for you all when we've done.'

Even moving from tree to tree had us out of breath. Joy quickly grew tired, not surprising given her age and the exertions of her hillside expedition, and so we persuaded her to take an easier part in proceedings: her job to check on the most delicate of plants, such as the crocosmias. Before the snow fell they had featured distinguished speared leaves and a display of fiery red flowers. Now, they were slumped to the ground, slowly turning into a reddish-brown liquid, staining the snow like blood.

After an hour's hard labour Joy surveyed the scene from a vantage point high on the hill. Satisfied that all the imminent danger had been averted, she called us into the house, where we were given towels and the option of removing whatever wet clothing we had on and placing it on rails in front of the fire. Such was the demand that Joy used the taller of the Minoan statues to act as an additional drying perch. She then fetched an assortment of dry clothes from her room and laid them out on the dining table.

'Don't worry, they're not my cast-offs. People stay and leave behind all sorts. Feel free to wear whatever. Doesn't matter what you look like, so long as you're warm and dry.'

She suddenly laughed, prompting Tom and me to look round. Pavlos had taken everything off but his thermals. They were a bright orange.

'Pavlos, you look like an escaped prisoner from Jane's Alca—' Tom broke off to give me a sheepish look. 'I meant Al Capone.' He gave Joy a quick look but she was too busy to notice. 'Jane loves prison dramas, she tells me.'

I nodded in wry amusement at Tom, who was grinning in embarrassment.

'So now you haves me,' said Pavlos. 'I can never escape Joy in these!'

And so it was that, in a bubble of good humour, we gathered for a reviving drink around the fire, dressed in an odd assortment of attire, shirts that were too long in the arms, oversize sweaters and, in the case of Pavlos's feet, a pair of black and yellow football socks. If Joy had wanted to create the jolliest of foursomes she could not have gone about it in a better way. She handed out glasses of warm wine, mulled on trivets in the fireplace, and toasted us for our sterling efforts, announcing that she was pleased, for once, to be without electricity.

She announced the treat. 'I'm going to cook you a meal over the fire.'

'Great,' said Tom, genuinely pleased. 'Log cabin

time.'

'Hmm,' rumbled Pavlos, doubting her. 'How, Joy?'

'You'll see.' Joy went into the kitchen and then returned wearing her chef's hat. She struck a dramatic pose. 'I warn you all this is my first open fire *inageiras*,' she said. 'You're all going to assist.'

We were only too eager to help. Pavlos even volunteered to take over the entire operation himself. 'Joy-bells, you are worn out. Go and sit in front of the fire. Just tell me what to do and I will do it.'

But Joy had no intention of letting anyone interfere with her plans, which she had formulated following a power failure two years previously and which had left her for a whole week without electricity.

Step one had been to get Spiros to make suitable utensils for cooking on an open fire. His first job had been to make two four-legged trivets on which to place pans and a kettle, one higher than the other so that she could cook close to the fire or several inches away. Then he had made a trammel, or hanging arm, fixed to the inside wall of the fireplace. This had three hooks on which to hang pots. He was not yet finished. In addition he had made, or procured, an iron spoon, a slotted spoon, six long-handled forks and two spatulas, one short and one long, and finally, a small long-handled shovel.

Joy handed each of us two long-handled forks. I now understood what she meant by us having to 'assist'.

'It would take hours for a roast to cook,' Joy said. 'But you're all starving, so you've got to muck in.' On hearing the weather forecast and warnings of possible power failures she had taken the venison out of the freezer, leaving it to defrost overnight. She was now cutting it into pieces and placing them in a pot, which she stood at the side of the fireplace.

Each of us had to skewer a piece of the venison with a long fork, then place it on top of a trivet, careful to position it where the fork could be turned by hand at regular intervals. Alternatively, we could prop it up against the front of the fire basket where, again, it could be easily turned.

'But not yet. The fire has to be made ready.' Joy bustled back into the kitchen and returned with four large jacket potatoes, at the sight of which we all made appreciative murmuring noises. Pavlos was then instructed to take the poker and small shovel to poke and push the burning logs to one side of the large basket, leaving the rest of it packed level with a mix of glowing embers and hot ash, ideal for the baking of potatoes. Our second long fork was the tool for this particular task.

Joy played a Louis Armstrong record as the work of cooking and baking began. We had a copious supply of crusty bread and olive oil and as much ouzo or red wine as we wanted. We turned the venison and potatoes while singing along to 'When the Saints Go Marching In'. Cooking and eating from an open fire, the competition in trying to beat competitors to the best spot for the placing of a fork, was fun in itself. This was the second time at Helikion when I wouldn't have wanted to have been anywhere else on earth. After a morning of cold, wet, hard labour, I declared it to be the 'best meal of my life'.

To a chorus of 'hear, hears' Tom stood up and raised his glass. 'Look,' he said. 'I once came here when I was a kid. I enjoyed it then but I'm sure enjoying it a heck of a lot more today. Thank you, Joy.' He raised his glass. 'To the best hostess in the world.'

We responded: 'To Joy.'

With a smile Joy made no reply. Instead she went back to the kitchen to return with four large crystal glass dishes full of homemade syllabub.

'Wow,' said Tom.

'Joy, this is *eygeystos*. Delicious,' said Pavlos.

It was a day to remember. And it gave me hope as I noted that Tom, for the most part, remained quiet and reflective. I hoped it was a harbinger of what might turn out to be good news, after all.

Three days later, the snow had melted under the winter sun and the water and electricity supplies were restored. It was good to smell the earth and see the plants again, released from their cryogenic suspension.

Joy and I went around the garden with notepads, jotting down the names of plants that had been damaged. Most affected were the two *Duranta erecta* shrubs that stood either side of the house. During the thaw slabs of wet snow had slipped from the steep sloping roofs onto the garden at the sides. The honeybush, one of my favourites standing proudly outside the alcove, had now lost its large leaves, giving it a miserable appearance.

Joy refused to be downhearted. She pointed out that the flower buds were unharmed and 'new shoots will come out of the rootstock'. It was all a matter of time, which nature had in unlimited supply, she stressed.

But she was unable to raise my spirits when I contemplated some of the cacti I'd potted in the nursery that were now sodden heaps. I said I felt as though my work had been all for nothing.

Joy was appalled to hear me say that. 'Jane, that's rubbish. I know it looks bad now, but in a few weeks you'll see most of the plants recover. Not the cacti, admittedly, but don't be disheartened about the rest. It's not the Arctic tundra.'

A week later I saw that Joy's forecast had, literally, borne fruit. We stood on the hillside, surrounded by a carpet of anemones. Even a few early marigolds shone brightly in the warm sunshine. Joy raised her face to the sun, exhaled and sat down on a rock to reflect.

'Everything changes, Jane, remember that.' She looked out over the garden and spoke slowly and softly. 'Whatever happens, remember to look at the view, Jane. Everything changes.'

\*         \*         \*

I saw little of Tom during the next few days. He spent much of the time in Athens, never talking much about what he did there, although he expressed his disappointment that the Acropolis Museum was closed, with work going on to move the artefacts to a new building further downhill. When I questioned him about his visits, he waved at me with a grin. 'OK, I had a meeting with a professor at the American School of Classical Studies. Now you don't want me to bore you with an account of excavations at the Athenian Agora, do you?'

I laughed with him. 'No, hardly,' I said. What I really wanted to know was how he saw Joy, the garden and its future. But I hadn't dared ask for fear of the answer. It didn't matter. I had the answer on the day of his departure, three days later.

Tom stood in the living room, his luggage at his side. Joy, who'd been checking to ensure he'd left nothing behind, came into the room to face him.

'Tom. It's been wonderful having you. I only wish your mother was still alive. I'm sorry about ... well, your decision can't be easy.'

Tom touched Joy's arm and spoke quietly.

'My mother wanted me to take over the running of this garden. We know that.' He hesitated. 'But it's not specified in her will. I don't have to obey it. But I want to. Believe me. I've just got to see how things go. Maybe I won't need to buy an apartment here. Maybe I can rent one. I'm talking to some people here. If they offer me a job I could take it. I might not. There's work in the States I may do. Nothing's settled. You do understand?'

Joy nodded. 'I do. If there's anything I can do to help ...'

Tom shook his head. 'The bottom line is money. OK, I know you're dying to ask. Why did I spend money on insulated windows? That *was* in the will. I had to. And I'm glad I did.' He suddenly grinned. 'We'd have all died of exposure if I hadn't!' We joined him in laughter.

It was in that mood of friendliness, streaked with sadness, that I stood outside watching him get into the Jeep. As he put on his safety belt Joy said something to him that had him rocking with laughter.

I waved continually as they went down the driveway, Tom's arm raised in farewell out of his side window. I thought I would never see him again and so I kept watching until the roof of the Jeep had disappeared from view.

I would be proved wrong.

# 14

# A Botanist is a Detective

It was late February. There were fewer cold nights now that the year had moved on. The dawn chorus provided my wake-up call; I had no need for my alarm clock. By 7.15 a.m. sunlight would stream through the gaps in the shutters, casting golden bands of light across the stone walls of my cell, a delight to see after the refrigeration of winter.

For the first time this year Orwell could lie on a terrace wall to greet the sun, while all around the inhabitants of the garden stirred from their winter slumber. The odd rock or wall lizard could be seen darting out from a shrub, or slipping between cracks in the terraced walls, pausing for a moment before another dash to somewhere else. The most dramatic-looking and adventurous of all was a green lizard with a bluish throat and spotted back. Joy told me that it was male and 'an unusually daring fellow'. On a warm morning he would crawl out from his rocky lair, scramble towards the bike sculpture and streak upwards to land on its seat, from where he regally surveyed his hunting ground.

Joy had told me that he was using the seat as a sun bed. 'Like snakes and tortoises,' she'd said, 'he's warming himself; raising his metabolic rate. It helps him digest his prey.'

Alcatraz was—at last!—a warm and pleasant place in which to live and I could enjoy eating without having to sit on top of the two heaters. I felt at one with nature simply because I, too, was coming out of hibernation.

After breakfast, always eager to spot and identify the latest sprouting plant, I would meet Joy for a pre-work tour of the garden. Armed with my sketchbook and gardening diary, I would accompany her on a trek around the hillside. She carried her magnifying glass and, in a small rucksack, a book on Mediterranean wild flowers and another on Greek flora—not that she ever needed to consult them. They were a learning aid for my benefit.

These morning tours were of a different nature to our earlier dusk 'walkabouts' when she used to snap questions at me and say, 'You'll never get into Kew if you don't buck up!' Now, Joy would quietly ask for my opinions on plant layouts, encouraging me to delight in an opening flower, perhaps informing me of its medicinal value. On more than one occasion, the sight of a plant or a curiosity—or even a question from me—sparked her into a passionate discourse on its relevance to anything from the ancient world of mythology, art, poetry or architecture. At these moments I found her utterly compelling. It was like listening to an international opera singer in their prime, a slow, beguiling overture building to a roaring and sensational climax.

Whenever I wander through a garden now, I can't help but recall the comical image of Joy eagerly bending down to a plant, magnifying glass poised, her long hair tumbling out of her straw hat and showing her excitement as she struggled to reconcile hair and hat. 'Remember, a botanist is a detective,' she would say, hopping to the next juicy annual.

\*       \*       \*

One morning, I found Joy sitting on a stone wall, ruminatively picking a few *Oxalis pes-caprae* flowers.

'This is one plant I don't mind putting in a vase, Jane,' she said abstractly, handing me the cluster of pretty yellow bells. 'Here. Brighten up the outhouse. Best to make use of our Attila the Hun weed. He'll be gone shortly.'

I followed her up the hillside path.

Joy stood at the hilltop looking down. 'Not long before watering time, Jane,' she said, almost as if it were of no consequence.

I stared at her in alarm. The note of resignation in her voice was not something I'd come across before. Water was the Holy Grail to Joy, her passion and the source of all creation. At that moment I felt utter dismay and, at the same time, a realization that she needed something to make her confront her fears.

'Joy,' I said, 'if you're worrying about Tom why don't you get Charles to email him again?'

Joy frowned at me. 'We're not talking about Tom,' she said irritably. 'Where were we? Oh yes. Tell me the size of a watering basin.'

Hanging my head—I'd recited it to her a number of times already—I began: 'They should have a diameter of sixty centimetres and a depth of twenty centimetres in order to hold twenty to thirty litres each—' I stopped talking. Joy had sat on a boulder and was gazing down the hillside, her hands settled on her lap, eyes unblinking.

'Sit down,' she said softly, 'and look at the view. It won't stay. Everything changes. So look now.'

I joined her and looked down at the clusters of waxy yellow crocuses tumbling down the hillside and jostling alongside the anemones. Vetches looped over the bulging dusky buds of grape hyacinths, while joint pine twisted its delicate stems through a mound of broom, creating a shape like Dougal from *The Magic Roundabout* of children's television long ago. Flowers, curving like shepherds' crooks, sprawling plants, lounging plants, plants that tangled in rampant profusion, irises, marigolds, alliums, mustard, purple goat's beard and many others, swooped over the ground, sending blooming hand grenades in and out of the garden's open boundaries.

Joy released a sigh and spoke slowly. 'With beauty like this, how can it belong to anyone, if not to all?'

Later, we wandered towards the boundary with the Neanderthal, my mind clouded with concern. Joy stopped to stare at his fence and then suddenly winced, put a hand to her head and turned to look at me.

'What is it, Joy?' I held my breath.

'You look worried. Why?' She was alert again, as if someone had thrown a switch.

'Do you realize,' she continued, 'that that man over there is draining the lifeblood of this land?'

'Yes, I do. I do.'

She took in a breath, squared her shoulders and turned to face the Neanderthal's fence. Raising her magnifying glass high in the air and glaring towards his house she shouted out, 'And gentlemen in England now a-bed, shall think themselves accursed they were not here!'

She broke off, turned and raised a finger at me and spoke firmly. 'When the time comes, Jane. When the time comes . . .'

298

She exhaled and put out a guiding hand. 'Come on. We're not soldiers. It's not marching that's to be done, it's mulching.'

For the rest of the day, we wheeled barrows of cotton waste from the heap at the side of the nursery down to the terraces. There, as I spread the waste around the borders, Joy worked it smoothly among the flowers and shrubs, sweat trickling from her brow with the effort.

*    *    *

She came out of the house after lunch, holding her hands, one cupped in the other, a familiar stab of pain on her face. Despite my pleas for her to rest, she waved them away. 'No, Jane. I'm all right. Touch of arthritis. You expect the odd twinge at my time of life.'

She turned away to reach for a barrow but was distracted by the sight of a broken stem on a cistus shrub. I watched her as she patted her pockets searching for her secateurs.

'Bugger. Where are they? Jane, be a love, nip back, see if I've dropped them?'

I retraced our steps, my tread slow and ponderous. She was always mislaying them. Pavlos and I had laughed about it at first. But now it was troubling. They would turn up in all manner of places, between the cistus shrubs in the terraced beds, in the potting compost tub, in the filing cabinet, in the garage and, at Christmas, on top of Zeus's head in the alcove. The day after Tom had left, Pavlos found them in the kitchen fridge, the blades stuck in a wedge of his favourite Greek cheese, Galotiri.

He had cried, 'Joy! This is the ends!' and went immediately to the village to buy a pot of Eco-safe 'Glow-in-the-Dark' pink paint. On his return he dipped the handles of the secateurs into the pot. 'If you lose them now, we'll be able to see them any times.'

Joy tried to laugh off her forgetfulness. 'Things on my mind, Pavlos. That's all.'

They joked about it, but it was obvious in the quick-fading smile, or the pauses between speaking, that they were both anxious, but in different ways. Pavlos worried for Joy's state of mind and Joy worried for the garden, not so much for herself.

In recent weeks Pavlos, I had noted, was visiting more frequently. There were times when I caught his expression, words forming on his lips, clearly feeling the need to speak to me, but unable.

I tried to make the appropriate signals in return, showing that I was willing to talk. But I had to remind myself continually that I was only an apprentice, still an 'intern', after all. I should do nothing that would mar my reference. Above all, I did not want to lie on my CV ever again.

And then I met him, quite by chance, in the village. Joy was at the dentist and I was waiting for her, sitting outside a taverna, drinking a cup of strong Greek coffee. It was the deep rumble of his voice that had me turning round. Pavlos laughed as our eyes met, something he always did on meeting. I had wondered if it was laughter wrought from nervousness, prompted perhaps by an innate shyness.

Pavlos joined me at the table and ordered a beer, then sat back, stroking his black bushy beard.

'Troubles with Joy,' he said. 'She forgets more. It's because of Tom, you know, Jane. Did you know that?'

'I suspected it,' I said quickly. 'Go on.'

'She's very worried. I want to help but she says no.' He spread out his hands. 'I don't know whats to do.'

I stared at him in surprise and felt a surge of frustration. I wanted to talk with him about Joy, but struggled to find an arrangement of words that I could put to him without breaking my promise to her. I wanted to say that if he genuinely wanted to help he had the means to do it. There must have been ways. Money laundering was well known as a means of transferring money without anyone knowing who owned it. But countering my excitement was uncertainty. Pavlos always appeared as a relaxed and big-hearted man, but I was ignorant of the social mores in Greece. I had no idea of protocol in these matters. Put simply, I liked him so much but, at the same time, was afraid of upsetting him. I ended up with a miserable question.

'Is there nothing that can be done?'

Pavlos, for the first time since I'd met him, looked at me seriously. 'Yes. I had some moneys from my father. I could buy the garden, but . . .' He made a gesture of the futility of it. 'Joy, she's . . .' He shrugged.

He had given me an opening. Quickly, I said, 'Is it because Joy won't let you help? Does she think it will cause you trouble of some sort?'

Pavlos shook his head. '*Ohi*. I think it's pride. She's a very proud woman.'

I sat back slowly, withdrawing my arms from the

table in disappointment. Pavlos was looking at me now, without expression. Clearly, it was time to change the subject.

*       *       *

When we arrived back at Helikion, I expected Joy to invite me to the house for a meal and a game of Scrabble. Despite everything, she had kept up this habit on a Friday night. But she didn't, just leaving me with a little nod and wishing me a good night.

I walked back to Alcatraz in a despondent mood, then sat on my bed and grabbed my diary:

*Pavlos is on the edge of talking about how to save the garden but clams up. Both of them want the same thing but it's buggered by Joy's worry over Pavlos's safety. There must be a way of transferring money without criminals knowing about it. Or is there something I don't know—that I should not be allowed to know? It's bonkers, Joy's scared of doing something that will get him kidnapped and Pavlos is scared of being kidnapped. And I'm worried about upsetting them both.*

I went out to sit on the veranda in the half-light and made a decision. If Joy hadn't made any contact by 8.00 p.m., I would go over to the house and make the excuse of wanting to borrow one of her plant books.

At five to eight I could wait no longer and slipped out of Alcatraz into a moonless, tar-black night.

I let myself into the house to find there were no lights on. Yet the Jeep was outside, so Joy must have been around. As I edged along the hallway, I had to stop for a moment to let my eyes adjust to the darkness. Now I could make out the black masses of the crouching furniture, then the table of hookahs and the outline of the Minoan statues. I moved slowly into the living area.

A hidden candle from an alcove shone some light into the room, so that I could see the dining table outside the kitchen. And then, as I moved on, I saw Joy seated at her desk. She was writing, the small Tiffany lamp at her elbow illuminating her work area, but little else.

She heard my approach and lifted her head quickly out of the pool of light into darkness.

'Is that you, Jane?' Her voice was hoarse, a cracked whisper.

'Yes. Are you OK?'

'No. I can't write like I used to. Come here, I want you to read something.'

I approached her carefully. She had drawn net curtains over the great expanse of windows, something she'd never done before. She loved to stare through them at the walled garden and beyond, no matter how dark the night. I came to stand by the desk. The ashtray was full of screwed cigarette stubs and the litter bin stuffed full with balls of crunched-up paper, others scattered around her on the marble floor. Joy handed me three sheets of paper.

'Read that. It's just a start.'

I scanned the pages. It was difficult to read what amounted to a letter, with words scratched out, stained with inkblots and lines overwritten. But I read enough to sigh quietly in relief. For one awful moment I thought I was about to read her last will and testament. No. It was a letter of appeal, trying to raise money for the garden. She was handwriting the letter, which meant that the people she was about to approach must have been those she knew already. I was uncertain, out of my depth. But, as with Pavlos, she'd given me an opening. I seized the opportunity.

'Joy, isn't—I mean, I know what you told me about Pavlos, but surely there must be a way?' The question came out strained, the pitch of my voice raised in tension.

Joy stared at me. In the lamplight her face was in part shadow.

'Jane,' her tone was heavy. 'Have we talked about the three daughters of Night?'

'Yes.'

'Tempting fate? No!' she snapped. 'I'm not going to allow it.' She paused, her voice softening. 'I love him too dearly. I'm not putting him in harm's way, even if it's a tiny risk.' She took a deep breath. 'I'm going to tell you something now and you must promise not to tell a soul. Promise.'

'Yes, I promise.'

Joy stood up and went to click on the lights. She entered the kitchen to return with two glasses of cloudy ouzo, ice tinkling inside. Handing me one, she asked me to sit down while she remained standing. Brushing a few grey hairs from her eyes, she took a breath and spoke steadily.

'Pavlos put his money into a secret account in Switzerland. He's talked about it with his English friend, who makes donations to us. They had a plan that Pavlos, his friend and his wife would create a company which had access to the money to buy the garden. Two years ago I would have said yes, thank you for the money. But since then European governments are now getting into these secret accounts. I know the UK has an arrangement with tax havens like Switzerland— and there's no guarantee Pavlos won't be named as a holder. Now if I was the cause of that investigation I would want to kill myself. Do you understand?'

I didn't quite. But I was thinking in my English mode. The 'go-between' in the L. P. Hartley book of that title had commented that the past was a foreign country where 'they do things differently'. And this was Greece and the same thing applied. What I wanted to happen was none of my business. I wondered whether I would be so selfless. I had to remind myself that I was merely an intern and needed a good reference. And Joy was the only person who could give it to me. All I could do was nod in submission and feel sorry for a woman who had all my respect.

Her eyes set hard as she lit a cigarette. 'Oh, I'm not a bloody paradigm of virtue, Jane, but to put a dear friend in that position?'

She held out her hand for the letter. 'Anyway, what do you think? Will it convince?'

'Yes.' I said. I took some comfort in the fact that she was back to her fiery old self and doing something practical.

'It would convince me,' I said, and meant it.

*     *     *

Another stench permeated Alcatraz, a more

potent affair than the malodorous whiff from the shower drain. This stink made my eyes water. Joy told me it came from the septic tank and said she would ring for the 'honey wagon' and—because I lived closest to the tank—perhaps I'd like to move back into the ghost room, a suggestion that I readily welcomed.

Two days went by and the wind shifted, releasing Alcatraz from the grip of the miasmic pong, but at the expense of the house, now held in its noxious embrace.

Then a toilet overflowed. Action had to be taken. Appointments for visitors had to be cancelled or rearranged. I was forced to ask Joy if she'd remembered to call for the honey wagon.

Yes, she had. 'Things are in motion,' she said, with a wry smile.

I said that was the trouble in the first place and we both laughed. It seemed she was back on the rails. Where we would go next, though, I had no idea. After the fourth day of no action, I wondered if Joy's sense of smell was affected by her being a heavy smoker. How could she stand it? In desperation I wrote reminders on post-it notes, sticking one on her desk and the other on an opened ouzo bottle in the fridge. Joy collected them and—while I was in the bathroom—pinned them on the back of my door.

She'd sketched a skull and crossbones on the top note in cartoon style and underneath written: 'Don't panic!! Honey wagon coming tomorrow. Sleep with this under your pillow tonight.' There was a small hessian bag of lavender attached to it with a safety pin. I used it. It helped.

On the fifth day, a Friday, with the wind blowing

away from the house, we were able to eat on the east patio. We had just finished when—oh, to what delight—the honey wagon finally arrived. The lorry lumbered up the driveway, two men inside, wearing sunglasses.

I watched her chatting to the men as they connected two sections of the large-diameter pipe from the lorry to reach the tank, which lay halfway between the tool shed and compost beds. Having raised the cover and plunged the pipe into the tank the smell was even worse. I fled inside the house and closed the kitchen window—which Joy always insisted had to be kept open—and busied myself washing up the breakfast dishes. Having finished and feeling tired, I sat down on the sofa with Titan, put my head back and was soon asleep.

I woke in shock.

'Jane! Jane!' It was Joy shouting from outside.

'Oh my God! What?' I jumped upright and, dizzy, had to steady myself.

'Come outside. Hurry!'

I dashed out of the house, an image of the septic tank exploding foremost in my mind. A blaze of sunlight dazzled me at first, forcing me to raise a hand to my eyes, but then there was Joy, all eagerness, standing at the edge of the terraces, her body inclined towards the garden, a trailing arm out towards me, her cheeks ruddy with colour.

'Come on, Jane, come on!' she beckoned, waving her arm.

I followed her along the gravel paths, past Orwell lying on a wall, past the small myrtle tree and then on to the phrygana to weave around a trio of almond trees covered in clouds of white blossom. Finally I rounded a rosemary shrub to

307

find her with hands on her knees, out of breath. She nodded at the place where I'd committed my cardinal sin.

The elm's stump.

I knelt to the ground and looked at the spurts of green poking from its bark.

'Remember, Jane,' Joy said as she fought to get her breath back. 'Keep this picture in your head. A lesson learned the hard way. If a tree is planted with love—' She broke off and sank down to sit by the stump, gently laying her hand on its flat top, lost in deep contemplation. I don't think she noticed me leave.

\*         \*         \*

Over the following weeks I divided my time between the ghost room and Alcatraz.

Joy didn't seem to mind and in the late evenings I would join her for a glass or two of ouzo. She would be reading, writing letters or staring out into the garden, a faraway look in her eye. If it was warm enough we would sit out on the veranda, extra clothing at the ready, watching the moon track across the sky and bats flitting between the trees.

One morning in early March I went out with Joy to tour the garden. When we reached the best vantage viewpoint, near the cistern, she turned to stop and stare, her voice breathless. 'Ah, Jane. Isn't that wonderful?'

This was no half-hearted spring. The 'view' which she'd told me not to miss had changed, but with a big ringing chime. Now the first poppies had emerged, bright red splashes dotted between carpets of daisies and rivers of blooming irises.

Sweet fragrances wafted on the air, vaporous oils surging through stems and leaves. Even the ancient boulders seemed to have a new lease of life, their wind-eroded tops now glowing pink and golden in the sun.

After I'd looked and kept looking, I spoke. 'The first job you gave me, Joy. I had to remove dead yucca leaves, then top off the irises and clear up debris over the whole garden. Five acres of it. Do you remember? I nearly quit.'

'But you didn't. Worth it, wasn't it,' she murmured, her eyes still fixed on the view, a knowing smile playing around her lips.

*      *      *

It was 10 March and still no news from Tom. It was also the first day of Lent in Greece, known as *Kathara Defter*—Clean Monday—and Joy was intent on forgetting her troubles for the day. In the morning we toured the garden and, from a safe distance, followed a lumbering tortoise around the balls of softly scented thyme. Joy seemed to be relaxed and I wondered if it was because of the imminent arrival of Pavlos. She always seemed to be happier when he was around. At lunchtime we were preparing a snack when he appeared, wearing a faded denim shirt, the colour of forget-me-nots.

'*Ya su*, ladies!' He gave his usual bass laugh and put both arms round me in his customary bear hug, then went to Joy to embrace her.

'Surprise. I have surprise, Joy-bells.'

She held him at arm's length, looking at him with

a suspicious smile.

'I know that look. What have you done?'

Pavlos chuckled. 'You'll see. Surprise for laters.' He uttered a groan and rubbed his belly, grimacing in mock pain. 'Fasting very hard, Joy. What are we eating?'

Joy laughed and pushed him away. 'Jane, he's been fasting from midnight to noon. And as a Greek Orthodox he's banned from eating food with a backbone. Which is why we're having octopus.'

With the lunch spread on the table, Joy opened a bottle of white wine.

'Should you be drinking?' I asked Pavlos good-naturedly, not expecting him to take the question seriously. Pavlos screwed up his face in thought.

'You're right. Clean Monday should be the leaving behind of all wicked ways.' He paused and twirled his wine glass, picking his words carefully. 'I believe in the Devil, which must means that I believe in God. But I don't believe in fasting. So I can allow myself some treats and not feels too guilty.'

He flashed me a mischievous grin, which Joy was too busy to see.

'Quite right,' said Joy. 'The world is painful enough.'

I smiled teasingly at Pavlos. 'I never know with you.'

Pavlos broke out into a belly laugh. 'Just hedging my bets, Jane. Not every day is goings to be a lucky one.'

He put his hand on Joy's arm. 'Some days are lucky, though. And this will be one.' He scraped his chair back and strode out, telling us to meet

310

him on the phrygana in ten minutes. He went out with an arm stuck in the air. 'I have ways of defeating the enemy!'

Joy watched him disappear, said that the lack of meat had gone to his head and proceeded to clear up the dishes. After the last bowl was safely stacked away, she put three ouzos on a tray and handed it to me to carry, then brought out an umbrella from the alcove.

'Best to be prepared, Jane. We might need cover. Pavlos does some crazy things. He tried to make honey wine last year without telling me. He left the bucket open to ferment and Wizard drank some. We had a drunken macaw, kept falling off his perch. That was his surprise. So, what is it this time?'

Outside, I followed her towards the phrygana, skirting around the tall yucca, where small birds darted in and out of its crown. We found Pavlos sitting on the low stone wall bordering the track, a model aeroplane in his hands. Lying beside him on the wall was a remote-control unit.

'Ladies,' Pavlos held up the aircraft, 'this is a radio control digital camera aeroplane.' He pointed at the front underbelly where a miniature camera was attached. 'The camera takes twenty-six pictures before needs to download onto computer.' He pointed to the remote control and a red button. 'You take pictures with this. Very simples.'

Joy looked solemnly at him. 'Are you intending to fly that over there?' She pointed at the Neanderthal's garden.

'I am skilled pilots, practising for weeks. A man who plays the cello can play this.'

'How much?' Joy wore her most severe expression. 'Did you buy it just for this?'

Pavlos waved a hand. 'No. I buy it to photograph very nice ladies sunbathing next door.'

I laughed. Joy gave a reluctant smile and crossed her arms. 'Go on, then. Let's see.'

Pavlos prepared the plane for takeoff. 'Centre of gravity very important. Control surfaces OK. Just like real planes.' Satisfied, he set the motor buzzing, then picked up the remote control.

Joy waved a hand to stop him. 'Wait a minute. Is anything coming?' She stepped out a few paces to peer down the track. 'Nothing.'

Pavlos raised the model high with one hand and with the other increased the motor speed into a fully powered high-pitched whine.

'Boreholes finder! Mission possible!' he boomed and released the plane. As soon as it flew off he grasped the control box in both hands, making rapid and skilful adjustments. The aircraft climbed steadily across the top boundary of the Neanderthal's garden. Once it had cleared treetop height it was trimmed to fly straight and level. Concentrating hard, Pavlos put the plane into a gentle turn to fly the length of the property and then turn for the hill-climb leg, all the time firing the camera button.

The plane flew two circuits in this manner with Joy and I watching in fascination, uttering tense exclamations and making instinctive hand movements, willing it to keep going.

Finally, Pavlos manoeuvred the plane to return, aiming its descent for touchdown on the camomile carpet, the softest runway in the garden. As the aircraft came in for landing, Pavlos reduced motor

312

power too soon. Short of the threshing floor he commanded it to perform the round-out by tilting up its nose. He overdid it. It was slowing down too much. The end looked inevitable.

'Oh no!' Joy and I cried out simultaneously as the aircraft stalled, plunging out of sight and clattering through the branches of a pine tree.

We rushed across to find the plane upturned on a large Golden Barrel cactus, the tail damaged and a wing crumpled. Pavlos shrugged it off. It wasn't that expensive, he said. He could get it repaired. The camera was undamaged, that's what mattered. If it revealed the borehole as an undisputed fact, then it was worth every euro he had spent on it.

'Now all we have to do is take the camera off and plug it into laptop.'

Pavlos, staring at the camera, broke off suddenly to clap a hand on his forehead in horror. 'The lens cover. I forgot to take it off!'

'Oh, Pavlos,' exclaimed Joy. 'You absolute cretin.'

He ruefully picked up the damaged model. 'I've got things and toolbox in the sheds. I'll make it OK. We'll fly tomorrow.'

He spent the rest of the day trying to repair the model aircraft, but failed, as Joy had told me he would. To reward his efforts and show sympathy she cooked him a *Yigandes plaki*, or a baked giant bean casserole, his favourite Lenten dish.

'A giant meal for a giant. Thank you, Pavlos.' Joy raised her glass. 'And sorry it didn't work.'

'Yes,' I said, raising my glass. 'Bad luck.'

The big man was no longer thinking about damaged aero models. He chuckled with delight, stuffed the napkin into his open shirt and began to

313

tuck in.

*    *    *

Along with the fluttering new leaves and the flower-filled scents that drifted around the garden, March also delivered a new regime for Alcatraz. I returned the fur-lined boots, rug and heater that Joy had lent me at the beginning of winter and returned to full-time sleeping in my warmer cell. I sensed that Joy found some relief in this, perhaps harbouring the suspicion that I had stayed overlong in order to keep an eye on her, an intolerable thought for such a stubborn and independent woman.

Out also, along with the 'winter warmers', went a livelier Orwell, who regularly decamped overnight to prowl around the garden. At dawn, with its orchestration of chirrups and tweets, he would return to be fed then go back out to doze on stone walls, keeping one eye on the birds.

Every evening around 6 p.m. I would find a small gecko, the colour of pale alabaster, suckered to the stone. He wouldn't move an inch, not even when the camera flashed, taking a picture of him. Overnight I would leave him a saucer of dead flies that I'd collected during the day. By morning the gecko and the flies would be gone.

Joy had told me to 'drop in' at the house whenever I wanted, saying she was happy for me to sit out with her on the veranda. And, of course, there were 'botanicals' to be scoured over, Scrabble games to be won and euros to be lost. Her enthusiasm for the game stemmed, I suspected, from proving that her mental powers were still intact which, in terms of word building, was true.

In the wider world March was also a month of strike action, another cause of worry for Joy. Journalists, newsreaders, banks, refuse collectors, trains, buses, electricity providers and postal workers all took turns to shut down or down tools to march through the streets of Athens; the main protest this year concerned the government's pension reform plans.

It was the threat to the mail service that concerned her the most. She could cope with the sudden loss of electricity and candlelight illuminating the room, her preferred method of lighting anyway, but was frustrated by the thought that her letters of complaint regarding the Neanderthal were languishing on a mountain of post in some abandoned sorting room.

*     *     *

And then there was Tom. A month had passed without news from him, each passing day adding to her woes.

One fine dawn, she knocked on Alcatraz's door and led me to Christos's bike sculpture on the hillside.

'Clean it up, Jane. The lizard deserves a tidy throne and Christos wouldn't like it looking so shabby.' She handed me a tin of Hammerite rust remover and a couple of rags then left, saying she was staying in the house for the day.

As the sun slowly rose from the horizon I shivered as I shook the tin. I was annoyed that Tom had not contacted her. No matter how much

I had enjoyed his company, at that moment a part of me hated him.

And then I thought of something. Why was I cleaning Christos's bike now? Then I remembered. It was 21 March and the metal tag on the tree that I'd cut down also had that date, 21 March 1991, the day he died.

But, despite all the upheaval and fretting, there came a day when Joy found something to delight in.

I was on the phrygana hooking out crown daisy, an annual that, if left to seed, would spread rapidly, when I heard Joy calling out to me. 'Jane, come here!'

I wound my way around the olive and pistacia trees, tiptoed over sprouting wild flowers, then ducked under the sharp leaves of a yucca to find Joy standing in the middle of the threshing floor, her feet hidden by white flowers.

She put a finger to her lips to silence me then flipped off her sandals and lay down on her back, striking out her arms and legs into a star shape, the sudden movement releasing the sweet scent of the camomile. She chuckled at what she saw as my bewilderment, not knowing that it was matched by my rising fear of her having succumbed, at last, to stress.

'Um' was all I managed to say.

Joy read my face. 'Jane, I'm perfectly sane. I'm not going bonkers. Don't be such a boring old fart, lie down. Do what I did. Take your boots off and get down to the smell of it. *Feel* the camomile between your toes.'

Relieved, I took off my boots and socks to lie down beside her.

Joy exhaled. 'Isn't it beautiful?'

I stared at a long wispy cloud trailing across the blue sky, one end curving upwards, like the prow of a ship.

'Kick your arms and legs out. Go on.'

I giggled as I did it, then took a breath and closed my eyes to the perfume of the flower. It reminded me of my days as a child in Derbyshire, rolling down the lush hills of spring.

Our strange behaviour acted as a magnet for the dogs. Titan came at us bouncing, tail wagging, thinking it was all a game, but Winston merely arrived to inspect my discarded boots as suitable rutting material. He sniffed in disdain, gave up and waddled off.

We lay in silence for some time. When she spoke it was as though she'd been speaking to herself, her inner debate now becoming a voiced continuation. 'You see, if my son, Josh, visits in June he'll bring my grandson Charlie. I haven't seen them for years. And you'll wonder why.'

I detected a slight quiver in her voice and looked at her, enquiringly.

She remained still. A deep frown crossed her face, as if she found it difficult, or puzzling. 'I may have told you about Josh and my daughter. I can't remember. Did I?'

'You just said you had a son and daughter,' I said. 'That was all. Oh, the son was in Ireland.'

'That's right.' She paused. It was clear that it was difficult for her to express her feelings. 'My first husband ... he was ... well, let's say unreasonable ... it got difficult. I was forced to leave him.' Her frown became more intense. 'Because I'd quit the family and gone abroad the court gave him custody of my . . .'

She tailed off, finding it painful. I struggled, thinking hard what to say.

Joy put out an arm towards me. 'I'm sorry, Jane. Not fair to tell you. Forget it.'

She slowly hoisted herself to her feet. 'Yes. It will be good to see my grandson,' she said forcibly, as if trying to convince herself all would be well. I looked up at her, shielding my eyes, to observe loose strands of her grey hair moving in the breeze and sparkling in the sunlight. She shuffled into her sandals without bending down. 'I'm going to look for something. I'll tell you if I find it.'

As she walked away she kicked the flowers, arousing the camomile perfume once again. I lay flat on my back, giving myself up to the sun, initially thrilled and happy. Now, more than ever, I told myself, I was part of her world.

Then, suddenly, I was filled with concern. To have her confide in me her painful memories had brought me closer to her, but at the same time only served to make me even more anxious on her behalf. I became angry, once again, thinking of Tom. How could he keep her on tenterhooks like this?

\*     \*     \*

Later in the day I received another urgent call from Joy. She took me to the hilltop, near to the cistern. 'Careful where you tread, now,' she said as I reached her. 'I want you to look among the grass. Go on.'

I followed her instructions and gazed at a small flower spike with four solitary inflorescences. It

318

was an orchid, but of a type I'd never seen before. Each flower had yellow-green petals and sepals. The 'lips' were purple-brown in colour with a velvety appearance and violet markings in the centre, shaped like a capital 'H'.

'What is it, Jane? What do the flowers remind you of?'

'They look like bees from one angle,' I said, then moved to another viewpoint. 'From here they look like ducks flying an alien spacecraft.'

Joy laughed and clapped her hands. 'It's called an early spider-orchid, the Latin *Ophrys sphegodes*.' She explained that the flowers were pollinated by male Andrena bees and, to attract their attention, the flowers mimicked not only the appearance of female bees but scent also, duplicating their pheromones.

'Fraudsters, really,' she went on.'The smell lures the male insects to settle on them. They copulate with the flower, then fly away covered in its pollen, dropping it onto the next plant they're attracted to. That's what the orchid wanted to happen. What's even more clever is that plant actually *knows* when the female insects are dormant. It's now, this time of year, so they can't be around to divert the males' attention away. It leaves the orchid free to con the males.' Again she clapped her hands. 'Bloody Machiavellian, isn't it?'

'How do they know?' I wondered, enthralled by the story as much as Joy was enthused in the telling of it. 'Is it a change in light or temperature?' I shook my head in amazement.

Joy smiled. 'Sometimes I like to believe it's magic. Next year there should be more of them than ever—' She broke off suddenly and lowered her head.

Next year. I felt her deep cutting anxiety. Next year . . .

\*       \*       \*

By the end of March the asphodels had thrown up their strong flower stems and towering flower spikes, most reaching above my waistline. With the increasing beauty of the garden, so Joy's stress increased further. Tom still had not rung or emailed Charles with news. And there had been nothing from Josh, her son, to indicate if he was actually coming or not. I wanted desperately to talk with Pavlos, for some reassurance if it was possible, or at least to get my feelings out in the open, to have him clasp me in his thick arms and offer me comfort. But Pavlos was unavailable, away it seemed on some undisclosed journey.

But Joy had one person who would definitely be arriving at Helikion later that year, a Japanese scientist and keen botanist, the first of his countrymen to visit the garden.

'Maybe he might help,' she said. 'You never know. These world scientists have links. And I'm sure he'd hate to know that we're in danger of being kicked out for lack of money.'

The first evening arrived when there was no longer any need to bring top-up clothing onto the veranda. Joy invited me to join her for a meal, after which we reclined in loungers on the veranda, sipping ouzo, leisurely clinking the ice while overhead the swallows darted in and out of the eaves. Winston lay curled on Joy's lap, while Titan splayed out on the large cushions against the window, one breeze-block paw resting on the lip of a planter.

Athens, earlier that day, had seen a big march, ahead of the usual 'labour day' protests. Immigrants demanding legalization and human rights had marched through the city, walking with their banners draped before them, to the accompaniment of whistles and megaphones.

It seemed all so foreign and meaningless in that calm repose of evening, when workaday worries had given way to a disbelief that life could hold any pain, all our senses luxuriating in the still, warm air, the perfumes that filled it and the little sounds that the garden made. The only intellectual activity I allowed my brain to indulge in was the pastime of identifying the sources of those sounds. Suddenly a chirrup-like noise rent the air. There, I heard it again.

'Joy? Can you hear it? It's the first cicada of the year, isn't it?'

There was no answer from her. She appeared not to be listening, just gazing at the pointed tops of the cypresses, lost in thought, stroking Winston's head.

When she spoke it wasn't in answer to my question, but again as a voiced continuation of her thoughts. 'And if Tom does decide to sell, he might help us with getting the kind of buyer we want.'

Then she surprised me with the answer to my question.

'Cicadas now, Jane? No. They usually start up in late spring, May or June. Did you know they spend most of their lives underground, feeding on plant sap? It's only the males that make the racket.'

A loud-hailer, a man's barking voice, startled me.

'Oh my God!' I sat up. 'What's that?'

'He's one of the males—a noisy sod in a van,' she laughed. 'He's driving around buying second-hand goods for his market stall, that's all.'

Joy composed herself again, settling back in her lounger, her gaze settling on a lemon tree in the walled garden.

'Jane.' She sounded decisive. 'Things are going to change. I hope for the better. We have to be positive. Be a love, can you pour me another drink?'

# 15

# Bitten by a Snake

EUROPEAN GREEN
LIZARD on CHRISTOS'
BIKE

The year moved on into April and Joy seemed back to her best—active, dominating and questioning me about plants. Christos's anniversary was over, but the future of the garden still hung over her like the sword of Damocles. I wondered if she'd taken Tom's silence so far to mean that no news was good news and that he was probably trying to put together some kind of financial support to keep Helikion going. These things take time, with contracts to be drawn out and studied. On the other hand, I feared his lack of communication could mark his reluctance to give Joy any bad news and that he, like Mr Micawber, was hoping 'something will turn up'.

One morning I noticed a change in the garden. As I entered I immediately felt and saw that spring had not only arrived but was at its most vibrant. The flowers were now host to clouds of butterflies dancing around the garden like windblown confetti. Bees, humming around the prickly pears, binged on the nectar, tumbling from flower to flower. When replete they would fly off like drunken helicopters. Others slept inside the petal cups, their legs twitching in the air, bellies dusted in pollen.

I was walking down the hillside with an armful of stem clippings when I stuttered to a halt, my trail blocked by lines of ants laden with flower seeds. As they marched across the sun-warmed path, a stormtrooper beetle, armoured in metallic black, ruthlessly crashed through their lines to clamber over a splitting log bordering the path. I watched the ants quickly recover, whipped back by regimental commanders into orderly supply columns once more. Keeping an eye on—and learning about—insects and spiders had become a habit of mine ever since Joy had first lectured me on their importance as excellent pollinators and predators of garden pests.

'Bugs are not going to inherit the earth,' she would often say. 'They own it now. So learn to love the landlord, Jane.'

One day I had a revelation about the actual nature of gardening. It came to me that the pesticide-free garden was, despite seeming to be in a state of near anarchy, in fact a finely balanced ecosystem. I put it to Joy, who was delighted in my perception.

'If one insect, bird or animal goes down,' she affirmed, 'the rest will multiply and devour the whole.' She gave as an example the processional caterpillar nests which were growing in number because their natural predators, the cuckoo and hoopoe, now rarely graced the hillside. I was surprised when the next creature I saw was not an insect, but a tortoise, plodding its way towards the house. Fascinated, I watched it lumber towards a low step, bravely try to climb it, but in the process become marooned with its back legs waving slowly in the air.

It was a Greek land tortoise of the Spur-thighed breed, perhaps on its first outing since its hibernation during the winter months. I picked it up, took it to the threshing floor and carefully placed it on a spongy bed of waning camomile. When I returned half an hour later it had disappeared.

Much of my time that day was spent in cutting

early-flowering bushes and perennials, the aim being to prevent the plants from becoming straggly or dying in their middle parts. Later in the afternoon, as the sun dipped below roof height, Joy came to see me with the light of the missionary in her eyes.

'You've been here six months. Now begins your initiation in the most vital of arts. What is it?'

It was a tease, but behind it lay a determination that contained a threat should I fail her. I knew the answer, instantly.

'Watering.'

'Yes. Your education starts now. I've drawn up a rota.' Joy produced a sheet of paper, which she handed me. 'No need to learn it. It's for reference. But what you do need to know is this: watering is like the seasoning of soup—too much and it's ruined, too little and . . . what happens?'

'It's also ruined?' I answered. I dutifully put on a solemn expression and concentrated on the lesson.

'Yes.'

Joy went on to instruct me that, dependent on inspection, each young plant should be watered every two weeks. Established plants would be left to their own devices, unless *in extremis*. Hosepipes, evil things, did not have any place in the garden.

'Water infrequently but *copiously* each time,' she warned, her finger raised. 'The aim is to water enough to form a patch of water deep in the ground, to draw the roots downwards towards where moisture lasts longest without evaporating. Then the plant's roots will be kept damp and be able to cope for two or three weeks. Do you understand?'

'Well, yes,' I replied. 'But how do I do this

327

without using too much water?'

Joy nodded sagely. 'I told you that watering is an art. You'll *know* when to stop. Look at the soil, the leaves. Go back to the plant. Observe, Jane, observe.'

That evening I must have trudged up and down the hillside at least ten times in a seemingly never-ending labour of hauling and watering. Worse, I worked in a mental fog—I simply could not foresee a time when I would 'know' intuitively how much water a plant required. I tried to 'observe' three established lavender plants. They looked ragged in the middle, some of their shoots wilting and dying back. Did that mean they were lacking water, and I needed to give them more, or was it because the roots were being eaten by a pest? It was maddening.

In the end I had to search out Joy for guidance. I found her working on an upper terrace. She returned with me without delay. After an inspection of the affected plants she let out a small sigh. 'It's lavender shab disease, Jane. Take them out. Burn them. We'll get fungal spores over the rest of the plants if we leave them. That must be stopped. For the good of the whole we have to be ruthless. You do that, I'll get the drinks.'

It wasn't the need for thirst quenching that sent her back to the house. If Joy had to destroy a plant without returning it to the earth through composting, she would toast its departure with a small glass of ouzo, whatever the time of day.

I set to, pulling out the lavenders. As I removed the last, I felt something sharp prick my hand. There, inches from my fingertips lay a snake, slowly uncurling itself from where it had been wrapped around the lavender root.

I was seven years old when I first saw a snake. My friend found it in the rough behind the goalposts at school and showed it to our teacher, who promptly appropriated it as a project. For the rest of the year, while my schoolmates scrawled crayon pictures of the beast inside its cage and wrote diaries of its dietary habits, I lived in fear of 'Bruce', as we called it, escaping.

My mum told me that I had a 'phobia' and showed me the definition of the word in a children's dictionary. With a hug she assured me that I'd get over my fear and made me rhubarb pie and custard, my favourite. It didn't work. I had still found it hard to look at 'Bruce' without coming out in a cold sweat.

My reaction to this much larger snake was, therefore, something off the planet.

'JOY! I'VE BEEN BITTEN BY A SNAKE!' Shouting in terror, I raced back to the house.

Joy, who was bringing out the two glasses of ouzo, put them down and hurried towards me. 'Calm down and show me,' she said firmly. I pointed to where I'd felt the prick and answered her sharply put questions. No, it didn't hurt and it wasn't swelling. No, it wasn't bleeding. The diagnosis didn't end there as Joy, to make sure, went back to the library and picked out her book on snakes.

'What did it look like?' she said.

'Greyish, with an orangey zigzag pattern across it,' I said, puffing and wiping my brow. 'I think it had some red as well.'

I waited anxiously, but not for long. Joy showed me a colour photograph of a snake. 'Was that it?'

she asked.

'Ugh! Yes, yes. That's it. Is it bad . . . I mean, will I be all right?' With horror, I imagined Joy sucking the poison out of my hand.

'Yes, because you've not been bitten.' She pointed at the picture. 'That, Jane, is a horn-nosed viper. Very poisonous. And I'm absolutely delighted. It's years since I've seen one. Well done!'

'So I'm all right,' I said, bringing her back to the purpose of the consultation.

Joy tapped the photograph with her finger. 'Jane. If that snake had bitten you, your hand would be swollen and bleeding and you'd be in agony. And I only have the antidote for dogs so you'd be dead within two hours. Just be pleased that you've seen one.'

'Oh. Yes, I'm very glad,' I said weakly.

I was about to go back to the garden, when I hesitated. 'Joy?' I said, suddenly feeling sick. 'It might still be there. What do I do?'

'We photograph it, I hope. And drink the ouzo. Now, where's my camera?'

\*       \*       \*

Oddly, there were to be two more snake alarms that proved false, but both had an adverse effect on the running of the garden during those first two weeks of April. Unaware that the garden's fate hung in the balance, four volunteers had arrived to cut down the hundreds of spent asphodels.

Just before lunch a local Greek woman, who was working alongside me on the upper slopes, suddenly screamed and jumped backwards into a

330

prickly pear. Joy came quickly. After examining her and getting a description of the creature, she declared that it hadn't been a snake at all, but a skink, a fast-moving lizard with two tiny legs.

She took the woman into the house, where she used tweezers to pick out the protruding spines from her back, then dabbed each of the puncture wounds with an antiseptic. The result, unfortunately, was that the unpaid worker couldn't bring herself to return to work in the garden. It would no longer be a pleasure, she said, delicately putting a hand to her bottom. There would always be the nagging fear of snakes. She offered her profuse apologies and left, Joy watching her depart with a sigh.

'You can't blame her. Those prickly pear spines really hurt,' she said sadly.

The second alarm occurred around noon on the same day when Angela, the freckle-faced American volunteer, also cried out in pain, fearing a snake bite. On spotting the offender, Joy saw it wasn't a snake but a huge centipede. On this occasion, she was quick to get the victim into the house, where she wrapped chunks of ice in a cloth, telling Angela to apply it to the infected area for ten minutes at a time until the swelling had subsided.

The swelling, however, remained painful and for the second time that day Joy lost a volunteer. Angela waved goodbye to me, but then stopped to demonstrate the size of the centipede. Placing her hands apart she assured me, 'It was this big!'

To make up for the loss of labour, I worked harder and longer than ever before. I needed the extra time because I spent so long carefully checking for snakes before I began any work. My ritual was to poke a stick in the undergrowth and wait for a reaction. If I didn't hear a hiss or a slithering noise, I would move on, pretending that I was an intrepid explorer in the jungle, rather than a cowardly gardener cutting down spent asphodels. As the sun set and shadows lengthened I remained out there, the remaining two volunteers having long gone.

'For goodness' sake, stop, Jane!'

I turned round to find a stern-looking Joy standing on the path, in her hand a tall glass with an umbrella cocktail stick poking out of its rim. 'Here. Pimms with lemonade. Do you realize you've worked for eleven hours today? Don't you tell anybody, else those bloody European pen-pushers, who don't know the meaning of hard work and commitment, will come and arrest me.'

'Don't worry; I won't. Thanks, Joy.' I took the glass with a tired smile. 'Cheers.'

Joy's expression relaxed. 'Now, there's another waiting for you in the house. No snakes in there, only Wizard. And you're eating with me tonight. Meal's on, already bubbling away.'

\*     \*     \*

One evening, mid-April, the cowbell clattered from outside the house and I went to answer the door. It was Nikiforo, his cap stuck on the back of his head, propped up by his mop of black hair. Otherwise he was smartly dressed in a white shirt and black trousers. In his hand he held a length of rope, at the end of which was a young goat. He pointed at it and said something like 'holy cotton'.

332

I pointed into the house, sign language for 'I'll get Joy'.

When I entered the kitchen and told Joy, she corrected me.

'He must be saying *holokautei*. It means a religious sacrifice.' She sighed and pinched the top of her nose in distress. 'Oh dear, Nikiforo's done this before at Easter. I tell him I can't slaughter an animal. I try to explain, but he keeps doing it, bless him. He's only being nice.'

Joy went outside to politely decline Nikiforo's 'offering'. After much debate, she accompanied him back to his van, into which the young goat leapt. He seemed happy enough as she waved him goodbye, his arm waving back as he drove down the driveway.

Joy returned to pick out a book from the library. 'Do you know, Jane, how we got the word 'tragedy'? It comes from the Greek word *tragodos*. It means 'the song of the goat'. They used to sacrifice goats to the god of fertility and god of wine. Nikiforo wanted to give me something really valuable as a mark of his respect.'

'What, a sacrifice to the god of fertility?' I laughed.

'Ha, ha,' Joy said dryly, peering at me over her spectacles. 'No. He meant the wine bit. He knows I worship that god. Not bothered about the other.' She chuckled throatily and brought out a dusty hardback book.

'So Nikiforo expected you to kill the goat,' I said, undaunted, watching her flick through the book's pages.

'Oh no, not me. Maybe he thought you could do it.'

I blanched. 'What! Hardly, Joy. I've been saving tortoises, not stepping on ants, careful not to harm grasshoppers, running from snakes.'

'In other words, a typical concrete townie,' Joy cut in, with a teasing smile. She showed me a picture of Dionysos, the god of wine.

'There he is. He's my god. You may ask, why worship a man? Why not a female? We love wine as much as men, don't we?'

*    *    *

It was *Megali Evdomada*, the Great Week of Easter, celebrating sacrifice and rebirth. For Greeks, Joy told me, it was a religious holiday, even more important than Christmas. Celebrations, customs and re-enactments would take place during the week.

On Good Friday, a public holiday, I was invited by Joy and Pavlos to see the village procession that took place that evening. As it was the weekend and I didn't have to get up early the next morning, I readily accepted.

We arrived in time to see a bier being carried ceremonially through the village centre, headed by a band, its brassy sound strangely appropriate to the slow and solemn music being played. Behind came the altar boys carrying liturgical fans, as well as scouts and guides in uniform. The air was full of the scent of flowers emanating from the perfumes on the bier and from the scattering of flowers by spectators along the route.

The next morning, Easter Saturday, Joy enjoyed seeing my reaction when she invited me to 'an earthquake'. We had to be in place by 10.30 a.m. in

334

order to get a good view. She refused point blank to answer any of my questions, except when I asked if it was another volcano sunrise?

'No' came the firm answer, feeding my curiosity.

I waited until Pavlos's arrival and tried to wrest the secret out of him, but he also refused, preferring to chuckle and seize me in a bear hug.

At 11 a.m. Pavlos, Joy and I stood among a crowd in the square outside the village church. As its bells started to ring there came the sound of thunder from inside the building. Pavlos told me it was caused by the congregation beating the pews with sticks. I was puzzled but not exactly impressed. Where was the earthquake?

Suddenly there was a loud bang on the edge of the square. A communal 'Aah!' went up from the crowd. It was followed by yet another bang. I turned with the crowd to see, on the flat roof of a building, a line of men reloading shotguns. I recognized one of them as Nikiforo. On a command they fired another salvo into the air. As they continued to fire, from behind the church came huge explosions that sounded more like bombs going off than fireworks. And still the church thundered with the rattling of their sticks.

With shotguns firing, the explosions and the church racket, I could be excused for thinking it was the climax of the event, but I was mistaken. From around a corner came the village band, playing their instruments as loudly and as tunelessly as they could, the drummer enjoying it most of all.

'But what,' I shouted amid the din, 'has it got to do with an earthquake?' The increasing noise prevented me adding the question, 'And what has it got to do with Easter?'

Afterwards, as soon as we were on our way home, Joy explained that the noise had been to celebrate the earthquake as described in the Bible, which took place following the Crucifixion. 'It's a celebration that was started by the Venetians.'

On impulse she said I ought to go back that same night to see something that was as dramatic in its own way as the earthquake. I told her I looked forward to it and meant it. Until now I'd believed that the Greek passion for drama had dissipated with the end of the era of myth and legend. It seemed I was wrong. I was eager to find out more.

Back at Helikion, Joy continued to mystify me. She placed three eggs into a pan of boiling water filled with red dye. The egg, of course, was the symbol of Easter to both pagan and Christian and I asked if it had anything to do with the English custom of children chasing eggs down a steep hillside. I was about to add that I would have no chance of catching up with an egg rolling down Helikion's hillside when Joy put a finger up. 'You'll soon find out,' she said.

I went back to Alcatraz to write in my diary:

*Looking forward to tonight. I want to come back for another Easter, this time taking in the whole week of it. Hope Pavlos and Joy will be there when I do. Still no news from Tom. I saw Joy this morning wipe her eyes with a tissue. Were they real tears or was she just tired? I'm sure she's not sleeping much. Now got smudges under her eyes. She'd never admit it to it, though. And she's not 'Neanderthal bashing' half as much as*

336

*before. That tells me something. Never thought I'd write this, but I miss her banging on about him.*

At 10 p.m. that night Pavlos drove us to the church. Joy sat beside me on the back seat clutching a paper bag containing three candles. As we neared the village I saw flickers of light in the darkness. Drawing nearer it became apparent that dozens of people were walking towards the village, all carrying burning candles. Although we'd arrived early, all the parking places in the village centre had been taken and Pavlos had to leave the Jeep in a side street. And still people flocked towards the square.

On our arrival all the candles that had been in flame were extinguished and the people stood quietly. Dogs barked from some faraway place in the hills. A parent shushed a small child rushing between the thick legs of two old ladies and a baby in its mother's arms released the odd plaintive wail.

I noticed that there was a wooden platform outside the church, although apparently not in use. I queried Joy. She put up her finger and whispered back, 'Wait and see.'

At 10.50 p.m. all the lights in the village appeared to be switched off. Then the church doors opened and the crowd began slowly to shuffle inside the darkened building to take their places. Shortly after we sat down, near the back and close to the aisle, the pews were packed, with many standing.

At five minutes to midnight there was the echoing noise of large iron bolts being withdrawn

337

from their clasps. There was a pause and then the doors of the sanctuary were ceremoniously flung open. After another pause, through the doorway stepped the priest, wearing a golden robe and carrying a lit candle, his long grey beard perilously close to its flame.

'*Defte Lavete fos*,' he intoned loudly, and walked down the aisle, the people nearest to him lighting their candles from his, which in turn were used to light those of their immediate neighbours. In this manner it took only a short time for every worshipper to carry the symbol of rebirth. The old man next to me, with an unlit pipe clamped between his teeth, clutched his burning candle in both hands, breathing hard as he concentrated on keeping it upright.

The priest then returned to the altar and slowly picked up the holy icon of Resurrection, a drape fabric threaded with gold and jewels. He turned and, holding it reverently in front of him, walked slowly out of the church. As soon as he'd passed a line of pews the worshippers there rose to follow him. In this manner everyone had vacated the church within minutes.

'Whatever happens, Jane,' Joy said, cupping her hand around the flickering flame of her candle, 'keep yours burning.'

Outside, in the square, the priest stood on the wooden platform. As the church doors were closed he raised the icon as high as he could reach above his head.

'*Christo Anesti!*' His voice rang out triumphantly.

Immediately the congregation chanted in reply, '*Christo Anesti!*' All of a sudden everyone was shaking hands and patting backs, but each watchful that their candle flame was not extinguished. Simultaneously, the village lights came on. At the same time a large bonfire suddenly blazed up on a nearby hillside. The noise and the display lasted for fifteen minutes, after which I shook my head, smiling at Joy.

'It's great,' I whispered.

'And not over yet,' Joy replied.

When we arrived back at Helikion, Pavlos parked the Jeep inches away from the alcove. Joy stepped out, her still-burning candle in hand. There was a whisper of wind and, very carefully guarding her candle, she went slowly to the front door. On reaching it she made the sign of the cross in candle soot. Then she blew out the candle.

'Right. Come on, you two. To Jane's place next.'

We huddled together, guarding the two candle flames still alight, and crept towards Alcatraz, where we performed the same ceremony.

'House and garden now blessed for year,' Pavlos said, putting his arm around Joy's shoulder. She looked up and gave him a quick grin.

The mystery of the three red-dyed hard-boiled eggs was revealed when, on Easter Sunday, Pavlos arrived for lunch. Beforehand, the three eggs were lined up on the table, one for each of us. I was invited to strike Joy's egg with mine as hard as I could. My egg survived, Joy's did not. Amid laughter I then had to strike Pavlos's egg. Mine survived, his cracked. I was the winner, by virtue of the most blows having left my egg undamaged.

'Good hits, Jane,' grinned Pavlos, hugging me. 'It means you wills be lucky this year.'

Joy planted a big solid kiss on my cheek.

'Stay lucky,' she said, using her fingers to remove

339

a smudge of blueberry lipstick from my cheek.

*       *       *

May arrived and with it warmer nights, a temperature which was tolerable outside, but unbearable in Alcatraz. Almost overnight my cell morphed from being an icebox into a sauna. It was ironic. Throughout the dark and freezing nights of winter I'd longed for this kind of heat, but now I was trying to cool myself before bed by rubbing ice cubes on my forehead and upturned wrists. I mentioned to Joy how hot it was and she naturally suggested that I sleep in the ghost room. Thanking her, I said I'd stick it out.

Alcatraz was where I experienced the seasons and the ghost room was so reminiscent of suburbia that I would rather suffer a bit and be closer to the garden.

In my diary I added a note:

*Joy laughed when I told her, but she seemed impressed by my decision. Said I was a true 'mud baby'. Then she fetched me an electric fan and various insect repellents. The fan isn't great and the repellents aren't doing their job. Things buzzing all around . . .*

After work, I would sit on Alcatraz's veranda, reading or just enjoying the sight and sounds of the garden. I was gratified and surprised when Joy deserted her comfortable chair on the house veranda to sit with me for the first time. It was significant in that she remained for an hour, sitting awkwardly on a wooden chair perched on an

340

uneven stone floor. I hoped that she was demonstrating her friendship but when she began to twitch and fidget, with tiny grimaces crossing her face, I feared that she had a worry and guessed that it was Tom's silence. Finally, I took a deep breath and spoke. 'Are you all right, Joy?'

'No,' she said suddenly. 'I'm worried. The swallows on the house have built their nests again in the eaves. Have you seen them going in and out?'

'Yes, I have. That's good, isn't it?'

'I don't know. They cleared off last year without producing any young.' She sighed with frustration. 'And I can't work out why.'

She lit a cigarette then kept quite still, her right ear cocked and mouth open. She spotted my querying look. 'What's that, Jane? That noise?'

There was an intermittent cracking or popping sound coming from somewhere close. I frowned and shook my head. 'I've never heard that before. What is it?'

'It's the seeds of the large Mediterranean spurge popping out of their casings.'

Joy sat back with a mixture of a smile and a frown. 'Do you think man has caused climate change?'

I replied that I was unsure and that scientists may have an agenda. 'Don't they want an excuse to get away from using oil and one way is to blame it on carbon dioxide?'

'I didn't know you could be sceptic.' She looked at me with a smile of surprise then squinted into the distance. 'You know, our lives exist in the thinnest of layers, a biosphere. It's been described as equivalent to a lick of paint on a football.

341

Ecosystems are such delicate things—the swallows not giving birth could be significant.'

She shook her head and stood up to leave. 'I suppose it's difficult not to get obsessed with things in such a small world.'

I watched her stop to rifle her pockets. Her choice of summer attire amused me, as it was at odds with all her cares. She had a wardrobe of long shorts and billowing Hawaiian shirts decorated with bold flower patterns and sunsets. Her feet were permanently clad in a pair of red flip-flops, the straps bleached by the sun and the backs worn down. Unlike me—I couldn't walk on the ground in flip-flops without feeling pain—Joy didn't seem affected by the prickly seeds and burs that littered the ground nor were her legs irritated by the waving plumes of grasses and wildflowers.

After her first visit to Alcatraz, Joy made a habit of coming over. I found it ironic—a role reversal if you like. I enjoyed preparing her snacks and pouring out the ouzo. She would bring a book to read and on the third evening lugged over a couple of large oriental cushions to settle on. With Orwell at our feet and a glass of iced ouzo to hand we would read or listen to the cracking sounds now made by the egg-shaped cones of an Aleppo pine. These, having held grimly on to the branches throughout the icy blasts of winter, were gradually cracking open to embrace the summer.

*       *       *

One hot and muggy morning Joy reminded me that Takashi—I couldn't recall his second name— the Japanese scientist, was arriving that day.

342

'He's visiting as many Mediterranean gardens as possible. He's researching the changes in species of plant over a specific period of time—are they blooming earlier and so on.'

On his arrival he showed himself to be an enthusiastic, talkative man in his thirties. He was full of chatter about his various interests, which included guitar playing, photography and supporting the Manchester United football team. It was this latter passion that caused him to worry as we started the evening meal.

'Manchester United play tonight,' he said in his high-pitched staccato accent. 'We play Chelsea in Europe Champion League final. Big game. Very important. Satellite television. Have you got—'

'Takashi,' interrupted Joy. 'You wrote in your letter about it. Didn't you get my reply?'

Takashi looked shocked. 'No.'

'I said that we don't have satellite television here. But I know who does—Charles, at the hilltop. He's got it. He knows you're going up there.'

And, coming from a family mad on football, I too had been invited. Takashi beamed and proceeded to eat his meal with gusto. Ten minutes before the kick-off I escorted him up the hillside, accompanied by Titan. Takashi talked constantly of the game to come. I was informed that Chelsea would have to be flawless in defence because Rooney and Ronaldo would seize on any loose balls and punish the Chelsea defence with ruthless efficiency. His forecast was that United would win by four goals to one.

In the event, sitting in Charles' living room and plied with beer, Takashi became alternately

343

desperate then ecstatic during the penalty shootout at the end of a drawn game. Rachel, although reluctant to watch the game at first, indulged in a few glasses of wine and soon became engrossed, caught up in Takashi's enthusiasm. Manchester United won by six goals to five, Takashi raising both arms in triumph.

On the way down the hillside he brought out his iPod and handed me his earplugs, insisting that I listen to the heavy metal band Motorhead. 'You like it, Jane. English band.' At this point I felt it necessary to tell him that I preferred the band Oasis and gave him back his plugs. He looked puzzled then gently pushed my hand away. 'Ah, but brothers Gallagher always fighting. Motorhead's singer, Lemmy, son of church priest.' Lost in his logic, realizing it was hopeless to refuse, I compromised and put one plug in my ear, handing him the other.

'Ah!' Takashi exclaimed, stuffing it into his ear. 'Yes. Listen together!'

Linked by Lemmy and 'The Ace of Spades', with arms round each other's shoulder to avoid losing an earplug, we arrived back at the house. Takashi thanked me politely for having him as my guest then went indoors chanting quietly, 'United! United!'

Takashi was a different person the following day. He explored the garden at a sedate pace and—because Joy was absent—took notes and kept coming up to me as I worked, asking many questions, some of which I struggled with.

When Joy returned I had fun in telling her of Takashi's histrionic celebrations following his side's football victory, as well as his love for heavy metal. I had hardly begun to tell her of his interest in the garden, when she said I'd made him sound like a 'football yob'.

When they finally met for a tour of the garden Joy was put off by his constant use of scientific jargon. She told him, quite bluntly. that when she started working at Helikion she'd ploughed her own course in water conservation, gaining knowledge through experience and trusting her own powers of observation. Then, suddenly, after taking him on a tour of the garden, her opinion of him changed. Later, she told me that he was the first visitor to the garden who had convinced her of the increasing role that science would take in horticulture.

Over tea she told Takashi about her concern regarding the garden's future. Takashi frowned and shook his head. 'Garden very important,' he said. 'Very important. Must not close.' He gained even more respect from Joy an hour later when his taxi arrived. I stood by as he bowed and shook her by the hand, saying that he had contacts who 'might be interested in funding, or even buying, the garden.'

That night, after the meal, I put it to her. 'Do you think he was genuine about his contacts?'

Joy raised her chin and paused before speaking. 'Japan is a world leader in the desalinization of seawater by nuclear energy. That's all I know about them. Who knows?'

It gave me hope. As I left for Alcatraz she told me not to keep worrying about her or the garden. She believed in fate and added that she felt like a character in a Dickens novel who had 'expectations'. I doubted her. She was too practical to be someone sitting in a room waiting for fate to arrive. Her anxieties, I was certain, came from not being in control of the situation. There was nothing she could do *but* 'wait', and that didn't suit her at all.

*      *      *

The hot weather of May continued into June. I scribbled in my diary:

> *It reached 45.4 Centigrade yesterday.*
> *Alcatraz is steaming. I'm being bitten to*
> *bits. Bites filling with fluid. Feel like*
> *Quasimodo. I want to be back home. It's*
> *raining and Wimbledon starts soon.*

One evening Charles, dressed in a panama hat and crumpled linen trousers, brought news that the forecast was for the heat wave to continue. It was a signal for Joy and I to become semi-nocturnal creatures, rising at 5 a.m. with the dawn and working until 10.30 a.m. After this we would eat, try and enjoy a siesta, then resume work in the evening, finishing when it became dark.

One night when Joy paid me a visit in Alcatraz she found me lying on the stone floor in imitation of Orwell. The fan sat between Zeus's paws, but only expelled air that was coolish to tepid warm.

She was annoyed at my silliness. 'This isn't being nearer the garden. It's you getting nearer to being unfit to work! I know you now. You want to prove you're as tough as anyone. Well, you've done that. I want an intern who can get a good night's sleep. Come on, girl, I'm taking you where it's cooler. It's

346

ghosts again for you!'

I first made a token protest and then obeyed.

'Bye, Zeus,' I said, and noticed that his mane was flat and limp with the moist heat. 'Sorry, can't take you with me. Stick it out for both of us.'

It was a great relief to sleep in a temperature that was tolerable. However, shortly after my transfer I suffered from another series of insect bites, worse than those I'd encountered in Alcatraz. Wide awake and deep into the night I found myself flailing around the room, batting at mosquitoes and murdering other mini biters with a rolled-up copy of the *Spectator*.

I woke up in the morning with a thick head and faced the unenviable task of cleaning splatters of blood from the walls. I told Joy I was a serial killer. It made her laugh, which was the objective. She provided me with Anthisan bite cream as well as more insect repellent and fragrant joss sticks. I lit the latter and applied the former each morning and night, but the itching and swelling still caused me distress. How I envied Joy's leathery, wrinkled skin, which—I was convinced—gave her immunity to insect bites.

'Joy,' I said, scratching my arm, 'why don't the bugs bite you?'

'Nicotine,' she said, offering me a Silk Cut. 'You don't have to smoke it. Just hold it, waft it about and you'll see.'

I wafted and waved, but maybe the insects that surrounded me were hardened smokers. I covered up every part of my skin I could, but still they came to the feast.

Joy was far more credible when it came to the business of eating in hot weather. She ordered me

347

to stop making my own meals and declared that she would 'take care of it'. At first I tried to talk her out of it but soon began to look forward to her light meals, which were always tasty and provided the essential vitamins and minerals.

Each evening we sat on the marble floor for maximum coolness and ate variations on the standard Mediterranean salad of tomatoes, red onion, cucumber, feta cheese, black olives and fresh basil leaves. The protein was provided by fish or small pieces of skewered lamb. The additions included artichoke appetizers, grilled aubergine with apricot pomegranate sauce, hummus with roasted red pepper, sea bass grilled in fennel, shellfish, spiced chickpeas and fruits of all kinds. Each evening was a gastronomic delight, with plenty of ouzo or red wine available.

However, after a few mornings of waking with a throbbing headache and a parched mouth, I grew to be cautious with alcohol and took Joy's advice: 'Drink a pint of water before bed and some between every second drink. You'll be up all night going to the loo but you'll feel better in the morning.'

After each meal we would sit outside, the perfume of honeysuckle and myrtle drifting over us on the lightest breeze. Sometimes we would share a hookah and listen to the chatter of the night-time garden, while watching fireflies dart hither and thither in the blackness. As soon as we sat down Wizard would always join us, perching on the back of a chair, muttering comfortable noises of approval. He enjoyed his perch so much that when an overhead climbing plant began to drop its petals, he became irritable and shook himself free of them, still refusing to move.

If anything showed that Joy was a gardener by vocation it was her readiness to observe or teach at any time of day or night. Late one evening she asked if I had noticed the lone caper plant that was growing in and out of a terraced wall. I told her that I had. It had produced its first flower, its long, violet-coloured stamens exploding from out of large white petals.

'It's beautiful, the first caper flower I've ever seen, Joy.'

A year ago I was ignorant about where capers came from. I told Joy that every day I made a pilgrimage to look at the plant's round and chubby plant buds, imagining them crammed in a jar and on a supermarket shelf.

Joy was pleased. 'Dioscorides,' she said, 'believed that its juice would "kill ye worms in the ears".'

I thought of Takashi and his love of heavy metal and told Joy he might benefit from its juice, at which point she broke into a smoke-choked bout of laughter.

One night a fierce wind blew up, welcome in its cooling draught, but too strong to sit out in, so I fetched my laptop and we watched an episode of *The Sopranos*. Fascinated as Joy was by the drama—saying that she was strangely attracted to the actor who played Tony Soprano—she declared that she would never be enslaved by television. She saw it not as a window on the world but as a drug. It shielded people from the reality of nature, creating values and expectations that were, in themselves, dubious and thereby endangering the fabric of society.

In the continuing heat, Joy returned her attention to the Neanderthal. His sprinklers were on most of the time and it was driving her to distraction. It brought me some relief to know that Joy, despite all her anxieties, was back to her 'Neanderthal bashing' ways, a welcome distraction. She'd written letters of complaint to all the municipal and community authorities, asking them to investigate, but so far hadn't received any reply. This was especially frustrating since she wasn't complaining about the use of water, but the likelihood of an illegal borehole. Finally, she wrote to the police and was still waiting for their response.

'Perhaps they won't reply,' I remarked when she gave vent to her frustration. 'Perhaps they've been to look at the garden and haven't told you the result. Maybe the law won't let them tell you.'

Joy nodded. 'Mind you, we might not be his neighbour for long. We might be out on our ear.' And then her mask slipped and left me in momentary shock. She rose to her feet, both fists clenched. 'The whole bloody thing!' she exploded. 'If only Tom knew how I feel! No, not how I *feel,* what I *grieve* for the garden!' She shook her head in despair and left me. All the hope and expectations she had talked about seemed to have vanished in an instant.

The next day I climbed an olive tree, which gave me a partial view of the Neanderthal's lawns. I was amazed to see that they were turning brown. I rushed to tell Joy, who was more than pleased. She wondered if that meant 'the dreadful man' had

350

vacated the place.

'That's a lot of water saved. That man probably uses a month's garden supply in one hour with his blasted sprinklers.' But something was to happen that changed the entire situation and made Joy's letters and complaints irrelevant.

# 16

# A Toast to Winston

Winston's teddy,
and Kalanchoe
mangini in
re-cycled container

It was late afternoon and the thermometer was pushing thirty-five degrees as I performed my drawn-out watering stint on the terraces. A sudden call from Joy took me back to the house. I was to meet her around 'the other side of the walled garden, pronto'.

As I rounded the wall an arm met me, holding out a thickly padded jacket. It was Joy.

'You'll need this. Put it on.' I stared at her. It was blindingly hot and she wanted me to put on a coat?

'Joy,' I said, fearing she had finally lost her sanity, 'it's sweltering.'

'Doesn't matter. I said you'd need it.' She pointed to a mandarin tree, its branches dense and overcrowded. 'It needs a trim.'

I was still none the wiser. And then it dawned. 'Oh, to protect me from the mandarin's spines. Of course!' I gave a laugh. Joy sighed and helped me on with the jacket.

'You see, Jane,' Joy said, 'the more you have on the less the sun and the mandarins can get at you. Carry on. I'll bring your water.'

As I set to work a spine tore into the jacket. It could have been my arm. There was method in her madness, after all. Since the start of the heat wave in May, Joy had taken it upon herself to provide and regulate my intake of fluids. Each morning, she would usher me out to work with only a small bottle of water. After that she delivered me a bottle for each hour that I worked, taking back the empty one.

To my irritation and amusement I had once caught her dipping her little finger into a bottle, dabbing the liquid on her wrist, like an anxious mum checking that her baby's milk was the right temperature. When she saw me looking, she'd pretended that a midge had found its way in.

'Trust me,' she'd said firmly, handing me the bottle. 'I've observed you just like I do the plants. I know what your body needs. Don't throw it down your throat. You must drink it slowly.'

I had tried to reason with her, stressing that her ration of water didn't work, that my thirst was definitely not quenched, that I needed a long cold drink and not sips of tepid water. I should have added that I suspected she'd subconsciously applied her theory of the minimal watering of plants to me, but faltered at the last moment, deterred by her deepening frown.

On this occasion, when Joy returned with the promised bottle, I watched her leave then greedily guzzled the whole lot down in less than a minute. Afterwards I sat down on the baked earth, shuffled into the shadow cast by the mandarin tree and tried to work out the conundrum that was 'Joy'. It was useless making a dash to Alcatraz or the house for more water. She would inevitably catch me out.

Trying to get a fix on her was like grabbing hold of a bar of soap in the shower. She was extrovert, introvert, funny, explosive, of strong conviction, with an eccentric or individualistic approach to a number of things, not least gardening practices. Although she revelled in reading horticultural books written by 'gardening greats', such as Christopher Lloyd, her favourite author, she was a maverick in preferring to rely on her own observations and intuition.

'Be confident in your own ability. Start with

observation: use your eyes, ears, nose and touch. Then tune in, *listen*' was the substance of the sermon that she regularly preached. Now, in the undying heat of summer, her horticultural canon was to be applied to me.

Well, I had been *listening*. And my body always screamed back, 'I want cold water, iced water, bloody well lots of it!'

I was just going to have to be patient. Joy was suffering from stress and perhaps the hot weather had added to it, that was all. Pavlos had made allowances for her strange behaviour and so should I. 'These things will pass,' I told myself.

\*          \*          \*

It was 7.10 p.m. and I'd just finished pruning the mandarin tree when Joy appeared, dead on time, with another fresh bottle of water.

'Can you smell smoke?'

Without waiting for an answer, she told me I shouldn't be worried because it was coming from the island of Rhodes, where huge fires had resulted in many British tourists being moved to safe areas. 'Oh, they're far too far away for smoke to get here.'

She waved a hand, dismissing it as though I'd voiced that fear in the first place. 'You see, what makes people really alarmed are the television pictures. You see these enormous planes, like gigantic pelicans, scooping up water from the sea and dropping it on the fires. Frightening.'

I took off the torn jacket, its lining soaked in sweat, and stared at the bottle of water still clutched in her right hand. It was the focus of all my attention. Nothing else mattered, nothing in the whole world.

Joy, oblivious, continued. 'The prefecture—that's our second-rate local authority, I mean the second tier, not absolutely useless—has the fire alert on code red, but it's normal for a hot and dry summer.' She was sanguine about the whole thing. 'You noticed that there's a firebreak around the garden? Pavlos and some volunteers helped clear the growth years ago. We'll be fine.'

While she talked I purposefully switched my focus from the bottle to her eyes and back again, hoping to draw it to her attention.

'In point of fact,' she went on, totally oblivious, 'fires aren't always a bad thing. Some of the forests we've got today are the result of fires over the centuries. And plant life often benefits from the odd fire. Cistus seeds germinate from the brief heat of fire. They colonize tracts of land cleared by burning—not that I want my garden to catch fire in *my* lifetime!' She gave a loud chuckle. My eyes followed the bottle being slowly transferred from her right hand to her left as she reached into her shorts to bring out a packet of Silk Cut.

'There was a time,' she said, 'when we had a close shave. Many years ago. That was when I had to use loads of water. I had a horrible hosepipe going for hours. Pavlos helped, and Nikiforo. We kept the road boundary as wet as we could as the fire was coming up that way. Fortunately, the wind dropped and we were saved.'

Joy reflected on what she'd said, then sighed and drew in a deep breath. 'Oh well, keep it up. You're doing a good job, Jane.' She trapped the bottle under her right armpit, freeing her hands to light a cigarette. After that she turned to go back to the house, but then stopped and took the bottle from under her arm to point it at me.

'I'll give you a reference that will get you into Kew, mark my words.'

Regardless of my intense thirst, my heart leapt into heaven. This was the first time Joy had alluded to a reference, let alone a *good* one. But the water—Joy was walking back to the house with it. I stumbled after her, my arm outstretched. 'The bottle?'

She turned quickly to look at me, her eyes narrowing. 'You look tired, Jane. You do look tired.'

'I'm just thirsty, Joy. The water. . . ' I indicated the bottle in her hand.

She stared at it for a moment, then her jaw dropped. 'Oh Lord, what am I doing? I'm so sorry, Jane.' She went back to pick up the empty bottle, while still holding the full one, returning with both.

'I'm so sorry.'

She held out the empty bottle then, quickly realizing her error, broke into laughter and gave me the full one. Thankfully I unscrewed the cap and took the longest, deepest drink of my life.

'Well, you were thirsty. Really thirsty, weren't you?' Joy shook her head, hands on hips.

Panting, I came up for air and nodded in agreement.

She watched me drain the rest of the bottle. 'Sorry, Joy,' I panted. 'A sip wouldn't have done the job.'

'You poor thing,' she said, scanning my face and sweat-soaked vest, her eyes suddenly lighting up as if she had come to a realization.

'I got it wrong with you. Yes. Stay where you are. I'll fetch you some more.'

She set off for the house, chastising herself. No sooner had I sat down than she was scurrying back again with a larger bottle of water. And it contained ice.

Joy watched me relish it. 'You see,' she said firmly, 'this is how we learn. I hope I've taught you that. It's all done by observation.'

*       *       *

Still plagued by insect bites, my throat sore from the abrasive meltemi wind, the days were difficult to get through. Although now fully watered, I was inevitably affected by lack of sleep during the sultry nights, even in the comparatively better conditions of the ghost room.

I wanted my own personal fridge in which I could stick my head and shoulders. I yearned for a grey, miserable day and the lash of an English winter downpour. I fantasized about walking across fields on a frosty day, breathing in the clean and fresh country air. To make me feel even worse I had news from family and friends, all bemoaning the fact that the weather in Derbyshire and London was still wet and cool. Didn't they realize how lucky they were?

Clearly anxious to make up for the debacle of 'Watergate', Joy took to working with me for long periods. She also kept up my spirits with a fund of amusing stories. One of the most memorable was about her father, a vicar with a passion for keeping reptiles and, by her account, as eccentric as Joy herself. His parish had owed six thousand pounds for repairs to the church roof. The builder had been tolerant at first but ended up appointing a debt-collecting agency. This had galvanized Joy's father into saving the sum total of the plate collection from a number of services and placing the lot on a 100–1 outsider in the Grand National. It wasn't entirely a stupid act. He'd been tipped off by a stable lad who worked with the horse. It having won, and his bishop asking how he'd managed to pay off the debt, Joy's father said that the money had come as an anonymous gift. He quickly covered his tracks by ensuring that the next Sunday sermon was about the evils of gambling.

Joy's anxiety to make amends extended to her volunteering to lighten my load by taking over the watering of the nursery plants every other day, if not every day.

The high temperatures, she told me, could heat up the pots to a point where the young sensitive roots were killed, leading to the death or decline of a plant from fungal infection. With this in mind, she double-potted the plants, filling the space between the small and large containers with perlite, a coarse, porous material that kept the roots insulated from excessive heat. Fine-textured sand or soil would not suffice, as the plant roots would only grow through it.

A week later, I was a tad concerned to see that Joy had arrived back from a bottle changeover without carrying a fresh one. But I needn't have worried. Speaking as she approached, she put up her hand.

'Jane, stop now. I've just heard the forecast. It's getting even hotter. They think it could go up to forty-plus. You can have the rest of the week off.

361

We'll just do the watering, that's all.'

*     *     *

One afternoon, we heard the rumble of a lorry. I hurried down the track to see a low-loader truck stop short of the Neanderthal's property, the driver waiting for the gates to open. Strapped to it by thick ropes was an uncovered religious shrine made of marble, the size of a small outside shed. I could make out some kind of inscription etched into it.

'Brown lawns. Now this. Maybe he's doing penance for his sins,' said Joy as I returned to the hillside with the news. 'Or the shrine's devoted to the god of water. Come on. Religious talk always makes me thirsty for the harder stuff.'

We entered the house to find Winston lying on the marble floor, his good eye closed. Joy went quickly to him. He was breathing rapidly, his stomach moving in and out quicker than I'd ever seen it. Joy placed a gentle hand on his head. Normally he would make an effort to stand and wag his tail on our arrival. Now he made no attempt at recognition.

'He's not well,' she said, and remained in thought for a while. 'It's probably the hot weather. We'll see how he goes.' She brought his water bowl from the living area and placed it by the side of his head, stroking Winston with her hand.

'Poor old boy. Not ready for the knacker's yard yet though, are we?'

Joy, before the evening meal, intrigued by the Neanderthal's recent acquisition, cajoled me into doing another spot of spying.

'Take the binoculars. Find out what he's up to.'

I hurried down to the phrygana. From my olive tree perch I could see part of the shrine tucked away under a pine tree. When I told Joy what I'd seen she shook her head. 'He might be conning somebody, pretending to be a priest or something. I wouldn't trust that man further than I could throw him. I'll be damned if he's found God.' But she was wrong in her guesswork, as would be proved the next day when we went shopping.

*     *     *

We set off early for the village to escape the high temperatures of later in the day. Our first call was to the small, wood-panelled shop piled high with cheese and olives. Joy marched in as usual and picked up two bottles of ouzo.

'*Ya su*, Joy.' The shopkeeper poked his turtle-like head from around a sack of pistachio nuts.

'*Kalimera*, Adelphos.'

As usual, he pulled out a litter stick from under the counter and pointed the pincers at the top shelf of the cabinet behind him. He first gripped, and then lowered down, three packets of Silk Cut. As Joy fumbled in her bag for the money he began to talk to her in rapid Greek, pointing in the direction from which we'd come. Joy raised her head slowly, opened her mouth and closed her eyes at the news.

She turned to me excitedly. 'Jane, you won't believe this but he says the Neanderthal was in here a week ago spouting off that he'd sold his house and was going back to England.'

'That's great,' I said. 'Ask him about the shrine.'

Joy did as prompted. She came back with the translation. 'He doesn't know, but it's bound to belong to the new owner.'

On our return home Joy slowed down the Jeep to a standstill outside the Neanderthal's open gates. Inside was parked a builder's lorry and, beyond, workmen boarding up the house windows.

'Wonderful!' Joy exclaimed, her eyes shining bright. 'Under Greek law, if a house is abandoned and somebody squats in it they can take legal possession after a few years. That could be me, Jane. I should squat there. Why not the two of us? We'd have a ball tearing up his lawns, filling in the pool.'

'Blocking up his borehole,' I added, to Joy's deep-throated laughter.

As soon as we entered the house she opened a bottle of champagne to mark the event. I was amazed at the transformation in her and was gratified and delighted by her jokey remark that 'we' should appropriate the Neanderthal's property. I think she meant it.

I had a sudden thought. 'But how do you know his house is going to be empty or undeveloped?'

'Jane,' said Joy patiently. 'In Greece if house windows are boarded up it almost certainly means that the owner isn't going to be living there for a long time, or perhaps never. It's the same in England, isn't it?'

That evening, Pavlos came round with his accordion and we celebrated the occasion. Joy was relaxed and full of good humour. But she wasn't to remain in a carefree mood.

\*        \*        \*

The next day, Joy looked in her diary, uttered an obscenity and raced around the room, Wizard fluttering behind her. 'Oh Lord, oh Lord. I'd forgotten. Josh and Charlie are coming on Friday. I've only got three days to get ready, Jane.' Immediately she snapped into her busy mode of trying to do more than one thing at the same time, the result being that she mixed up everything and achieved little.

And then, as quickly as her anxiety and excitement levels had mounted, they dissipated with Charles bringing an email from Josh saying that he wasn't coming after all. Josh, as head of an art department at a Dublin college, had to give up his week to help with the reorganization of the department following a budget review.

But far from being relieved, I found her dabbing her eyes with a soft tissue. When she saw me looking she crumpled the tissue into a ball, hiding it in her closed fist, and gave me a fixed and bright smile. She took a deep breath. 'Good news, Jane. The day after tomorrow the temperature's dropping below thirty.'

\* \* \*

It was a day that I'd longed for. A comfortable day preceded by a good night's sleep. The sun was shining and wildflowers swayed in a tender breeze, a pleasant relief from the scouring meltemi wind that had plagued us for so long. I was on the hillside pulling out grasses to prevent them going to seed when I noticed Joy trudging up the path, her head lowered. I smiled to myself, remembering

365

when she had first set me the task of removing the swathes of grass populating the hillside. It had been another Sisyphean task requiring infinite patience and, in my opinion, pointless. A strimmer could have finished the job far quicker and more efficiently. It was like picking out salt grains from a jar of sugar.

Of course, Joy had an answer. Using a strimmer, she said, would inevitably 'topple' some wildflowers, disturb or kill insect life, and the whole balance of the garden would be upset. 'And how can you learn anything if your nose isn't hard to the grindstone?' She was correct. Bent on all fours, while patiently removing each blade of grass by hand, small flowers were revealed as well as curious insects.

As Joy approached I found two stones, one white and one black, the former round, the latter flat-bottomed and long, curving upwards at both ends. The two fitted perfectly together and looked like a miniature Henry Moore sculpture. I knew Joy would be delighted with them and I imagined where they might sit on her desk, when suddenly she stood before me, her face set like the stone in my hand.

Winston had died, she said. She had found him behind his Zulu warrior stool.

She pursed her lips. 'It's the natural scheme of things. I rang Pavlos. He's coming round.'

I couldn't speak, just nodded, full to the brim.

An hour later Pavlos arrived and insisted on carrying Winston's body to the pet cemetery. As we set off up the hillside, I carried a spade and pickaxe while Joy lugged up two bags, one of them holding two bottles of champagne and three glasses. She didn't say what was in the other bag.

When we reached the spot, Joy put down the bags and said, 'You know the vet reckons he was about a hundred and ten years old in human age. You can't mourn that. He had a good life.' We watched Pavlos use a pickaxe on the hard ground, first managing to break up the surface of stones and packed soil, then taking a momentary breather, at which Joy stepped forward to take the pickaxe herself.

'I must do a bit,' she said. She raised it above her head and drove the blade some way into the softer soil, but gave up after another blow struck a hidden rock. Titan came up to Joy and rubbed against her legs as if in consolation.

Pavlos took the pickaxe back. He began the toil of breaking up—and then digging out—various-sized rocks mixed in with the soil. When the hole was deep enough Joy insisted that she, alone, lower Winston into his grave. She then turned round to take out her village shoes and teddy from the second bag, carefully lowering them to rest on Winston's body. After Pavlos had filled in the hole with soil we each picked up rocks and piled them on top of the grave.

When all was done, Joy led us to sit under a carob tree overlooking the pet cemetery and opened the first bottle of champagne. 'To Winston' was her toast. Only when the last drop had been extracted from the second bottle did we stand up and walk slowly back to the house. Cicadas chirped in their hiding places. Around us the small purplish-blue flowers of the Persian hyssop had begun to wane, although the perfume of their leaves was still pungent.

That evening, as swallows and house martins swooped and circled around the veranda, we sat in silence. It was broken when a bothered-looking Charles appeared, slightly breathless and sweaty.

'Joy. Just had this.' He handed her a computer print-out. 'It's from Tom. He's got a buyer for the garden. Says they want to keep it running and keep you on as curator.'

Joy stared at him. He looked worried and uncertain. Slowly, she moved a straggle of grey hair from her eyes. 'What's wrong?'

Charles puffed out his cheeks. 'There's a problem.' He paused. 'Mind if I have a drink?'

# 17

# Maltese Cross

Wizard
and the
cross

Joy, cigarette in her mouth, held the print-out of Tom's email close to a burning candle, while waving away the light-attracted moths and insects. 'It's a couple. Helen and Mark McGregor. Both American.'

She looked at Charles, an eyebrow raised in query. 'They've got the money, Tom says. So, what's the problem?'

Charles took back the print-out. 'You've not bought property in Greece, Joy. I have. Listen to what Tom says.'

He read the message aloud. 'Their funds for buying Helikion are offshore which is great because they won't be paying any taxes on withdrawal. In my book it makes them good buyers.' Charles raised his eyebrows at Joy and shook his head. 'I'm afraid he's wrong.'

'Offshore,' Joy echoed, staring at Charles. 'A tax haven.'

Charles nodded. 'Yes.' He broke off to take the drink I handed him. 'Foreigners sending money here must do it through a Greek bank and show where the money's come from, the country, the bank, the name of the account holder. But . . .' he paused, stressing what he had to say next, 'if it's from an offshore bank, from a *tax haven*, they may refuse to send those details. Oh fine, the buyers can still bring the funds into Greece, but if they do all the money will be taxed here as income.' He paused again for effect. 'That's at forty per cent.'

Joy's face fell. Then she said, 'Tom's selling at four hundred thousand, isn't he. What's that at forty—'

371

'He'd have to pay tax of a hundred and sixty thousand euros.' Charles shrugged at Joy's expression. 'Sorry, but there it is.'

Joy stubbed out her cigarette and rested her head in her hands. 'That's awful.'

'Yep,' Charles sighed. 'Well, I'll go back and tell Tom that there's no option. Either they pay the tax or drop out.'

'Charles. Don't go just yet.' Charles was stepping off the veranda when Joy stopped him.

'Do you think it wise for Tom to warn them? Won't it put them off? Wouldn't it be better if they came here first and we talked about it then?' She grimaced, waiting for his reply.

Charles meditated and finally nodded. 'OK. Of course we could consult a tax specialist. You never know. Maybe there's a way. I'll brief Tom, ask him to fix up a date for them to come over, but not to say anything about tax. Perhaps he can speak to a tax adviser in America and I'll try and do the same here, yes?'

After Charles left, Joy downed the remains of her glass of ouzo and went to her room.

In my diary that night I wrote:

*2 a.m. Can't sleep for worrying about Joy. Tom's sent news—at last! Here's the good— he's got a couple who want to buy Helikion. Now for the bad—they might get taxed heavily. If gardeners were paid a decent wage I'd buy Helikion. God knows how Joy will be tomorrow.*

The next morning I found her vigorously raking up piles of pine needles scattered over the driveway.

'Jane,' she greeted me urgently, brushing hair away from her face. 'We've got tourists coming. A party of Germans. I forgot to tell you. Can you tidy up the nursery?'

After ten minutes Joy shouted for me to join her in collecting almonds from the top of the phrygana. The grey-green husks were splitting open and she was worried mice would ferret them away. Halfway through that task she let out a cry and pointed to the house.

'We need to tidy the living room! Wizard's scattered the Scrabble pieces everywhere. And there's all that mess on my desk. Nobody, let alone a German, likes a mess on—'

'Joy.' I spoke faintly in face of her passion. 'Don't you think it would save time if we finished this job first?'

'No! They'll be here any time. They have to sign the visitors' book and pay for the plants in the house. I can't have it looking like a rubbish tip.'

As we stepped into the alcove, Joy stopped dead and turned to me. 'Get back to the nursery.' She shook her head. 'We haven't got any plants in the house to sell.'

I about-turned and quickly marched outside. Joy followed me out, slamming the door behind her and shooing me on with a wave of her arms. 'Go on, get the herbs out, rosemaries, oregano—anything with a scent. They sell the best. I'm coming. Well, don't just stand there; go on, off you go!'

I jumped over a large pile of abandoned pine needles and dashed ahead. Joy, on arrival, went straight into the work of checking and collecting the plants to be sold.

She stopped to look at her watch then, ears pricked, peered around the shrubs and down the hillside. The sound of a diesel engine could be heard, growling and labouring up the track.

'Gawdstrewth, they're here already. Should have guessed. Towels on sun beds at dawn. Come on, Jane, *ela, ela!*'

She set off down the rocky path, while I panted behind, pushing the heavy wheelbarrow full of potted plants. After ten seconds or so she suddenly turned to me and flung her arms in the air, knocking her straw hat off.

'Jane, they're not allowed to take plants into Germany. It's illegal. Nothing for it. Take them back.'

I froze. Faced with Joy's agonized expression, I swallowed an urge to swear then turned the wheelbarrow and—

'No. Leave it!' Joy picked up her hat and waved it in the air. 'Run to the house and get some seed envelopes. They can buy those instead. We'll do it outside. Tea, cakes, the lot. No need to tidy up the house. Oh, and bring out the visitors' book.'

I dumped the wheelbarrow and raced past her with Joy's *'Ela, ela,'* ringing in my ears. As I neared the driveway the Germans, mainly retired couples, were gathering outside their mini-coach and taking a first look at the garden.

On reaching the alcove, I paused to collect my breath and looked back at Joy descending the hillside. She stopped to bundle up her hair carefully and put her hat on. Then she lifted her head high, took a deep breath and composed her face before walking serenely across the driveway towards her assembled visitors. She clasped her

374

hands together and, having got their attention, voiced the greeting she'd been practising so assiduously.

'*Guten Tag, Sehr geehrte Damen und Herren.*' She spoke with warmth and confidence. '*Willkommen zu Helikion!*'

\*      \*      \*

The next morning passed quietly, without Charles bringing a reply from Tom. Joy was very quiet and I saw nothing of her after our breakfast meeting.

After lunch I was completing one of Joy's unfinished tasks, raking up pine needles near the house, when a Mercedes estate car, a man driving and a woman in the front passenger seat, came up the driveway and stopped outside the Neanderthal's gates.

The driver got out, a middle-aged man with greying hair, wearing khaki-coloured trousers and a white T-shirt. He unlocked the gates and, returning to his car, caught sight of me watching him. Without hesitation he smiled, took off his sunglasses and strode towards me. Wary of anybody associated with the Neanderthal, I tentatively walked forward to meet him halfway down the track.

'*Ya sas,*' he said, extending a hand. He said something else in Greek, raising his eyebrows in query.

'Hello. Sorry, I can't speak Greek. I'm English,' I added, feeling stupid and taking his hand.

His smile grew broader and his brown eyes, filled with gold flecks, sparkled in the sunlight. 'Wonderful,' he said, in perfect English. 'My name's Aleko—my English friends call me Alex. Do you live here?'

'I'm Jane. I'm at the house up the track, working as a student horticulturalist.'

'Even better.' He indicated the woman still in the car. 'My wife. We both love gardening.' He gestured to the phrygana. 'It looks lovely. I'm glad I shall be living next to it. We're putting furniture in today.'

He turned to follow my gaze. A tall removals van was crawling uphill. He turned away to jog back, waving a hand in apology. 'Sorry. I have to go. We're not moving in for a month or so. When we do, I'll come round and introduce myself properly!' He returned to his car, got in and drove through the open gates, the removals van trundling behind.

I hurried to find Joy, eager to bring her the good news. In the heat of the day she was still working, slowly picking up almonds.

'Joy, I've just met the new neighbour. He's nice. Likes gardening. Doesn't look the sort who'd waste water.'

She stood upright and nodded her head in a tired fashion. 'Good. I didn't really want to be a squatter. With any luck we'll find out about the borehole. Let's have an ouzo, Jane.' She was weary in voice and manner. 'I suppose we have to celebrate.'

Once on the veranda Joy put her head back to try and sleep, found it impossible and poured herself another glass of ouzo. I sat looking at her with anxiety when the telephone jangled. Joy made to stand up.

'No. It's OK, I'll get it.' I returned ten minutes

later with a written recording of my phone conversation. I offered it to Joy. 'Charles. I told him you were asleep. This is what he said.'

Joy grimaced and shook her head. 'No, Jane. That was wrong of you. I'll ring him back.'

'Joy, please.' I put a hand up to stop her. 'You're very tired. Please rest. I'm very worried about you.'

She looked at me, saw that I meant it and sat back to wave a tired hand at me. 'Oh, go on then. Read it.'

I exhaled. 'Right.' I read from the notepaper. 'He's had a reply from Tom. He agrees not to tell the McGregors about the bank conditions. He's arranging for them to come over. He hasn't found out any way to get round the tax thing.'

I looked at Joy. 'I said I hope they can come over as soon as possible.' I paused. 'That's it.'

She sat still for a few moments and when she spoke it was in deep reflection.

'When something's your whole life, Jane, something that's more important than your life, and it is, at my age . . .' She wiped a hand over her face and looked at her watch. 'Oh dear. I have to go shopping.'

No amount of protest from me would stop her. With the sun falling behind Mount Hymettos we set off for the village, the sky streaked violet and red. Titan sat in the back seat, occasionally nudging his wet nose against our necks.

Joy was re-energized behind the wheel. I was amazed as to where her new-found energy came from. She even showed her traffic-light phobia. 'At last,' she said, banging her foot down on the accelerator as the lights changed to green. 'Got some sense into them.'

377

Arriving at the village she parked the Jeep in a place from where it was easy to reverse and switched off the engine, frowning at the dashboard.

'Jane?' Her voice had suddenly lost all its authority. She turned to look at me, appearing frail and exhausted. 'Am I all right? No, be honest, tell me, am I?'

I let out a forced laugh. 'Why do you say that?'

She shook her head. 'My memory. Not so good. No doubt you've noticed.'

I told her I thought that people who feared they had a problem usually didn't. 'You remember all the Latin names for the plants. I think it's because ...' I hesitated, searching for the right words, not wanting to upset her. 'I think it's because at times you do too many things at once. It's easy for anyone to forget stuff when that happens. But you must rest. You really must.'

'I'll rest when I've done.' Joy climbed out of the Jeep.

On our return to Helikion I was scared that Joy might fall asleep at the wheel, but once again she received a sudden and inexplicable renewal of energy, stopping the Jeep in a narrow lay-by. 'Want to show you something. It doesn't grow on our hillside.'

She got out of the Jeep, closing the door quickly to avoid traffic coming from behind, and walked a few yards into the scrub, crouching down at the side of an unremarkable wildflower.

'Look at those small yellow flowers. Don't they glow, Jane? So tiny a survivor. Some call it a Maltese Cross. Do you know what the Latin is?'

'*Tribulus terrestris*,' I said, pleased with myself. It

might be nondescript but I'd learned that its nutlets were sharp enough to puncture bicycle tyres and would cause considerable pain to anyone walking on them in bare feet.

Joy stood up slowly, staring at me as if I'd somehow changed my appearance, as if I were a revelation. 'It's true, Jane,' she said, searching my face, looking frail once more but childlike in her wonder. It reminded me of the moment in the film *ET* when the alien creature stares in tenderness and wonder at the boy's face.

'I shall probably cry when you go. You know that, don't you?' Joy said slowly.

A momentary hesitation and then I embraced her. She pushed me away, firmly holding me by the shoulders. 'Why don't you stay for a while longer? You don't have any work organized at home, do you? You could live in the house. We could— oh no!' She broke away to scramble to the Jeep and yanked on the driver's door. It was locked. She dashed round the other side, having to pull back immediately as a van, with its horn blaring, sped past. She tried once again, only to find the passenger door, as she feared, was also locked.

'Joy!' I screamed, racing towards her. 'Don't move!'

Alarmed, she flattened herself against the side of the Jeep as a truck roared by within centimetres. One of the flour bags it was carrying had split and was spewing out its contents. After the initial blast of displaced air I nipped round the back of the Jeep to drag her to safety.

We stood looking at each other. I started to laugh, pointing at her face. 'You look like a clown.' My face must also have been like Joy's, a grey pancake with red lips and nose protruding, because she too pointed at me and began to giggle. Then I let out a sob of relief.

'Don't you blubber, you big Jessie.' Joy hugged me back.

We stood in a laughing, crying embrace.

'Jane. Have you brought your phone?'

'No.'

We stared at each other, in the knowledge that we were stranded on a dusty, dangerous road.

'When we sort the Jeep out we're going to get sloshed,' Joy said, her face now fixed in confident resolve. 'Come on. Let's run to the garage for help.'

'Please rest first. Please just sit down and rest.'

Joy stared into my face again, not in childlike wonder, but in recognition. Without a murmur she sat down with her back to a wheel.

She was still sitting there, having fallen into a doze, when Charles's car pulled up behind the Jeep in the lay-by. He hopped out, his mouth wide open.

'Good Lord, Joy. I saw the Jeep. Have you broken down?'

'Yes. Well, I have,' Joy croaked. 'I owe my life to Jane.'

I helped her stand upright. 'Don't be silly, Joy,' I said.

'May we have a lift?' Joy asked Charles with a smile.

On impulse he embraced her. 'Jane told me you were exhausted. Let's get you home.'

\* \* \*

It was mid-September. The doctor had seen Joy, ordered rest and prescribed her various pills. I doubted that she took all of them, but it served to dampen down her exuberance and save energy. A brief tonic came when Charles reported that Tom had emailed to say that the McGregors intended to make the journey to Helikion and hoped it would be towards the end of the month.

But as the days passed Joy reacted to the vague promise and became withdrawn again and less talkative. 'Hope,' she said cynically. 'What does that mean?' Her depression had an effect upon her work and I found myself working longer hours to compensate. Nevertheless, she was appreciative and a 'Well done, Jane' comment accompanied by a touch on the shoulder or an appreciative smile of gratitude was payment enough.

But her warm reception to my work in the garden did not extend to my nagging that she consult the doctor again.

'No, Jane I will not. His jacket squeaks. I can't stand it.'

One morning I found her sitting at the kitchen table, head in her hands. When I said, 'Morning, Joy' she dragged her head to look up at me, black smudges under her eyes. She raised a hand at my concerned expression.

'You win, I've called the quack,' she said. 'No need to worry.'

The doctor arrived and Joy insisted I stay with her during the examination. 'I may need a witness in case I have to sue.'

He took her blood pressure. 'A hundred and forty over ninety-five. Not bad, Mrs Strataki. You'll live, for now. Are you taking the pills I gave you?'

'Some. But I've an aversion to blue capsules. That's why I called you.'

The doctor grunted, continued his examination, then wrote out a prescription.

'Temazapam is a sedative that should knock you out. But it's only good for a fortnight of constant use. Use it sparingly after that. Promise that you'll take them for a fortnight, exactly as I instruct.'

'Fine. Yes, I promise.'

He handed Joy the prescription and stood up to leave. 'And stop smoking. You don't want to die before you're too old to dance.' Joy scowled at him as he went and reached for a packet of Silk Cut.

A day later she informed me, as though chalking up a victory over the medical profession, 'I'm only taking one of the little sods. But I am sleeping. You see, doctors? Useless.'

There was another email from Tom, this time carrying much more encouraging news. He said that if the garden was seen by the McGregors as he'd described it—and they'd seen the photos, garden layout and house plan—they would definitely buy.

'In which case,' said Joy, 'why aren't they here?' She didn't dare bring herself to ask Tom what his next step would be if they failed to make the purchase.

Charles came back later with the news that the McGregors had been held up by the wedding of their daughter, but that they were 'still on track to come over'. The reply, rather than reassure Joy, cast her back into depression and more anxiety.

\*　　　\*　　　\*

It was late September before we heard again from Tom. He apologized for the lack of action, but assured Joy that the McGregors' arrival was imminent. On reading this she exploded with frustration and sent a message back asking him directly what he would do if the deal fell through.

Tom replied with the admission that he would be forced to sell in the general market. At this Joy sent back suggestions, the first being to make contact with Takashi, who had already intimated he might be able to find a buyer. Then there were organizations the world over that might view Helikion as a little jewel in the world of water and plant conservation.

Tom kindly 'noted them' and promised each would be contacted if the McGregors backed out. 'But,' he wrote, depressingly, 'I'm running out of time.'

'Buddhists,' Joy said, taking Titan for his walk, 'have the right approach to life. They believe that if you don't *hope* you can't suffer disappointment.' The world, she affirmed, was driven by desire for material wealth. 'The world is too much with us,' she said, once again quoting Wordsworth. 'It drives me insane.'

'You're not insane. Never will be,' I said, with a pang of guilt, thinking of my earlier diary entries, which were scrawled with 'she's mad' many times over.

She gave a short laugh and allowed Titan to pull her towards the hillside. On her return, half an hour later, she once again looked exhausted but, on seeing me, squared her shoulders and gave a bright smile. 'Cheer up, Jane,' she said. 'Not dead yet.'

Joy's gregariousness belied her sensitive intuition. The next day I stopped the work I was doing on the hillside, lost between reflection and deliberation. Three weeks remained of my year as an intern and the question of whether I could abandon Joy in her present state was troubling. I thought of ways of saving the garden, which largely boiled down to dramatic demonstrations of my loyalty to a woman whom the world should extol, rather than reject.

'Jane. It's not for you to worry.'

I turned round. There was Joy looking at me. She lifted her chin, as she often did when challenged.

'If Tom's buyers don't buy, then we'll mount a campaign in the press. *Athens News*, *The Times* and television. I'll go on. I'll make the case. We've got lots of friends in the world. I'm not finished by any long chalk. Come on, it's tiffin time.' She made a pretence of walking jauntily back. I followed her, but noticed that her shoulders had dropped as we neared the house.

I felt another twinge of guilt. While I still worried about her, in one way I was feeling better about myself. I'd lay my head on the pillow each night, warm in the knowledge that our relationship had taken a seismic shift. It was clear that I had her full respect. I was no longer given orders as such. Instead of jobs being allocated to me, we discussed what needed to be done on an equal footing.

Joy put the final seal on our friendship when, one evening on the veranda, she said that in the event of all else failing, then I must join her, Charles, Rachel and Pavlos to discuss a strategy for saving the garden.

Impulsively, I said that if all else failed I would go home to write about the garden to show the world its importance in the changing world climate. Inspired by two further glasses of ouzo, I went further in my fealty, flinging my arm in the air and declaring that I would assail the House of Commons. I would stand on Nelson's Column. I would storm the BBC . . . I stopped my tirade to join Joy in laughter.

When she recovered she poured me another ouzo, croaking, 'Jane. You're an absolute treasure. I didn't know you had it in you.' In her relaxed and ouzo-lubricated mood she puffed a cigarette and began to talk about her days with Christos. 'You know, Jane, you *must* have thought me mad to give you a stuffed lion as a room-mate.'

'Pretty much,' I smiled.

'It was because I couldn't bring myself to get rid of him.' Her expression changed and her voice fell. 'Christos was injured by Zeus, but he didn't die because of that. He died because he had an operation for his injuries, which left him in an even worse state. I blamed the doctors . . .' She faltered a little. 'Then Pavlos—he was a dear friend to Christos—he taught me to paint. He's as good a painter as he is a cellist. From that I started a small gallery in Athens—not far from the Art Centre. It made some money, but not enough. I'd met Marilyn in the hospital Christos was in. She told me about the garden, gave me her phone number. And I rang her. It would be a nice day out, I thought, a bit of respite from worry over Christos.

385

The day I visited we got on like a house on fire. Out of the blue she asked me if I would look after the garden, be its curator. She never said why, but she had to leave for America. It was all such a rush. She would visit for a month each year, keep tabs on things, pay the bills and a small stipend, Christos could recuperate ... I jumped at the chance. And both of us fell in love with—here.' She raised her glass to the garden. 'Here, my place on God's earth.'

I watched her light another cigarette. She drew in deeply and shot out a plume of smoke before continuing. 'Christos died shortly after we arrived. I moved from the house to the outhouse for a time. It was like a retreat for me. Plain and stripped bare, far from the madding crowd. As you know, it sorts out the frivolous from the serious.' She chuckled a little, then frowned. 'What was I talking about?'

'Zeus.'

'Ah, yes. Zeus. I had him stuffed because he hadn't hurt Christos on purpose. He was only playing. And Christos loved him dearly. But when I moved back to the house I couldn't have him with me. It hurt me to look at him but I couldn't let him go. You see, I loved Christos more than the lion. Does it make sense? Is it silly? Am I making any sense?'

'Yes,' I said. 'And I like Zeus. He's somebody to talk to.'

\*      \*      \*

Diary entry:

*Finally everything makes sense. The mystery of why Joy was angry with me the day I asked her about the paintings was because I'd brought back painful memories. My chopping down of the Chinese elm was just as upsetting. Christos was the love of her life. She felt extreme guilt at leaving her kids and he must have meant everything to her, helped her through. And when he died the garden became 'him' in effect, that's why she's so passionate about it. But when will Tom bring the McGregors? I'm scared for Joy. Really, really scared.*

# 18

# Under a Greek Sun

Joy summer 2008

One late, sultry afternoon, as I began watering on the terraces, Joy appeared, Titan huffing and puffing at her heels.

'The McGregors are coming a week on Wednesday,' she said flatly, and sat down on a stone wall.

'Oh, Joy, that's great!' I punched the air in delight. 'I never believed they'd come.'

Joy gave me a wan smile. 'Neither did I, Jane. But I'm not letting myself get carried away with it. Tom says he hasn't found a way round the tax situation. He's had to tell them about it. The good news is they still want to come, see if there's any way round it.'

Later that evening, the news of the McGregors' forthcoming visit seemed to have sunk into Joy's consciousness as she came to Alcatraz and invited me to go for a walk. She seemed—once more amazingly—to possess renewed vigour. We wandered down the phrygana and around the olive trees to find the ex-Neanderthal's gates open. We stood in the entrance, staring into the garden. The mock-classical Greek columns had all been removed and one of the lawns, part of which we'd seen with its water sprinklers, had now vanished. In its place was a large area of gravel dotted with pots of flowers.

'I hope the other lawn's been dug up as well,' Joy said, feeling for her hat as a breeze got up.

'It has.'

We wheeled round to find Alex stepping clear of the shrubbery, a pipe in his mouth.

'Just having a wander.' Smiling, he raised his

eyebrows at me, indicating I should introduce him to Joy.

'Oh, sorry. Joy, this is Alex. Our new neighbour.'

They shook hands. 'I'm delighted you're here,' said Joy sincerely. 'Absolutely delighted.'

Having established that Joy and I were his immediate neighbours, Alex wanted to know who lived at the top of the hillside. When we told him about Charles and Rachel he suggested that we brought them round for a meal. 'How about Saturday night?'

*     *     *

After months of inexorable heat, the garden looked much the same as when I'd first seen it, when Joy had raced me around it after the 'Queen of the Night' party and the worm hunt. Then I had likened it to a stately house that was in disrepair. Now I loved its frayed yet dramatic display. Whenever I entered it I was conscious of its silent battle for survival. No longer did I see the plants as the fantasy characters of last autumn, among them the 'mischievous', the 'exuberant' and the 'shy'. Instead, I feared that a Greek tragedy could easily become a reality in the relentless drought.

The fight to prevent the debilitating effects of water evaporation was carried on in different ways. Summer-deciduous plants had long since shed their leaves, whereas other shrubs, such as the grey, dusty sage, produced an oily armour and rolled its leaves inwards, pointing them upwards to prevent exposure to the sun.

Joy, over the year, had enthusiastically pointed out plants that used other strategies to prevent

392

water evaporation, ending her lecture with a familiar refrain. 'All life on earth, Jane, no matter how small, depends on water, or it will disappear.'

My worries for Joy, her future linked as it was to the garden, were put into perspective by the article she'd shown me in the *Athens Plus* newspaper and kept repeating:

'Can you believe it, Jane? The government says that Greece's water reserves are so low it could take ten years of proper management for levels to get back to where they were. And—listen to this— scientists from the Hellenic Committee of Hydrogeology have announced that there are around three hundred thousand boreholes, many illegal, that have to be checked as soon as possible.'

It was another reminder of the garden's true purpose. Surviving on a scorched, windy, stony hillside with little rainfall it was a call to gardeners the world over to experiment, to grow indigenous plants, and not resort to unwise watering. In Joy's mind, Helikion was, in its own small way, at the forefront of the quest to find a solution to global warming, and it was doubly important it be saved, not just for her sake, but for that of all plants and, consequently, human life everywhere.

As for me? Well, I was more selfish. I wanted it saved for her sake alone.

\*         \*         \*

As we made our daily tours it was a pleasure to see the large bulbs of sea squill thrust aloft their curling flower spikes, and the Cape plumbago, climbing through a small, wild olive tree at the rear of the house, had produced a fine display with its soft blue flowers, something I hadn't expected after the snow of February. However, it was in a sheltered position and Joy, in her wisdom, had covered it with protective fleece. A few frost-damaged stems had to be removed, but that was all.

On the Saturday evening Joy and I marched triumphantly through the gates of the departed enemy. Alongside us were our co-fighters in the struggle, Charles and Rachel. Joy, in fear of upsetting our hosts, had decided to withhold any question about there being a borehole or not until she spotted an opportunity. We would simply have to 'bite the bullet and wait'. Patience, while participating in the chatter of small talk that often follows the meeting of strangers, was at a premium.

Alex's wife, Chrysanthe, a woman with strong classical features and deliberately tousled curtains of blonde hair, led the way into the first topic of conversation, flowers.

'Chrysanthe,' she said, smiling at me, 'is the flower chrysanthemum in Greek.'

She and Joy spent the next twenty minutes talking about their mutual passion, wildflowers. During the conversation she expressed the hope that she and Alex could look forward to being given a tour of Helikion.

Joy seized her opportunity. 'Of course. I was going to ask you round anyway. But after this you'll get a special tour. I'm dying to look round your garden,' she said, looking at me with a glint in her eye. 'We've always been intrigued about what's in here, haven't we, Jane?'

We exchanged quick, conspiratorial smiles.

'We'll go round with drinks after we've eaten,' Alex promised.

After the meal, coffee was served. Coffee and more talk. It seemed interminable. The sky was darkening when we eventually went outside, the air cooler than I'd felt it for a long time. I thought of England in the autumn. Home was only a few weeks away and I looked forward to it, but knew that I would never be truly happy until Joy's fate had been decided. I prayed that the answer would be positive and arrive with the McGregors. As we rounded the corner of the house, there was the swimming pool, or rather its shell. It was empty. The tiled bottom was full of stone sculptures and pots with succulents cascading out of them.

'We thought of filling it in,' said Alex. 'But it's saved us the cost. And we like it like that.'

Joy looked at Alex in renewed interest. 'Is it because you don't swim?' she asked cautiously.

'No! It's because of the waste of water. Aren't you against them?'

Joy smiled, her body relaxing. 'I am. We all are. Anyone who's got any sort of conscience.'

I could sense Joy holding back about the borehole. Alex, like most Greeks, was a proud man and he might have resented another question about water, suspecting that Joy was ferreting—as she was.

In between bouts of conversation Joy and I looked around quickly and carefully, covering as much of the ground as we could without giving overt signals to our hosts. At one point I surreptitiously held a shrub back for Joy to peer behind, but there was nothing that suggested the presence of a borehole.

Alex led us into that part of the garden farthest away from Helikion. As we passed by an arbour, its wooden sides and roof clad in climbing plants, I saw the marble shrine sitting at its head. Alex saw me looking. 'It's to our son. He was in the Hellenic Coast Guard. On holiday in Italy he was killed on his motorbike.' As he spoke he put an arm around his wife. Charles went close to it, reading its inscription. We stood in silence for a while, then Alex quietly moved us on. 'Come on, I want to show you something.'

We came to some more shrubbery. Partially hidden was a square shape in the ground covered in small rocks. Alex bent down and removed a few of them to expose part of a metal pipe and a blue plastic casing, serving as a cover.

'I suspect that this was an illegal borehole. Did you know there are nearly three hundred thousand boreholes in Greece, many of them criminal?'

Joy gasped, threw her head back and laughed in delight. Alex and Chrysanthe stared at her in surprise.

'I'm so sorry.' Joy patted her chest as she started to cough. 'I did know. We did know, didn't we, Jane? Dreadful things.'

Alex smiled. 'Well, we've poured loads of concrete down there. It won't be used again in a hurry.'

As he stood up Joy gave him a big hug. '*Efharisto*, Alex. Thank you so much. You've made my year.' Alex blinked, overwhelmed by her enthusiasm.

I smiled, glad to see her so happy. I hoped that after the McGregors had been she would be even happier.

*     *     *

The following Friday evening Charles brought news from Tom, as usual in the form of a print-out. He handed it to Joy without a word, but this time with a smile suffusing his face.

Joy held it up to a lighted candle and read it aloud. 'The McGregors will be in Athens on Monday night. They will need a day to rest from jet lag but look forward to meeting you on Wednesday. I will be there on Tuesday. Hope we can all meet up together for some of your delicious cooking. All the very best, Tom.' Joy held her breath for a moment, clutching the print-out to her chest, then put her head back and softly sighed.

The next morning Joy's turbine was revved up, back on full power. For three days she embarked, once again, on her madcap round of jobs, leaving no time for worry or reflection.

On the eve of the most important day in Joy's life she began to prepare for the meal. Everything had to be right and in its place. The food she was serving had to be of the best and cooked to perfection.

'If you want something badly,' she told me, flicking through a thick Greek recipe book, 'if you really need something, then you have to put everything into it, one hundred per cent. I'm not going to fawn on them or butter them up. But what I do intend to do is show us in our best light. They're going to see the garden at its worst time of the year. We'll need my photos to show them the best. And yours, Jane.'

I suggested that I got a picture board and placed the best photos in seasonal order, so the McGregors could follow the year and quickly see the splendour of spring and summer fading into autumn, all sustained by a careful use of water.

Joy was delighted with the idea and got Pavlos to go into the village and choose a board from an art shop. He was back in time for me to spend most of the afternoon carefully arranging the photographs for display. I cut out strips of white cardboard and with a black felt-tipped marker pen carefully headlined each photograph with the title of the appropriate month. When I'd finished I went to the kitchen and asked Joy to take a look.

She stood before the board, which I'd placed on a chair for easy viewing.

'Oh, Jane.' She put her arm around my shoulder. 'It's marvellous. I'm lost for words.'

She broke off with a short laugh, her eyes moist. Fanning her face with her hand, she waved me away from her emotion and scuttled back into the kitchen, berating herself. 'You soppy old bat.'

The telephone rang. I took the call. It was Tom, at the airport.

'Hi, Jane. Great to hear your voice again! How are you?'

'I'm fine. And you?' I couldn't help but sound a little terse. He'd kept Joy hanging on for so long.

'Never better. I'm on my way. See you in an hour. Oh, I spoke to the McGregors. They're here, looking forward to tomorrow night.'

An hour later Tom arrived by taxi. He looked even fitter, more of the American jock than when I'd last seen him. Joy made him dump his luggage and go straight to the veranda for a reviving ouzo and, of course, a close quizzing about the McGregors.

The briefing gave Joy promise. Tom kept it concise and specific. He'd tried to sort out a way of keeping the garden while taking a job in Athens, but had not been encouraged by what he'd learned about his prospects and so he outlined the situation regarding the McGregors. It was his best hope, he said.

I saw Joy flicker at that but allowed him to continue. Tom stressed that the McGregors had retired from dealing in real estate to help develop some kind of technology in water conservation. That was now up and running, so they were looking for something 'green' in which to have an interest, like the enterprise at Helikion. Mrs McGregor hoped to write about her work and horticultural interests in any journal that might be interested. They didn't want to live in the house. That would remain for the curator's sole use.

Joy was relieved to hear that. 'How old are they?' she asked.

'In their fifties. Don't worry, Joy, they've got lots of life yet.'

'But what about the tax on their money?' Joy looked candidly at Tom. 'Are they willing to pay forty per cent more than your asking price, because that's what it amounts to.'

Tom fell silent a moment. 'Joy, I can't bring the price down forty per cent.'

'I know that. I didn't ask that. I said—'

'These two people are serious. My hope is they'll find a way. They're going to talk to an investment adviser in Athens. Charles fixed it up, didn't he tell you? Look, let's get them round the garden. Get them hooked first.'

'Yes,' said Joy heavily, lowering her head. 'We'll do our best.'

Poor Joy. I could see that she wanted to maintain the drive and enthusiasm that she had brought to the problem, but it was so difficult for her knowing that it would all come to nought if the money wasn't forthcoming. When I offered my sympathy she mentioned Buddhists again.

'Hope, Jane. How it blights lives.'

She shook her head and opined that she was determined not to indulge herself with 'any expectations'. Instead, she would rely on the fates. 'We trust the fates, don't we, Jane?'

I returned her brave smile but she'd failed to reassure me. Failure was not an option. I couldn't imagine how she would react if she lost Helikion.

As I left for Alcatraz that night the repetitive hoot of a scops owl came from afar. On that particular evening it sounded melancholy and echoed my mood of increasing gloom.

\*       \*       \*

Pavlos had kept quiet in the matter of Joy's troubles during the past month. I had noticed the odd moment when he'd raised his head suddenly as if to speak, but had then lowered it again. I guessed that he was troubled, so I wasn't surprised when he came to the house just after breakfast, asking to talk with Joy, alone.

The next day, while I removed spent geranium flower heads from pots huddled around the corner of the house, I spotted them walking down the path. Pavlos was gesticulating and talking rapidly, while Joy held a hand to her hat, protecting it from flying off in the wind.

When they reached the plateau my heart sank. Joy was tearful, dabbing under her eyes with a soft tissue, while Pavlos looked mournful.

'Jane!' He put on a big smile when he saw me staring at him. 'I wills see you tonight!' he called out, passing out of view as he went to the driveway and his moped.

After he'd gone, Joy came to me, biting her lip.

'Oh, Jane,' she said in anguish. 'Pavlos wanted to pay the tax that the McGregors would have to pay. I'd told him Tom's asking price, four hundred thousand euros. The dear man said forty per cent of that was only a hundred and sixty thousand euros. Only! I can't do it. I can't do it.'

'But it's his money, Joy. He must know how much—'

'No!' Joy clapped hands over her ears. 'No. I'm not endangering him even a tiny bit. And that's final.'

The irony was that, at the last, it would be Pavlos who would play a key role in the failure or success of her meeting with the McGregors.

\*     \*     \*

The moment had come. Tom, driving the Jeep, had been to the hotel to bring the McGregors back to Helikion. Joy and I stood on the driveway waiting to greet them. Titan sat obediently at Joy's feet, his coat newly brushed and gleaming in the late afternoon sunshine.

Joy wore a long, flowing dress, beaded necklaces and a purple silk scarf loosely wrapped around her neck. She had taken an inordinately long time to pin her hair into a chignon and apply make-up, all made more time-consuming by Wizard having whisked away her magnifying mirror into the roof space. In between trying to get him down from the rafters, she'd insisted that I wore 'something nice'.

'Something other than those gardening rags, Jane,' she'd said. 'It's time for us to dress like ladies.'

After months of wearing the same garb, I threw myself into the challenge. There were clothes that I'd packed and never worn, partying garments that I'd never had the chance, or occasion, to wear. I put on my favourite skirt and a posh vest, arranged a silk pashmina around my shoulders, took almost as long as Joy to fix my hair, then put on dark, shimmering eye shadow, mascara and eyeliner. After scrubbing my fingernails clean, I contemplated the reflection in the cracked mirror above the sink. I didn't recognize myself.

Joy nearly choked on her cigarette when she saw me. 'Jane, you look absolutely fabulous!'

I returned the compliment and we stood together, shoulder to shoulder, our mood lifted. Suddenly, I grabbed Joy's hand. I could hear the Jeep coming up from the road. She looked at me and smiled. 'Do you remember last January when you pruned a viburnum and said you were sorry that you hadn't done a good job?'

I nodded. I'd pruned a few stems back too hard and left a gaping hole in the shrub. Joy had titivated the stems around it, thereby covering the gap and my error.

'Well, what did I say to you?' persisted Joy.

'That I was a silly nincompoop and that the last

402

remaining freedom to man was—I think you said—"attitude"?'

'I did. Whatever life throws at you, keep a good attitude. I know I don't sometimes, but I know you can.'

'Yes,' I laughed. 'Regardless of the blasted fates or not.'

She joined me in laughter then lowered her voice as the Jeep drove into view. 'Don't you forget it.' She lifted her eyebrows at me knowingly and gave a little nod before stepping away to greet Tom as he jumped out of the now stationary Jeep.

'Tom! Welcome back!'

He kissed Joy, then myself, on both cheeks. 'You look fantastic!' he said. 'Both of you.' He winked at me, then turned and opened the Jeep's rear door. A man effortlessly hopped out with a smile on his face.

'This is Bill,' said Tom.

Bill McGregor was in his early fifties, a tall, slim man with silver-grey hair and a tanned face. He wore a lightweight cotton blazer in pale blue, cream chino trousers and Italian brogue shoes.

Tom helped Bill's wife out from the Jeep. 'And Helen.'

She was beautiful, with piercing blue eyes set above prominent cheekbones and a firm strong chin. Her flaxen hair was tied with a black bow at the back of the neck and she wore a fitting black linen jacket over flared white trousers. On first impression, they looked like a couple straight out of the society pages of *Tatler*.

After the introductions, Joy urged them to the veranda for drinks, then took them out onto the hillside, with Tom and I walking discreetly behind.

403

Joy pointed out that it wasn't the best month in which to see the garden. The McGregors seemed unfazed, even murmuring to each other their appreciation of her comment. However, as the tour progressed Bill's fixed smile began to worry me. It was either a mask, or the sign of a man who was so rich that he worried about nothing.

Helen was much more animated, having keen eyes for many of the plants, quick to comment, ask a question or crouch down for a closer inspection. Her knowledge of wildflowers was excellent and I could see that Joy was impressed. I noted that she wore 'comfortable' shoes in leather and her hands were jewellery-free apart from engagement and wedding rings. She also had square fingernails that didn't protrude past the fingertip. I could well believe that she was a gardener of sorts.

In rising optimism Joy led Helen into every corner of the five acres, pointing out the differences between the same type of plant, according to its position. By now, it was plain to see that Helen McGregor betrayed every sign of wanting to buy the garden. For me, worry remained in that her husband's smile had not changed from start to finish. I could readily see that she was the driving force behind their interest and he was a businessman who dealt with their money and—therefore—made any financial decision. I noted that Joy, as she finished speaking about a plant or shrub, would often give him a cautious glance. It didn't bode well, even when the tour had ended and Joy and Helen walked onto the driveway, chatting and laughing like old friends.

Joy and I had agreed beforehand that the

strategy during the pre-meal drinks would be for her to stay talking with the McGregors as long as possible while I would check the progress of the cooking. As soon as Pavlos arrived I would serve the appetizers or mezethes, basil and feta cheese rolls. The main course was to be a glorious moussaka and the sweet was a splendid-looking almond pie.

Pavlos arrived, as usual chuckling and bubbling, stroking his black beard and impressing the McGregors with his great charm. Helen, I could see, was immediately attracted to him.

'Are you a singer?' she asked. 'You've got a great voice.'

Pavlos waved a hand. 'A littles,' he rumbled. 'Bass, in choirs.'

'Pavlos is a great cello player,' I nipped in to say.

'Really?'

It was no coincidence that Pavlos had brought his cello with him. Joy had cast him as entertainer following the meal. I brought out the mezethes, the setting sun casting shadows all around as I first offered the tray to Helen. I heard a loud laugh and looked round to see that Bill McGregor, for the first time with an animated look on his face, was conversing easily with Tom and Pavlos. I felt a surge of expectancy, knowing that Joy had planned to start 'selling' her love for the garden and its importance after the second champagne. As that began I would go into the house and return with the board of photographs, standing it against a pillar on the veranda wall.

It was that very moment. The sun flooded the veranda. Helen and Joy were together in one corner and Alex, Pavlos and Tom in another. And

405

Joy's 'pitch' to Helen seemed to be working. She was hanging on every word. Having digested the history of the garden she was now fascinated by Joy's tales of visitors from abroad and the scientists who had written about Helikion, their treatises published in botanical journals.

I caught Joy's eye. She gave a little nod and, reading the signal, I went immediately to fetch the photograph board. I returned and placed it as arranged against the pillar and said nothing, just continued to look at it. It was Helen who was drawn first.

'Joy, excuse me.' She went to stare at the board. 'Bill, you've got to see this.'

Bill came to stand with her, staring at the photographs.

'Isn't it beautiful?' said Helen. 'It's the garden the whole year round.'

Bill, Tom and Pavlos stood around Helen staring at each photograph to the accompaniment of a number of 'Oh, isn't that gorgeous' and 'Just look at that' remarks. Joy's strategy was working. Helen was now communicating her enthusiasm to Bill. And Joy, in topping up their champagne, was clearly 'oiling the wheels' before she set off down the main line.

But, on the debit side, I'd noticed that Bill McGregor, although having lost his fixed smile, was careful in his intake of alcohol. It strengthened my view that he was a shrewd and careful man and would not enter an agreement without assessing all the angles. It was after we had sat down to the meal and dug in to the tasty moussaka that he surprised me.

'Joy.' He held up his glass. 'I'd like to thank you

for taking us round your wonderful garden. I really mean that. It was inspirational.'

The sincerity in his eyes seemed genuine.

'Helen, darling. Is it everything you expected?' He raised his eyebrows at his wife.

'Yes. Absolutely wonderful.' Her Massachusetts accent was cultured, certain words oddly denoted by the very British way in which she pronounced them. 'Without a doubt.'

I saw Joy close her eyes for an instant and then, finding me looking at her, gave a flicker of a smile. I could sense that her life and passion lay on the table midway between the McGregors. I wondered as to which of the McGregors would make the first reference to money. I bet on Bill.

'What Joy has done here,' Helen continued, 'is nothing short of marvellous.' She raised her glass. 'Joy, may you be here many years. To Joy.'

We touched glasses with the toast.

It was at this point that Pavlos, who had been relatively quiet through most of the evening, spoke up. 'Joy-bells is my special friend. She is one of the very best persons I know. Everybody should know that.' My heart dropped to see him giving a rather challenging look at Bill McGregor.

'Oh, shut up, Pavlos,' Joy said with a smile, but I could see she was, like me, suddenly panicked.

'No, Joy. You deserve to stay as long as you want here, in this garden.'

I tried to give him a warning look, but mercifully the McGregors hadn't shown any reaction.

'Hear, hear,' said Bill McGregor. 'So you should, Joy.'

'To a great lady,' said Tom, backing up Pavlos, but careful not to put the McGregors on their guard. 'Joy is the best of the best. Look, Bill.' His grin was gone, in its place a determined look. 'I know how difficult this tax situation is. Let's leave it till you see the investment guy in Athens. We all know it's tough. But let's—'

'It is tough,' cut in Bill McGregor. 'I make no bones about it. We're not multimillionaires. We have money, but it's all been earned and saved. We pay taxes back home, don't forget. And I can find things in plant and water conservation in the States without having to shell out all that tax. Helen, tell them about the Wildflower Research Center work in Texas. She's been talking with them. Together with Texas University they're set on conserving our native wildflowers. We could fix up our own garden there, doing just this here, no problem.'

Nothing was said as we digested the import of what he had said. An icy hand gripped my heart. Pavlos had made a bad move and in prompting Tom to cover up had started what Joy had feared, negotiations at the table. She had wanted to keep it as relaxed as possible and leave any discussion about finance until well after the meal. The evening, which had started so well, now threatened to implode. I glanced again at Joy. She was looking down at her dish, her mouth open and lips trembling a little. I looked at Tom in anger. It was Helen who broke the tense atmosphere.

'That's all true, Bill,' she said slowly and calmly. 'But right now I want Joy to know that's not what I want. I can easily work back home, in Texas or wherever, but Greece is where my heart is. It always has been. You know that.'

Joy and I looked at each other, eyes wider, hope resurfacing.

'You love the country, the mountains, the sunshine,' said Pavlos, nodding. 'The classical tour. Everybody does. The magic of Greece, of course.'

'Yes,' said Helen. 'That's true. But I have a special reason. You see, I have a vested interest.' She smiled broadly. 'My grandfather was Greek.'

'Really?' Joy looked astonished.

Pavlos had his fork halfway to his mouth but froze at what she'd said.

'Yes,' Helen said. 'He was a doctor in Kavala—it's in the north. His son, my father, emigrated to America, met my mother, Josie, and never came back. Grandfather used to tell me tales about Greece and I never got bored with listening to them, again and again. I was brought up to love Greece as much as America. I've always wanted to be here, doing something in gardening.'

Joy began to ask Helen a series of questions, eager to exploit the moment.

While all this was going on I noticed that Pavlos had an intense look on his face as if he was trying desperately to remember something. Suddenly, he stood up, breaking the conversation.

'Joy, excuse me, everybody. I have urgent calls to make.' He pulled out his mobile phone. 'Back soon.'

I looked at Joy, puzzled. Had it, could it possibly be anything at all to do with the garden?

Joy, who obviously had the same thought, dithered and then finally stood up and made to leave the table. 'Back in a minute—the pudding.' She and Pavlos were gone for a long ten minutes. Tom, who had sensed that something important was happening, kept up the flow of conversation whenever it threatened to stall. Helen was starting

409

to look uncomfortable at the prolonged absence of the couple. Finally, she looked at me. 'Jane. Is everything all right with Joy and Pavlos?'

I was thinking of an answer when Pavlos returned with Joy. They both sat down, Pavlos beaming, Joy looking excited.

'My dear Pavlos,' she announced, 'has something to say.' She gave me a warm, thrilled smile.

Pavlos looked around the table. 'Ladies and gentlemans. I have a text message here.' Pavlos showed his mobile phone. 'I have a friend, a public notary. He knows lots about property. I spoke to him and asked if someone had a Greek grandfather would they be able to get Greek citizenships. He said yes. I asked if a Greek citizen brings in money from tax havens and not earned moneys here, there is no tax. He said yes. I asked him to send me text message so I can proves it to you. I give you his answer. Joy can translate.'

Pavlos handed Joy his phone. She looked at it and spoke in a clear loud voice. 'Yes. Anyone with a Greek ancestor is entitled to a Greek passport, making them a citizen. They are allowed to bring in money without having to pay tax on it.'

Bill and Helen looked at each other. Pavlos took back the mobile phone from Joy.

'Let me get this straight.' Bill paused and spoke deliberately. 'He's saying that if Helen gets a Greek passport and the money's in her name when it's brought here, there's no tax to pay?'

'Yes, that is correct,' said Pavlos. 'Any foreign person who buys property here must declare it for taxes. They must have proof where the moneys come from. It comes with a pink slip or bank statements. Tax haven bank might not send pink slip or bank statements. Then taxes must be paid. But Helen will have Greek passport, so . . .' The big man shrugged his broad shoulders. 'Everything OK.'

'You're positive. We're talking about coming from a tax haven? There's no tax. That's definite?'

'Not if Helen's grandfather is Greek and has a passport. Not a euro.'

Bill was smiling and shaking his head. Joy, meanwhile, had both hands to her face.

'Joy?' It was Bill.

Joy took her hands from her face to look at him, a desperate hope against hope in her expression.

'This is incredible.' He had all our attention. 'I contacted an investment adviser in New York by phone and internet. He made no mention of us maybe having a Greek ancestor. So neither did we. Would any of you? We had no idea! We're Americans, for God's sake! Thank you, Pavlos.' Bill got up to shake Pavlos by the hand.

Joy rose and went to put both arms around Pavlos's neck.

'Dear, dear Pavlos,' she murmured.

*       *       *

I stood inside Alcatraz. My rucksack was packed. I looked around my living quarters for the last time. Life had often been hard and unpleasant, sometimes sad and lonely, but I felt a strange affection for the place, now that I was leaving it.

I placed a hand on Zeus's head. 'Thanks for listening to me. Take care.'

I stepped outside, lugging out my rucksack. There was a cool breeze. I looked at my watch. My

411

flight left in five hours. Joy and Pavlos were scheduled to take me to the airport in an hour's time. Before that, she had given me one last order, to report to her in fifteen minutes' time for a last walk around the garden, not to talk about plants but just to feel the *genius loci* of the place. She wanted to remember me, she said, always recalling that moment.

I went to the three sunken compost beds and tossed bits of torn-up airport leaflet into the first pit then walked up the hillside and sat down on a boulder to stare over the garden. I dwelt on the year I'd spent at Helikion.

Financially I was only six hundred euros better off than when I arrived, through buying little, apart from food. But as a gardener I was leaving enriched, not just in terms of knowledge and skill, but also with a deeper and fuller understanding of the nature of plants and their role in sustaining life on this earth.

In the microcosm that was Helikion, the outer world had taken on a greater significance in teaching me that conservation of the soil, water and air were far more important than raising living standards. My growing tolerance of Alcatraz itself had helped convince me of that.

Then there was Joy. My admiration for her was unbounded. I would miss her comical ways, her indomitable spirit and strength, her passion, even her dottiness. Mostly, I would miss her friendship which, to a pang of inner pain, I realized I'd not enjoyed until late in the year, probably my fault in being either too afraid or too wary of her. Above all, she had taught me to regard death as an occasion for rebirth. She had given me a purpose in life. I would carry on in my horticultural career and, no matter how many knock-backs I received or how tough it got, I wouldn't run away again, ever. And as for water . . .

Then there was Pavlos, the gentle giant. I would miss him nearly as much as I would Joy, but I was happy and glad that, just as she was fearing failure, it was he who had come up with the solution of saving her world without endangering himself in any way.

And I would miss the reflective moments that I'd enjoyed sitting on the veranda, smelling the perfumes of the night, watching Orwell chase the birds, the swallows wheeling, the flitting bats and the fireflies. I would miss all of it.

Why, then, was I going home? Was it because Joy after inviting me once to stay had never pressed me again? I dismissed it. If Kew Gardens would have me, I would be living near to central London with its pavement cafés, pubs and theatres. And then there were my friends back home. As much as I loved Joy—and felt for her—I had to return.

Inside my rucksack, carefully packed away, was the reference she'd given me at my leaving party the previous evening. She had assured me it would impress the people at Kew. It was sparsely written, but all the more impressive for it.

I thought about the party the previous evening. All the other people who had made my stay at Helikion so memorable were there: Pavlos, Charles, Rachel, Demetri and Vassili, even Spiros. He had turned up with a luminous pair of secateurs that he'd found on the passenger seat of his van, provoking much hilarity when he

413

produced them.

At the last moment Joy had invited Alex and Chrysanthe, expressing her apologies for the late invitation. Only she and I knew that she'd simply forgotten them until I'd made the suggestion. Pavlos had played his accordion and had us dancing. Later, when a wine-induced lethargy was upon us, he had treated us to yet another moving Elgar concerto, which I'd listened to and hid my tears.

'Dear, dear Pavlos.' Joy had put her arms up to him as he finished. 'What would I have done without you?'

Pavlos chuckled. 'You would have done it, Joy-bells. You can do anything. It was just time. All you needed was time.'

*       *       *

I looked down over the garden. I could see Joy emerging from the house, her slim, taut figure leading out Titan.

As I made my way down to meet her I felt nothing but apprehension. I was afraid of breaking down. And I didn't want her to cry, as she'd said she would. I wanted to leave her as Joy the indomitable. I wanted to go, not in distress, but in gratitude. It would be difficult.

She was smiling as I approached. Wizard sat on her shoulder, murmuring. My eyes locked with Joy's. I hesitated. She grasped my arm firmly and tucked it under hers and we set off without a word. At the pet cemetery Joy broke the silence with a laugh about Winston and his odd habits. And then we fell back into our own reflection.

414

As we reached the house there was just time for Joy to take me to the veranda for a final glass of ouzo, toasting my future. Then she insisted I sat down a moment while she fetched something.

She returned with a small painting. It was of me working in the garden, surrounded by olive trees and wildflowers, under the Greek sun. She had painted it without me knowing, just at a time when I thought she was being sharp-tempered.

'Thank you, Joy,' I said, my voice quavering. I stood up and put my arms round her. 'It's beautiful.'

I could hear Pavlos's moped buzzing up the driveway.

'Jane. I must tell you something.'

I didn't like how she sounded; her tone was urgent.

She spoke quickly and quietly.

'Listen. The reason why I didn't beg you to stay here was because you wouldn't want the worry of living with somebody who was losing her marbles. I couldn't let you, as much as I couldn't let Pavlos pay that money. Please tell me you understand.'

The moped had stopped. Pavlos was coming, whistling a tune. I nodded, holding back the tears.

'Do you remember the Queen of the Night party, Gordon and the hunt for worms?'

I nodded, still unable to speak. A few drops of rain began to fall as Joy smiled at me and took me by the hand.

# 19
# Joy Strataki's Letter #2

*10 January 2009*

*Helikion*

*To my dearest Jane,*
*Happy New Year! I hope I find you well. I*
*know you will enjoy the enclosed book. I saw*
*you dipping into it many times and couldn't*
*think of a better home for it now that I'm*
*leaving the garden. I'm going to live in*
*Ireland with Josh, Anne and Charlie. They*
*have plenty of space for the rest of my books*
*and a large garden in desperate need of my*
*care. It's time to go. I've seen the wretched*
*doctor and have had to go to hospital for*
*some tests. They tell me I'm suffering from*
*old age. I keep telling them they've made a*
*mistake but Helen and Bill have talked to*
*them and they think it's for the best. They*
*have nothing but good intentions for*
*Helikion and now it's saved I can rest and*
*leave with some feeling of contentment.*
*Titan and Wizard can come with me. I want*
*Orwell to stay in the garden. It's his territory*
*and he'd miss it terribly. Although he will*
*keep harassing the sparrows he's never*
*caught one yet.*

*Now, I must attend to the meatballs.*
*Pavlos is here. He sends a big hug. He's*
*already planning a visit to Ireland. I gather*
*that ouzo's hard to find there and his supply*
*will be essential.*

*I hope my reference helps at Kew. If they*
*don't accept you, tell me, and I shall give*

*them a piece of my mind!*

*I enclose my new address. Keep me informed and visit soon.*

*Remember to look at the view. Everything changes . . .*

*With fondest love,*
*Joy*

# Epilogue

The week after I left Helikion, I felt like a deep-sea diver coming up to the surface too fast. I was completely disorientated. London seemed huge—the traffic and the noise were alarming and everyone seemed to walk so fast. It was great to see Mum, Dad and Bubski the cat, and to catch up with friends, but I found it hard to answer their questions about my time in the garden—it felt as though I had the 'social bends'. I made jokes, told everyone what a character Joy was, how hard it was living in Alcatraz, how I was relieved to be back, etc., but then I clammed up, wishing I was back in my cell at Helikion or out on a 'walkabout' with Joy. I even found myself, when alone, talking to Zeus!

I was in complete shock when I received Joy's letter. To think she was actually leaving the garden—and after all that worry! But in a way I was glad and I understood. She needed someone to keep an eye on her full time. And as she said, she would be leaving with contentment as the garden was now in the hands of people who loved it. It also meant she had finally put Christos to rest.

In July 2009, Joy sent me a book by Wordsworth. She'd outlined the poem 'Lines Composed a Few Miles Above Tintern Abbey' in red. It was great to hear from her, although it made me sad. Her handwriting had become less decipherable—it took me ten minutes to work out that she was helping to whip her son's garden into shape, and deadhead a few roses. I wondered what she was doing with herself all day. I liked to imagine her reading poetry and sitting in the garden with her battered sunhat askew. I hoped she was being cherished.

I wished Pavlos would send letters, but he's always been a secretive one. I'm happy just to have met him. Then there's Tom. There's been no contact between us; I think we both knew nothing would come of exchanging phone numbers. He's out there, I'm here—still as single as ever. I'm thinking of trying internet dating then I imagine the look on Joy's face if I were to tell her, and think again. Of course, she'd be horrified.

It's been a year since I left Helikion. Since coming home I'm a lot happier, and definitely more observant. I can always spot a 'survivor', as Joy always used to say, growing in the bleakest of streets, a small flower or a spread of leaves lying flat on the ground doing its best with the conditions available.

My gardening rounds are doing OK. People seem happy with my work. I feel ready to apply to Kew now. It's a long process, though; I won't know if I even get an interview until next May. Whatever happens I will have Joy in mind, and her most inspirational of Churchillian quotes: 'Failure isn't fatal, it's the courage to continue that counts.'

# Acknowledgements

A big thank you to my agent, Gordon Wise at Curtis Brown Ltd; Angela Herlihy; Kerri Sharp, senior commissioning editor at Simon & Schuster; Ian Allen, copyeditor; Rory Scarfe, junior editor; Arianne Burnette, proof reader; and Liane Payne, art director.

Hugs to my mum, olive trees, and all the cats—Jose, Daffers, (on loan, but in a league of their own) barkin' Bee (your release dates soon) and especially Georgie 'Bubski'.

Lastly, love and gratitude to 'Joy'—every time I take a 'walkabout' in a garden I can't help but think of you and smile . . .